Missions to China's Heartland

The Letters of Hazel Todd of the China Inland Mission, 1920-1941

Missions to China's Heartland

The Letters of Hazel Todd of the China Inland Mission, 1920-1941

Edited with Notes and an Introduction
by
Robert Gardella

MERWIN ASIA
Portland, Maine

www.merwinasia.com

Distributed by the University of Hawaii Press

ISBN 978-0-9836599-9-0 (paperback)

Printed in the United States of America

The paper used in this publication meets the minimum requirements of the American National Standard for Information Services—Permanence of Paper for Printed Library Materials, ANSI/NISO Z39/48-1992

Contents

Preface

This book is dedicated to the memory of Winifred Todd, who passed away in February 2006. Without the cooperation and support of the Todd family, in particular Winifred Todd, Sergio Perez and Isabelle M. Perez, this project would never have commenced. Professor Sergio Perez, my colleague at the U.S. Merchant Marine Academy, inspired its origins in the spring of 2003. Sergio suggested that, as a China specialist, I might be interested in reading his copy of a book entitled *Letters from Hazel*, edited by Winifred Todd. The younger sister of Hazel Todd, Winifred became her family's archivist, preserving, editing, and in 1977 publishing a judicious personal selection of Hazel's correspondence from her many years of missionary service in China. That private publication, in very limited circulation since it was primarily intended as a commemorative record for family, friends, and community, served as the essential documentary scaffolding for the broader range of materials included and annotated in the present book. Winifred Todd subsequently donated Hazel's manuscript letters to Whitworth University in Spokane, Washington, where they were carefully compiled and processed by the able team of H.W. and Mary B. Johnston. In early 2005, thanks to the gracious assistance of Janet Hauck, Whitworth's archivist, I was able to access and copy these original documents and also carefully compare them for discrepancies with the published text renditions. Tad Wisenor, Whitworth's Director of Development and, as Winifred's nephew, the direct donor of the manuscripts, generously allowed full reproduction rights to the numerous original photos included with the manuscripts, and also provided his own digital images of several intriguing curios that Hazel had sent home from China.

Appreciation is also due to Wayne D. Weber and the staff at the Archives of the Billy Graham Center, Wheaton, Illinois, for their research assistance, to Dr. George Billy and Donald Gibbs of the Bland Library of the U.S. Merchant Marine Academy for arranging key interlibrary loans, and to Professors Murray Rubinstein, Theresa Kelleher, and Joseph Lee for their helpful comments and suggestions. Finally, a special vote of thanks is due to Doug Merwin and Professor Kathleen Lodwick for their encouragement of this project, as well as to the United States Merchant Marine Academy for providing the timely sabbatical leave in 2004-2005 that made it possible.

Introduction
China, the Missionary Project, and the Career of Hazel Todd

This is a firsthand account of the convergence of three historical realities—turbulent Republican China, an undaunted Christian missionary project, and the self-recorded experiences of a single American woman missionary. The first half of the twentieth century in China witnessed a series of revolutions, chronic political instability, military and ideological contests for power, and the awakening of modern mass nationalism in reaction to national weakness and the inroads of foreign imperialism. Unreconciled to the possibility of failure, a few thousand foreign missionaries, about half of them Americans by the 1920s, sought to bring Christianity and as much modern education and medical care as seemed compatible with it to "China's Millions" (not coincidentally, the title of a prominent China Inland Mission monthly periodical). Leaving her native California in 1920, twenty-seven-year-old Hazel Todd joined the interdenominational China Inland Mission (hereafter, CIM), and for most of the next two decades dedicated her life to the rigorous evangelical project conceived of by her sponsoring agency. At the time of her arrival, China was a nation in search of itself, a brutal process that inevitably defined her own life and missionary career.

China in Turmoil

In the past few decades the unthinkable has happened again and again: major states have undergone political disintegration, generating prolonged periods of localized armed conflict and strenuous efforts at political and social re-integration. Perhaps such evidence of contemporary turmoil—whether in the former Yugoslavia or ex-Soviet Union, or present day Iraq and Afghanistan—will lead modern readers to a more sympathetic understanding of early twentieth-century China's even more protracted search for political stability and accountability, social justice, cultural revitalization and a sound pattern for economic development. The history of the period from the aftermath of the 1911 Revolution to the Sino-Japanese War of 1937-1945 is notoriously complex. Only its broad outlines are presented here as basic background information.[1]

The Qing dynasty's last decade saw the final unraveling of an autocratic monarchy which had ruled China with a considerable degree of effectiveness since the mid-seventeenth century. An ultimately fatal combination of *nei luan wai huan* ("internal disorders and foreign incursions"), as an ancient Chinese expression has it, challenged the dynasty. Western powers humbled the Chinese Empire in a series of lopsided wars (the second round of which fully opened the country to Christian missionary activity in 1860), while internal unrest and massive civil strife further undermined Qing legitimacy. As a result, China's sovereignty was compromised for a century (from 1842 until 1943) by a series of "unequal treaties" that conceded disproportionate advantages to foreign powers.

China's late nineteenth-century efforts at "self-strengthening," the term for strategic modernization projects such as ordnance factories and shipyards to cope with foreign and domestic threats, proved inadequately coordinated and woefully unequal to the task. Following a decisive military defeat by Meiji Japan in 1894-1895, reformist political activism grew among Chinese elites while an anti-Manchu republican revolutionary movement began to emerge from below. Imperialist demands for spheres of influence, naval coaling stations, territorial concessions, and railway rights presaged "The Breakup of China" (the title of a popular British book of the era). Such foreign pressures provoked the desperate xenophobic reaction among both Qing officials and the masses known as the Boxer Uprising (1899-1900). With the occupation of Beijing by Allied foreign armies and the imposition of punitive peace terms, China's humiliation seemed complete. In fact the Qing dynasty's last decade (1901-1911) exhibited a series of major institutional reforms ranging from the creation of modern government ministries to the planning for a constitutional monarchy. The contest between controlled dynastic reform from above and mobilized revolutionary action in society at large was short-lived, however. An opportune collaboration of provincial elites, regional military leaders, and republican revolutionaries brought an end to China's two thousand years of imperial rule in 1911.

Although the 1911 Revolution ostensibly transformed an empire into a centralized parliamentary republic, China rapidly fragmented into a crazy-quilt pattern of regionally based military regimes, several of which lasted well into the 1930s. Practical politics in this so-called "warlord era" degenerated into shifting alliances and protracted rivalries among coalitions of militarists, punctuated by frequent resort to armed conflict. Within less than a decade after 1911, China's new political framework seemed both irrelevant and inadequate, leaving the way clear for more radical attacks on traditional Chinese culture (the real or presumed basis for national weakness) and more radical, broad-based movements for political change.

While World War I and the 1917 Russian Revolution exposed the fissures in Western civilization, a New Culture movement led many Chinese intellectuals to question the conservative values and institutions of their past (such as Confucianism, the Chinese family system, and the injustices of the social order) as well as China's perceived domination by imperialism, capitalism and warlordism. As a conspicuous import from the West, Christianity could not escape guilt by association in the growing opposition to these impediments to national unity and national renewal. The May Fourth movement of 1919, a wide-ranging popular protest against both domestic and foreign betrayal of China's national interests at the Versailles Peace Conference, marked the dawn of a new era in Chinese politics.

The new era encompassed the 1920s and early 1930s, and it featured the emergence of two modern political organizations that bitterly contested the future of China. Reorganized in the early 1920's with the military and political assistance of the Soviet Union, Sun Yat-sen's Nationalist Party (the Guomindang) was for most of this period the dominant political force in China. Founded in 1921, the Chinese Communist Party grew in influence as the junior partner of the Nationalists between 1923 and 1927. The two parties collaborated during these years in a mass-based campaign against warlords and imperialism (amid the political insecurity of these times, many Protestant missionary activities in China had all but come to a temporary standstill by 1927). During a military campaign to liberate and unite China known as the Northern Expedition (1926-28), the ideological goals and political strategies of the Nationalists and Communists became completely irreconciliable. Under Chiang Kai-shek (the party's leader after Sun Yat-sen's death in 1925), the better-organized and well-armed Nationalists all but destroyed the Chinese Communist movement in China's cities, driving its remnants into remote mountainous enclaves in central and southern China.

The Nationalists consolidated their power from 1927 to 1937 in China's new capital of Nanking, while the Chinese Communist Party struggled both to survive and to develop effective political and military operations in some of the most backward regions of the country. Nationalist efforts at nation-building, while significant, were curtailed by budgetary stringencies and skewed by the military and political imperatives of the party's leadership. In any case, they inevitably fell far short of China's immense needs. To cite an example of particular relevance to the present study, one authority on the period notes that "By 1920, it was estimated there were about 1,500 modern doctors in China, of whom 600 were either missionaries or foreigners in private practice." The same source then adds that the entire country had less than 2,000 nurses and only 500 hospitals by the mid- to late 1920s.[2]

Destruction of the Chinese Communist movement remained Chiang Kai-shek's chief domestic priority during the early to mid-1930s, a goal that was almost achieved when relentless Nationalist military pressure forced the Communists to evacuate their rural "Soviets" or bases in the famous "Long March" of 1935-36. Unfortunately for the Nationalists, Japanese aggression in China between 1930 and 1937 was much more difficult to deal with, in that it exposed China's relative military weakness, negated Chiang's diplomatic temporizing, and eventually forced yet another temporary alliance between Communist and Nationalists. When all-out war broke out between China and Japan in July 1937, few could have forseen its ultimate consequences: the slow erosion of the legitimacy of the Nationalist government, the reemergence of the Communist Party from the caves of Yan'an as China's most convincing political alternative, and the tragic disruption and devastation of much of the country in eight years of total war.

The Missionary Project

Christian missionary activity in China, as classically documented by Kenneth Scott Latourette, may be traced as far back as the T'ang dynasty (618-907). Its heyday lasted only a century from the Opium War of 1839-1842 to the Communist Revolution of 1949. A Roman Catholic presence in China that dated to the mid-1600s was rapidly overshadowed by an explosion of Protestant evangelism, with its multiplication of mission societies and the expansion of related institutions such as schools and clinics. As the names of these organizations reveal: the [Anglican] Church Missionary Society, the American Baptist Missionary Union, the Basel German Evangelical Society—they were commonly organized along the lines of national affiliation, denomination, or a combination of both.[3]

What difference, if any, did this dramatic proliferation of organized expatriate religious energy make? The question lends itself to many responses, and the issue remains contested.[4] Speaking directly to the issue of American Protestant missionary influence in China, however, John K. Fairbank's comments two decades ago are still worth reiterating: "Protestant missionaries by their calling were aggressive individualists in thought and attitude. To be sure, their aggressiveness was shared by the merchants seeking profits and by the Western officials seeking to open China. But only the missionaries sought direct contact with the common people in the two civilizations. They were the principal if not the sole link between village China and small-town America. Only they sought to change Chinese minds and hearts. They penetrated farthest into Chinese life and became among all the foreign invaders the most deeply involved on the local scene."[5]

The missionary project by definition sought "to change Chinese minds and hearts," but what this actually entailed in terms of day-to-day activities in China gradually tended to change over time. At the turn of the century, the majority of workers in the field were still generalists who devoted much of their effort to propagating the gospel. This steadfast concentration on evangelical activity is quite evident in the letters and diaries of Eva Jane Price, who served with her husband Charles and their children in Shanxi Province from 1889 to 1900 on behalf of the American Board of Commissioners for Foreign Missions (the Prices were among numerous victims of the Boxer Uprising).[6]

By the 1920s and 30s, much had changed. Separate studies by Kathleen Lodwick and Lawrence Kessler have both pointed out that most missionaries were then being recruited with professional qualifications in mind as educators, physicians, and the like.[7] Lodwick notes that, in the absence of objective attainments, including college degrees, a fervent religious commitment or "calling" in itself was no longer sufficient justification for enagaging in missionary work.[8] As Kessler emphasizes, mainstream American missionary activity was by then subsumed by the social gospel paradigm which emphasized transformative good works in the world. A concentration on medical and educational functions meant "increasing professionalization and secularization." The unambiguous approach of an earlier era equating missionary service with resolute evangelism was increasingly displaced, yet not totally rejected, as "an outmoded and impractical conception of mission work."[9]

Followed by two unforgiving decades of worldwide economic depression and global war, the early to mid-1920s proved in fact to be the high water mark of the modern missionary enterprise in China. Some 6,500 people, representing hundreds of sending organizations, served in virtually all regions of the country.[10] About one-sixth of these people (a total of

1,185 workers at the end of 1927) belonged to the CIM.[11] Founded in 1865 by the English evangelist James Hudson Taylor, the CIM had more missionaries operating in China in the early twentieth century than any other single Christian agency, Protestant or Catholic.[12]

The CIM was the outstanding exception to the mainstream tendencies of the Protestant missionary movement as outlined above. Consistent with its founder's intentions, CIM recruitment was nondenominational, international, and relatively undemanding respecting the educational background of candidates for service. The mission further distinguished itself operationally from peer organizations in a number of significant ways: by situating the direction of CIM activities in China rather than abroad; by requiring missionaries to conform to Chinese social and living conditions as much as possible (including wearing native dress); and by reliance on ad hoc "faith-based" funding rather than on regularly planned budgets and guaranteed salaries, a financial regime that in itself would have largely precluded excessive "professionalization and secularization."[13] The financial practices of the mission were clearly stated in each issue of its monthly journal *China's Millions*: "The Mission does not go into debt. It guarantees no income, but ministers to workers as funds sent in will allow. All members are expected to depend on God alone for temporal supplies. No collection or personal solicitation of money is authorized."[14]

Theologically speaking, the CIM was perhaps best known for consistently proclaiming Protestant evangelical orthodoxy at a time when theological modernism was vigorously challenging biblical verities and spiritual certainties.[15] Candidates were screened for their adherence to CIM's doctrinal guidelines, and were expected to resign from service whether at home or abroad if their views on any aspect of these fundamentals subsequently changed. The basic doctrines involved were those common among conservative evangelical Protestants by the early twentieth century: the divine inspiration and authority of the canonical Scriptures; the Trinity; man's fall, sinfulness and need of salvation; Christ's death as vicarious atonement for man; justification by faith; the resurrection of the body, and eternal life for the saved and eternal punishment for the damned.[16]

The primary role of CIM missionaries, sustained over virtually a century of activity, was to diffuse the knowledge of the gospel as widely as possible among the masses throughout China. True to the organization's name, this particularly involved the CIM in penetrating the ordinary villages and rural towns of the vast interior of the country, rather than concentrating on converting influential elites such as the traditional scholar-gentry and the modern urban intelligentsia.[17] A vigorous proclamation of the gospel through sustained itinerant preaching and local teaching, and distribution of the Word through sales and donations of bibles and tracts ideally led to lasting individual conversions. These CIM activities certainly enabled the later formation of denominational churches, and the organization characteristically deferred in this regard to the long-term interests of other Protestant missionary bodies.[18]

In practical terms CIM missionaries found that they could not purely confine themselves to ambulatory preaching and conversion of the countless pagans in China's unchurched hinterlands. By 1928, for example, in addition to operating 269 principal mission stations and 1,987 outstations, the CIM also managed seven hospitals, 64 medical dispensaries, and 280 native schools.[19] As the career of Hazel Todd can serve to illustrate, the actual day-to-day lives of CIM missionaries in the field might embrace a limited version of the social gospel without undue deference to the fact.

The Career of Hazel Todd (1893-1941)

The Call, John Hersey's epic fictionalized narrative of an American missionary's spiritual odyssey in early twentieth-century China, began with his hero growing up in and eventually transcending a disadvantaged rural environment. Hersey's protagonist secured his missionary "calling" along with a prestigious college degree and a relatively desirable Y.M.C.A. position in China dispensing the social gospel, in his case, lectures on basic scientific and technical knowledge.[20] In the present case, the exigencies of Hazel Todd's life not only differ from the novelist's art, but also from the comfortable bourgeois backgrounds shared by many American women missionaries in the late nineteenth and early twentieth centuries.[21] Born in Minnesota in 1893, Hazel was raised in the wheatlands of North Dakota in a large Presbyterian farming family with very limited resources. She developed her "calling" from childhood contacts with an uncle, then on furlough, but serving at the time as a Protestant missionary in the then British colony of Sierra Leone, West Africa. The family subsequently moved to southern California, where her father took up fruit cultivation and hay farming in the San Joaquin Valley. Hazel was by then determined to pursue her missionary vocation without the personal expense and further delay of obtaining either a high school diploma or a formal college degree. Given its deserved reputation as an organization that "valued spiritual sincerity over academic preparation," the CIM was Hazel's logical choice for an immediate and lasting affiliation.[22] In a Register of Candidate Information, 1898-1934, the CIM's U.S. Council simply noted that Miss Todd was accepted on June 16, 1920, with three years of high school credits and an additional two years' study at the Bible Institute of Los Angeles (hereafter, Biola) behind her. Her required medical and theological screenings were both listed as "satisfactory," and her references "satisfactory on the whole."[23]

Hazel Todd arrived in Shanghai on October 10, 1920. Except for two extended furloughs in the United States (from early 1927 to early 1929, and from mid-1937 to late 1938), she spent the rest of her life in China, where she died suddenly of typhoid fever on November 17, 1941. Her experiences, whether humdrum or dramatic, over twenty-odd years of military strife, localized banditry, mass nationalist awakening, growing communist revolutionary activity and brutal Japanese aggression were recorded in a weekly to monthly stream of letters to her family in southern California. This correspondence discloses a determined, vigorous individual with what seems to be an uncomplicated sense of both herself and her mission in China. She faced daily hardships, episodic isolation, and the generalized insecurity of early twentieth-century life in the rough hinterlands of Hunan and Anhui with little complaint, doubtless schooled and skilled by the demands of her early years in rural North America. She was unshakably secure in her evangelical Christianity, and thus inherently antagonistic to the Chinese religious traditions it sought to displace. Privileged by treaty rights that nationalistic Chinese abhorred and soon would eliminate, she accepted the protected status of an American expatriate as a necessary political condition of her missionary work.

Hazel Todd's letters are artifacts of a deep-rooted historical connection which has hardly ceased to color Sino-American relations. In more personal terms, they recall the career of a remarkable woman reporting on extraordinary times from an alien society she eventually came to call her own. She routinely walked many miles each day to sell scriptures in the countryside, fended off the frequent incursions of gun-toting warlord troops, treated the sick with the limited means at her disposal, attempted to teach rural women to read their own language with the gospel as a primer, and came to manage all of the complex routines of a CIM mission station. Without any Sinological background before arriving in China, she attained basic competence in two quite dissimilar varieties of Mandarin, and also acquired some command of the difficult classical or literary language. During her first furlough from early 1927 to early 1929, she completed a course for medical missionaries at Biola, which gave her the nursing training that she turned to good account on her return to the field. With typical unadorned forthrightness, Hazel remarked in 1936: "Is there anything a missionary does not need to know? Bookkeeping, housekeeping, gardening, nursing are a few of the skills required in addition to a good thorough knowledge of the Bible and its practical applications."[24] She amply justified the conviction, going back to the mid-nineteenth century, that single women would eventually emerge as the most essential human factor in carrying out the Protestant missionary enterprise in China.[25]

Missions to China's Heartland

The Letters of Hazel Todd of the China Inland Mission, 1920-1941

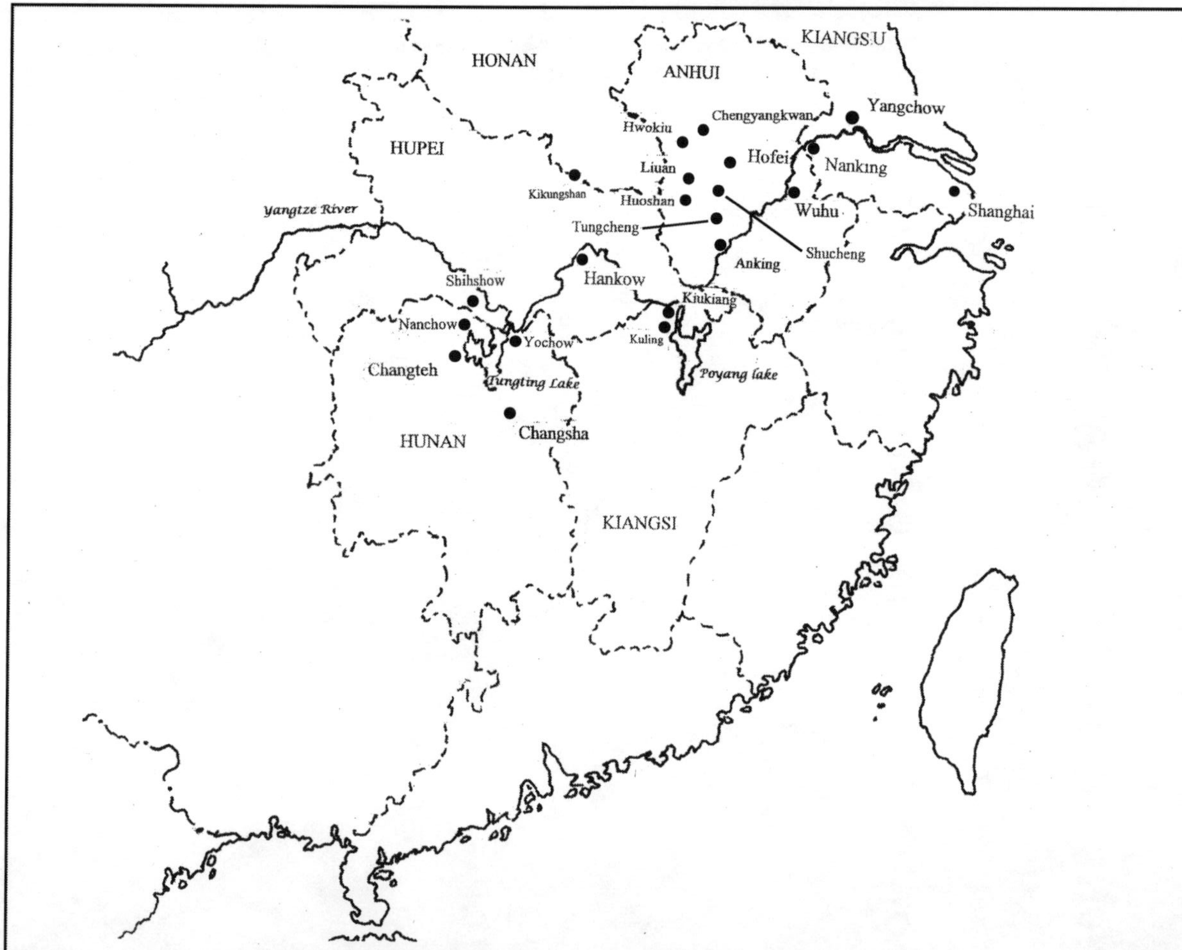

Hazel Todd's China, 1920-1941

CHAPTER ONE

From Yangzhou to Hunan: The Early Years, 1920-1930

Hazel Todd arrived in Shanghai on October 10, 1920, and soon proceeded to her assigned destination for the next six months, the CIM's language center for women located in Yangchow, about a hundred miles upriver from Shanghai.

Yangchow, November 3, 1920

There are twelve of us women in this home studying the language and they expect about five more. Four are from England, five from the States, one from Canada, and two are from Australia. We have three Chinese teachers, one woman and two men. We each have a private lesson and three group classes every day. I have a woman teacher for my private lessons. She is wonderfully patient but very exact with me. Getting these tones, when to aspirate or not, and those idioms is quite a task. Fortunately they do not have declensions and conjugations like Latin, and the numerical system is somewhat like our own. They have one character they attach to all verbs to make it past tense and one they use to attach to nouns to make them possessive. The order of the words while very different than ours is not particularly hard to catch.[1]

I suppose you people at home are thinking about how the election is turning out. We are more interested here about what kind of Chinese officials we are getting. Some provinces have a very good stable government. Others hardly have any government at all. However we new workers have not much cause for fear as they shield us from so much just at first. At present the Chinese christians are getting up a petition to ask them to prevent the breweries from coming over here. I often feel like being very much ashamed of my native land that such a thing should be necessary. Also that the most common thing for sale here in China from the USA is cigarettes. Why does the Lord so continue to favor us when we are such sinners against the poorer and more ignorant people of the earth? God be merciful to our sinful nation.

I feel very unworthy of the love and respect of these Chinese. The

Chinese christians always stand when we missionaries enter the room. They call us "teachers" or "big sisters."

Yangchow, November 6, 1920

Today three of the English young women with one of the servants went out into the country. We never go out without an escort. The others had never seen sweet potatoes or cotton growing. The servants are always quite willing to escort the "chiao-shih" ("teacher") if they know beforehand we want to go. My Chinese last name is pronounced "Tao," and they put the last name before the title. Hence when they call me by name it sounds like "Tao chiao-shih."

Passport photo of Hazel Todd, January 24, 1929.

Yangchow, November 9, 1920

There are two things you always seem to want to know about. In the first place I have plenty to eat but miss the fruit and the fresh water. No water in China is fit to drink without its first having been boiled. The Chinese know this and never offer water that has not been boiled. Of course water that has been boiled does not taste fresh. The question of money is not likely to bother me very soon. Expenses in many directions are cheaper than at home. In some others they are much higher. They aim to allow each of us $750 a year although they may fall short of it. Some of our travelling expenses will have to be paid out of this but not all of it.

This Chinese may be almost as much a stumbling block to me as Latin was; however, I am here now, and I simply have to get this. In many ways my study of Latin helps.

Of course on every side I am reminded that this is a heathen city and not California, but I do praise the Lord having brought me here. The fields are little and queer, and the streets are narrow. But we live in this comfortable house enclosed by a high brick wall. There is a large garden but some times it makes one feel a little like a bird in a cage not being allowed out of the gate without an escort. One reason for this is that the streets are so narrow and crooked it would be very easy to get lost, and our Chinese is as yet so limited that in case we should get lost, we would not be able to inquire the way home. This place is about as large as Los Angeles.[2]

"The chairs we had on the way here."

Yangchow, November 12, 1920

It may not always be possible for me to write so often, but one can not study Chinese all the time, or the characters would start playing hide-and-go-seek in our brains. Besides that, as my Chinese vocabulary only consists of about a hundred words I can not make much head way talking with the people in fact, so yet I do not try. We study Chinese most of the time. We do go for a walk most days which most of the time I would enjoy more if my eyes were closed or if I could strike out at my own gait and go so far as I want to. They have the ugliest looking dogs I have ever seen here in China. The cats are not quite so bad. There are so many beggars and blind too. The other day we took a walk on top of the city wall. There we could look over down into the gardens and also see the trees. When we walk in the street, brick walls prevent us from seeing gardens. That day we saw more loquat trees than almost any other kind. Days when we do not go outside we walk around in the garden.

Yangchow, November 14, 1920

I attended Chinese church service today and caught a word now and then and once in a while two or three words together but could not catch the general drift of what was said. The minister did use the word for knowledge or knowing very often, and I found out later that the sermon was on divine wisdom.

Yangchow, November 17, 1920

This week I bought a pair of Chinese shoes. They are black satin trimmed with braid. They are lined with flannel and warmly interlined and are very much warmer than our shoes. There is just one fastener on each, a buckle like on overshoes. They cost $2.20. I thought I could save my more expensive shoes by having them. I am planning on having some Chinese trousers to wear under my skirts when it gets colder. I already have a Chinese wadded jacket but I have to have it altered a little. A suit of brocaded poplin lined with cambric and wadded heavily with cotton costs five or six dollars. Most of the Chinese goods are more durable than ours The trousers will of course be wadded. You will see that you will not need to worry about my keeping warm.

Two of the servants went to celebrate their mother's seventieth birthday last week. While there the good time they had expected was very much spoiled by some evil men who came daily demanding money, saying that their brother who is now dead owed them a large sum of money. It worried the mother considerably and it was so unjust. They did talk about going to law about it but it was finally settled outside of court. They say going to law in China is much worse than at home.[3]

Things are so different here than at home. Most of the hauling here in Yangchow is done by wheel barrow. You can usually know when a wheel barrow is within a block or two of you or is going by for it protests because of the lack of oil every step of the way. They haul all hours of the day and night and often in the very early morning one begins to hear the squeak.

Perhaps you would like to know what the men wear. Beggars wear garments which look like a dirty ragged old bed quilt. The main color the poorer class wears is a very bright blue. The beggars' garments though are faded. Rich men wear black satin caps which fit tightly, black brocaded satin jackets of a very rich and beautiful quality such as we almost never see at home, black satin slippers and white stockings. Their skirts are usually of ankle length and slip at the sides to the knee. Buddhist priests wear a drab-colored garment which opens in front and reaches clear down to the ground. The sleeves usually extend about six inches below the hand. Buddhist priests look like rascals to me.

Yangchow, November 28, 1920

Five of us went from here to the home of some American Episcopalians for Thanksgiving dinner which was in the evening. There were twenty-four of us there and all but one were missionaries. There are two other American missionaries in Yangchow but they could not be there, and that is the total number, not counting some children of Americans in this city of several hundred thousand. We went a few minutes before six, and the first thing we went to was a Thanksgiving service held in the chapel on the compound.

They are having such an awful famine in some parts of China; they say that millions are in need of food. At the Thanksgiving service a collection was taken up for famine relief which amounted to ninety-one dollars. The salt merchants here in Yangchow, or what would be the chamber of commerce at home, have given a hundred thousand dollars for famine relief and other cities have done very much the same.[4]

Yangchow, December 9, 1920

It really did used to bore me to hear missionaries telling about the Chinese way being the right way, and even after arriving in China I still felt the same at times but I am beginning to see their viewpoint. My coming to China was not my choice but I now am glad to be here. In time it may become almost as dear to me as my own native land. I like to eat Chinese food for it really is delicious and their way of serving it does have this to commend itself in that there are so few dishes to wash. I did not come to China to get out of washing dishes but it seems to be a natural consequence.

There are several reasons why I like Chinese clothing. The first reason is that one can so cheaply hire them made. I have just had a garment made of an unusually good grade of percale. The cloth and all the hand work cost

$1.71 for the cover that almost reaches my knees. There is no style to choose, for they are all made alike. The Chinese do not use buttons but make loops and knots of the goods. Then they are all in one piece, and there are no extra collars or belts to think about and have straight. They are not tight anywhere. Last but not least the Chinese prefer to have us wear Chinese clothing, and when we get into the work, they are less likely to be thinking of our clothes when we want them to think about our message.

Yangchow, December 14, 1920

Chinese from first to last means the hardest kind of digging but that is most of my job these days. We have had about two hundred characters but the worst is yet to come.There were a number of things they want us to have that are too bulky to pack and can just as cheaply be bought here in China.

One thing I have had to buy was a mattress and an oil skin cover and mat to wrap it all in for use when traveling. The mat and cover could not have been bought at home but it would be very handy even there for camping. In China one takes their bed with them and they wrap all their bedding in one bundle. Wherever you stop for the night, you spread out your bed on the floor of the inn or house-boat or on the ground once in a while.

I heard some one say the other day that the two chief characteristics of the CIM are kindness and common sense and I believe it is true if the little I have seen of it is correct.

Yangchow, December 19, 1920

Yesterday I went to Chinese Sunday School. We can not all go every Sunday because there is not room, and too many foreigners would attract too much attention. One of the older missionaries spoke, and for the first time I heard the gospel presented in simple enough Chinese so that I could understand. It sounded even better than it does in English. Just to understand the drift of it was a great joy to me.

Saturday we went for a walk to what is known as the Five Roofed Bridge. It is a beautiful thing and one of the sights of Yangchow, but is hard to describe. On the way we saw some beggars. One little girl not much older but no bigger than Winifred followed us a couple of blocks and knelt clear down to the ground every few feet. We are always told never to give to the beggars for if we did they would surround us from all sides and would stop at nothing to get money. We are never supposed to carry money with us nor to try to buy things. The servant sent along always to escort us carries the money for rides on the canal if we cross or for those who ride on anything else.

Yangchow, December 24, 1920

We are beginning to celebrate Christmas already and it is so good to be here although I would so much enjoy being there at home just for Christmas. Tonight about thirty Chinese girls came up on the veranda and sang "Hark the Herald Angels Sing" and "While Shepherds Watched Their Flocks by Night" while we were eating supper. They sang in Chinese, of course, but oh how I wish you could have heard them! They sang so beautifully, and some were singing alto. After supper we went over to their school and sang for them in English and they came where they could hear without our knowing it.

Tonight one of the teachers came to my room to tell me I am doing much better with Chinese than at first and my Chinese teacher makes favorable comments every now and then, but to me the glory does not belong. Only the Lord can ever give me this language.

We girls have gone together to buy books for the three missionaries in the home. But most of the money this year must go for famine relief. We do not see much of it here but millions are starving and it does seem more terrible to us here than it would at home. Perhaps I have already written that a man was on the street of Yangchow trying to sell his boys who were from the famine district. We hear and know more about it than at home.

Yangchow, January 22, 1921

Saturday four new young women arrived, one from Norway, one from Germany, and two from Switzerland. This is the first woman to come from Germany since the war began. Of those from Switzerland one is French Swiss and the other German Swiss.

Yangchow, February 26, 1921

There is no place quite like China for me now. California may have its climate and a lot of other great advantages, but if the Lord tarry "I hope when I die, I shall breathe my last sigh" in China. It would suit me to be learning the language more quickly; however, that is coming gradually, and perhaps by another year it will be possible to show the Chinese that the only way to God the Father is by our Lord Jesus Christ. They already know that there is a God and that He made all things (which is more than some of the people at home know) but that can never save them from sin.

Today I went for a short walk into the country. We saw them plowing with a very crude plow which was drawn by one ox. Since coming to Yangchow I have not seen a horse nor an automobile. If you want to go anywhere from here you have to go by canal, ride a little donkey scarcely as big as a burro, go by sedan chair carried by two men, ride a rickshaw or a wheel barrow, or walk. By the way the women do travel by wheel barrow. They are not like ours though, for they have a large wheel in the middle and a small platform on each side. So many of the women here in Yangchow especially of the upper classes have bound feet not much bigger at the bottom than a baby's, so it makes it very difficult for them to walk much. I have seen coolies haul two women one on each side of the wheel on a wheel barrow.

They reap their grain just as they did in Bible times with the same kind of scythe, then they gather it in large bundles and tie two of these each to a stick. They put the stick over their shoulder and sometimes the bundle is so large it nearly goes down to the ground. They thresh the grain by first sweeping the dust off the ground or else spreading mats on it and then they drive an ox over it. Another method they have is to take small bundles at a time and hit them hard on a table or frame until the grain is pounded out of it. This is the women's method. They still grind with stones here. Here in the home the servants make the peanut butter by grinding the peanuts with stones. It takes one of them a half day to grind us a week's supply. It certainly is delicious peanut butter.

"Yangtse River boat."

They do not have many wells and so many of the men make it their occupation to go around carrying water. Water is also carried on a pole put over one shoulder or else on a wheel barrow. Principle streets which lead down to the canal are always wet by the water they slop over. This is not strange for so many of the water carriers are blind.

A great many of the houses are bamboo plastered over with mud with a thatched roof. There are brick houses but they are all enclosed within brick walls. Chinese try in every way to keep out evil spirits. They have an idea that the spirits can only go straight, so you often see a high brick wall a little wider and higher than the door built in front of it.

Hankow, April 27, 1921

My time and my strength have had to be put on my studies recently. My first examination was just finished this afternoon. Now I am free to answer letters.

The past few weeks have held much excitement. So many of us who had been together and had become such friends this winter were packing up to leave for many different parts of China. We left Yangchow Wednesday morning, April 20. We went by launch to Chinkiang and arrived there at noon. From there the three young women going to Yunnan had a very short time to wait to catch the train for Shanghai. In the afternoon the rest of us bought some things to eat and went for a walk. We went to the graveyard where Hudson Taylor and so many others are buried who did so much of the pioneer work here in China. Many babies and little children are buried there. It has cost tremendously to bring the work in China to where it is now.

The next morning we stopped at Nanking but could see little of the place from the boat. The second morning the Canadian woman got off at six o'clock at Anking. A native boat came out to meet us and fastened to the steamer. She scrambled down into the boat, and we watched her baggage being put into the boat. We parted as the boat was untied, the steamer never stopping at all.

That afternoon we stopped at Kiukiang where much of the most beautiful china is made. Displays were brought right onto the steamer.

The river, of course, that we were traveling on is the muddy, dirty Yangtze; however, when the moon shines on it, there is a certain beauty about it that is very hard to describe. Some of the way we must have been miles from either shore.

When traveling in China, one must keep an eagle eye on his baggage which includes his bed. If one runs out of anything, there is no place to buy. There are no faucets either. If one wants to wash his face, he must have something of his own to get water in.

We arrived here in Hankow at the CIM home on Saturday. This is a nicely furnished house set in the midst of the foreign concession. After being on the dirty, smelly steamer, it seems good to be here where there is hot and cold running water. In the afternoon we enjoyed a walk partly on the wide cement walk along the river front. Here there are even automobiles, the first I have seen for six months.

From here I am to go to Changteh which is on the largest lake in China. There is a couple there with small children named Mr. and Mrs. E.J. Bannan and a young woman from North America named Catherine Chaffee. The plan is to prepare Miss Chaffee and me to take over the work in Nanchowting when Mr. and Mrs. G.F. Draffin who are there, go home on furlough.

Changteh, May 16, 1921

Changteh is a fine place to be, and the people here are splendid. If only I could describe things so you might see it as we see it. There is a brick wall about twenty feet high and about eight to ten feet thick around the main part of the city, an area of about a mile and a half long by three quarters of a mile wide. Of course this is only the part inside the wall and it is a very thickly populated city. The wall is about twenty feet high. There are steps at each gate so that we can climb up and walk on the top of the wall. At each gate there is a tower which is convenient for a look out. The gates are lifted by ropes into the tower during the day. The gates are very heavy, giving me more meaning to: "Lift up your heads, oh ye gates, and be lifted up ye everlasting doors, and the King of Glory shall come in."

Just at bedtime last night someone quoted the verse: "There shall no evil befall thee neither shall any plague come near thy dwelling place." How little did we realize the need to claim that verse before morning. At half past three we got up because the second place from here was on fire. The blaze gave us light to dress by. The building occupied by the oil company was burned, and ten families were made homeless. The fire caught in the upper storey of a chemist's shop. Some men were gambling and upset a lamp. The proprietor of the place has been put in jail. They put a great deal of the furniture from the burning houses and those they were afraid would burn in the courtyard next door. And even we had water handy upstairs to throw on the roof or veranda in case they set fire. They do have a great advantage in having the high brick walls and they do have a kind of fire department. Men carry water by the hundreds and they have a crude kind of engine to shoot water into the air. These most of all appeal to the Chinese by the amount of noise they make when hauled over the stone pavement.

Saturday a baby boy was born to the Draffins. This is their third child.

They had come to Changteh for its arrival. Mr. Draffin and Mr. Bannan have each written to Shanghai to ask them not to send Miss Chaffee and I to Nanchowting because they think it is too big an undertaking for two young women so new in the work. But so far the only reply is that there is no other way to provide for Nanchowting. Things are so unsettled because of robbers and soldiers not having been paid that it really is a man's job but there are no men to send. It is a hundred miles from here and is twenty miles from the nearest station worked by any other mission. There are ten or eleven out stations and three or four hundred church members. Of course there is not another foreigner in Nanchowting. Miss Chaffee who will be my companion there is a few years older than I and has been in China a year longer.[5]

Changteh, May 17, 1921

We were invited to an English gun boat this afternoon. It probably would not have come if the water had not been unusually high. But the occasion for their coming was some robberies, firing on a British boat, etc. It was American missionaries who have been robbed. Really England and America get along together very well except at home where the wool has been pulled over the eyes of the people by yellow newspapers. They served tea on board and showed us around. They keep about eighty men on board.

My medicines are now beginning to come in handy, my boric acid especially. A German nurse, who could afford to bring very little with her, thanked me over and over for giving her boric acid for her sore eyes. I have shared the pound I brought also with two missionaries going farther inland. The other day my oil of cloves stopped the tears of a little girl crying with a toothache.

Changteh, May 19, 1921

People in China make such a lot of noise over doing things. At school the teacher shouts the lesson out, and the pupils bawl it out after him at the top of their voices. This must strengthen their lungs at any rate. You can always tell when nearing a Chinese school by the sounds. The men who carry things always make much noise, but this does warn anyone to clear the track.

Changteh, June 1, 1921

Today I started helping two women who want to learn to read. One is a widow who weaves for a living. She says others laugh at her when she asks what the characters are. They want to know why an old woman should want to read. What seems strange to me is that I am helping grown people of another country how to read their own language.

Changteh, June 10, 1921

It is just eight months today since we landed In China, and not one day or hour when I have not been glad the Lord let me come. We who know him never have to depend on environment or any outward circumstances for happiness.

One of the biggest nuisances here in China is that when one buys anything you ask the price and the shop keeper nearly always asks more than he expects to get or else asks you to name your price. The Chinese call it "chiang chia." Here they pronounce it "jang" and it means literally "to discuss the price." But I think we got our word jangle from China. About the only thing they do not "chiang chia" on is postage stamps so I made a try at buying some the other day. It was my intention to get two dollars worth and have some three cent as well as five cent ones. But to my sorrow in Yangchow they call postage stamps "hsin p'iao" and here they are called "in hua." But by the time the man had counted out a dollar's worth, after offering me post cards and some other things, so many had gathered to see the "foreigner" buy stamps that I concluded it was time to get away from there.

Changteh, June 25, 1921

Besides attending Chinese prayers and a women's meeting today, I went for a walk and studied the rest of the day. The studying is just what I want to do. I am still on the gospel of John. On two of the chapters I have found fewer than ten characters to look up after my first time through it. The Lord has done great things for me, but how I do long for the day when I can be a greater help to these people!

There seems to be no way to avoid a trip to Kuling for the summer. The doctor who was here Sunday evening said it would not do to stay from the health point of view. With no more language than I can use I could hardly manage being the only foreign woman in a city this size. The main thing to consider is Chinese "kuei-chu" which means they would not consider it proper for me to be here alone.[6]

Kuling, July 1, 1921

This is a beautiful place about four thousand feet above sea level. It is the summer resort for business people as well as missionaries. Many sick people from all over China are sent here for their health.

We came by steamer to Kiukiang. From there we came part of the way by automobile, then up the hill in sedan chairs. Those who weighed less than 175 pounds had to hire four bearers. Those who weighed more had to have more.

Since coming here Miss Chaffee has been ill. She has had the attention of a doctor and a nurse. Evidently she has malaria.

Kuling, July 21, 1921

Miss Chaffee went to the hospital. The doctor doesn't seem to know what the trouble is, but her stomach is upset, and she has a temperature.

Up here there are many conferences and fine speakers, but studying the language is the most important thing I have to do. Also I must do plenty of walking to be strong enough to do things this fall. There are some very

"Scene at Kuling."

good trails for walking here. The trouble is that they nearly all start going down. Then one must climb up. The views of the plain from up here are wonderful. The Yangtze, which is wide enough to float good sized steamers, looks like a yellow ribbon. There are lakes and rivers and water falls to add to the beauty up here, and I'm enjoying the lovely flowers.

Kuling, August 15, 1921

Miss Chaffee is back after three weeks in the hospital. She is a very good natured person, very easy to live with. She has an abundance of reddish golden hair long enough to sit on the ends even though it is wavy. We are so glad she is feeling better.

There is one thing I cannot understand. Why should men settle down in such tiny little churches at home? Out here in China they do not put a missionary in a little town like Lindsay or Porterville let alone a place like Strathmore. They have so much territory and so many out stations besides. I wonder at times what the people at home are thinking about, or if they are really thinking. We do have twenty-seven missionaries in Changteh for instance, but six stay at out stations one of which is eighty miles away. Some are in educational and medical work. But, as I have said before, the population is fully one hundred and fifty thousand. The task before us is simply tremendous. I am glad to be out here to help even a little.

Kuling, August 30, 1921

Most of the meetings are over, and the people have gone back to their work. I will be glad when my turn comes to go. The only boats now going through to Changteh are escorted by gun boats. One missionary accused me of wanting excitement. But business people do not give up because of some little thing in the way, so why should we who are on the business of the King?

We just heard of another bad earthquake up in the north. The first official reports, in fact all reports of famines and such things from the officials, are as bad as they can make them so that government and foreign appropriations will be as large as possible so they can pocket some of the money. Politics in China are corrupt to the core. And probably the majority of the officials in China would actually sell the country to get some money for themselves, and that is almost what they are doing with Japan. The soldiers besides are unpaid, some not having been paid for a year or two. Then when they bring too much pressure on the officials, they give the soldiers permission to loot a city and take everything they can lay hands on. The officials are immensely wealthy and the people pay taxes enough but the money goes in the wrong direction. Talk about class distinctions and corrupt politics and labor problems—as far as the laborer is concerned it surely does not look very encouraging. They need not tell us that education will help matters, for the officials of China have always had education, and some who have gone through the Western schools are the most corrupt of all.

Up here this summer we have often heard such severe criticism of the Bible Union, which above everything else stands for the inspiration of the whole Bible. Some say we are dividing the missionary forces, and in separating ourselves from the others we are not showing a Christlike spirit. Perhaps the people at home do not care that young missionaries are being sent out who tear down the faith of the Chinese which the older missionaries gave their lives to plant. The Lord cares though, and we do need to pray that the right thing shall be done. We ought to love the people who do not believe the Bible, but the Lord forgive those who come out and tear down faith in the Bible and our Lord for they know not what they do.[7]

Miss Chaffee is some better after her hospital stay. Now the doctor is sending her out to walk. I am one who thinks he is on the right track. Since being in China I am known for the way I walk.

Kuling, September 17, 1921

Even though it is so late in the fall I am still stranded up here at Kuling, and they may want me to stay until the end of the month. It is getting a little cool, especially now that we have not seen the sun for a week. In the middle of the summer there were about two thousand foreigners up here on this hill but now there are about two hundred. There are some people who stay up here all the time. There is a good hospital and two boarding schools. One is a private school and one is for the children of American missionaries.

Some parts of China have had too much rain this summer, causing floods again. So there will be almost as much talk about famine again this winter as there was last. In other places there has not been enough rain. People were compelled to dig up their rice to plant opium and now these places are lacking food. In districts where the soldiers have not been paid, they often have divided in bands and systematically looted every place they came to. If the people would not or could not give the soldiers what they were asking for, their houses were burned. Besides all this there is a large district that has been seriously damaged by earthquake. That however may have been a blessing in disguise. The Mohammedans were just planning a great uprising before that, and the earthquake completely swallowed up one of the main leaders and several hundred followers. They, being very superstitious, were then afraid to go on with the undertaking. Those in that district say that never before has it been so open to the gospel. China is in a sad state, but it would not take you long to wonder if you saw the hideous things they worship. Of course another explanation is that there are nearly four times as many people in China as in the United States, but it is only two-thirds as large. If there were six times as many people in the United States as there are, what would become of them?

Kuling, September 22, 1921

A very sad piece of news came to us yesterday. Mrs. Bannan passed away from cholera. She had eaten some bananas which must have contained the germs the night before she boarded the steamer in Shanghai. Word has now come that the wife of one of the Presbyterian doctors in Changteh will keep the two girls along with her four children for a year until she and her husband are due for furlough.

Probably Mr. Bannan will go back alone to work in Changteh, and I will be sent to work with the Draffins in Nanchowting. For me this would be a great tumble from working with people like the Bannans to be with the Draffins.

Some of our things left this morning. We are leaving in the morning. Where I go is in the Lord's hands, and I realize His ways are best though it is difficult to understand the removal of a person like Mrs. Bannan. She knew the language and how to work with people. Her Bible woman knows how to take complete charge of the women at Changteh. Some of her former servants are evangelists, and some are in training for definite Christian work.[8]

Changteh, October 10, 1921

In Hankow on the way back I had my eyes tested, and I now have new reading glasses. Chinese characters have been hard on my eyes.

The Chinese are very sad about the death of Mrs. Bannan. They are working very hard elaborately decorating the chapel for a memorial service with all the missions in Changteh working together. We foreigners are not asked to help. Most everything will be done in white, the Chinese mourning color. They have made bushels of paper flowers. They do know how to make those.

This has been a sad day. Mr. Bannan returned bringing word that I am to go to Nanchowting soon. Still I am thanking the Lord on this first anniversary of my arrival in China. You remember I landed in China on my birthday. Seeing Mr. Bannan again and seeing the women cry and so many things remind me of the deep loss in losing one I loved. My desire is that the Lord will permit me to live to have the Chinese love me and see Him through me as she did. The way the Christians here praised the Lord that Tao Chiao-shih had peacefully returned was more than worth coming here in the first place. Things are dirty and smell worse than I remembered they did, but I am happy in His service.

Nanchowting, October 21, 1921

This letter was started on the "Ark," a rickety little boat Mr. Draffin received money from a fund to buy supposedly for a preaching band but which is often pressed into service for their convenience. On this boat besides the Draffins is their cook, a woman to help look after the children, a Bible woman, the wife of their evangelist and three young men to work the boat. There is also a preacher on board. So we are squeezed in like sardines in a box now and right next to the Chinese for nearly a week. My choice would have been to stay longer in Changteh. My choice would have been to work with someone other than the Draffins. My choice would have been to keep the Chinese girl Mrs. Bannan hired to be my personal helper and teacher. I will now be in Nanchowting with the Draffins without my helper. I am the first unmarried missionary to be assigned here. The Draffins are good to me in their way, and they think I like them and I do. But they are not the people if I had my choice that I would work with.

We met a family of church members who are having trouble with the officials. A murder occurred next to them last year while they were away, and in China the neighbors are held responsible for what happens . Last year this man paid a lot to get out of trouble and this year he has been summoned again. He can not afford to let them have more money. He was asking Mr. Draffin what to do. We can only tell them to pray. According to CIM rules we can do nothing even in a case like this.[9]

A greater knowledge of medicine and how to use it would be worth nearly everything to me. We see such awful sores on children. I am going to see what can be done with sulphur or iodine. Someone the other day said something about Tao Chiao-shih having "ai-hsin" or heart of love. Some way that is worth many times as much to me as being told I have "tsong-ming" or wisdom. That is what they tell me about my ability to cook or to recognize Chinese characters.

Nanchowting, October 31, 1921

Nearly all this day has been spent out visiting for my first time with the Bible woman, it being the first time everyone wanted to give us something to eat. We had tea at most places. I lost track of how many places after I counted twenty.

If my observations of the women's work here are correct, only a small beginning has been made. Nearly all the work has been done by men for men, and you can never make me think that is the correct way. According to my opinion as much or nearly as much should be done for the women

"A Christian young couple."

as for the men. If the men come into the church without their wives, the wives can prove such a hindrance. This much is certain: the soul of every one of those woman we met today is precious in the sight of my Lord.

They have a school in connection with this place here, but I have not yet had time to visit. So many things around this station need doing. One has reason to wish they could do a dozen things at once. As a result of our calling yesterday there were many more women out at meeting today. I wish there was time each week to spend a day like it. If this place does have a population of thirty thousand, we ought to have more than thirty women out for a women's meeting and far more than a hundred out Sunday morning. I told Mr. Draffin we were only touching the edges of women's work, but he hemmed and hawed trying to push the idea off. We had the chapel full Sunday morning. There were about fifty women and girls there and about twice as many men. Our calling helped the attendance of the women. I stationed myself in the back of the room and tried to usher. One baby in the back started to cry and was nearly scared stiff of me, a foreigner. One old woman left a basket containing two or three chickens in the chapel before the service began then came in during the service to get it. Two or three came inside the door but left when asked to sit down. Some of the children ate peanuts, scrapped, visited, and read out loud, their only way of doing it. Some women drank tea and ran back and forth with babies. There is more that would not look well on paper.

Nanchowting, November 16, 1921

Since my last letter I attended my first wedding in China. It was part foreign and part Chinese. Our chapel was decorated with red and white flowers. A large piece of red cloth was placed on the chair of each one who took part. Mr. Draffin performed the ceremony, and Mrs. Draffin played the wedding march on a folding organ. The bridegroom wore a purple broadcloth gown, a purple satin coat, a red sash that came around over his shoulder, and a foreign hat. This hat was considered special and was kept on during the service. He is a church member about twenty years of age. Since he had never seen the bride before the service, he kept looking sideways to get a good look. The bride was a bright looking girl in her teens. The bridegroom's parents had paid one hundred and twenty dollars Mexican to her parents for her. She wore a blue satin blouse of Chinese style and a beautifully embroidered black skirt. Around her hair she wore a black satin band decorated with flowers. Her shoes were red satin. Red is the color for Chinese brides.

Today the Bible woman and I were invited to visit two homes of the richest clan in Nanchowting. This is the first time missionaries have been there. They listened and were interested in the tracts. Four of the women could recognize characters. I could understand these better educated women, and they could understand me because as yet my language is from books rather than from people. They felt of my dress and were not satisfied until I took my hat off to see my hair.[10]

Nanchowting, November 28, 1921

I feel like having a good cry tonight instead of writing. In the middle of the afternoon a small boy came for quinine for a baby less than two months old. He said the baby was having something like chills. Mrs. Draffin called me from my books and we put on our hats and went. The mother worked for Mrs. Draffin last year and this is her third baby. Mrs. Draffin said she had wanted to tell her how to take care of the baby and save this one. We found that they had only sent for us as a last resort. They had called in a Chinese doctor first, and he had so cruelly burned a place on each side of the mouth and two or three places on the stomach of the baby. If they had called us in when they did him we might have done something. As it was we were afraid to do anything for fear if the baby died on our hands we would be blamed. So we left saying we could do nothing but pray.[11]

Last week we made a trip out into the country six or seven miles to a village somewhat bigger than Strathmore in population. The evangelist, two older men who preach (one employed and one at his own expense), the Bible woman, the school teacher with twenty-seven school children, Mr. Draffin, and I went. The Chinese themselves had done some good work there, but Mr. Draffin and I were the first missionaries. They were quite curious about us. We thought we were going to help them burn idols, but we found in several places that the idols and the mantle piece where they had stood had already been destroyed. We put up some gospel posters on the blank places left on the walls. In the few days we were there we held a number of services. At the one held on the street there was a large crowd. At the end of some of the services I tried to talk with some of the women. They kept interrupting though to ask me questions. The Chinese polite way of doing is to ask your name, then your age, whether your father and mother are living, whether you have grandparents, older brothers or sisters, then your younger brothers and sisters. Then they ask what all these people do and their ages. It is most polite of them to ask and not at all polite not to answer. What amazes them most is that I have four brothers! One time I was trying to talk to the women after the service was over and one of the preachers came along. He really meant to help me by telling them all about me. One thing he said was that I could talk and read in three languages: Chinese, English and American. Anyway one can understand that it is difficult to get in a good word for the Lord sometimes.

Changteh, January 13, 1922

We did go out calling this week of course. At one place there was a woman whom they say is demon possessed. It is the second case I have seen in China. The Bible woman has been there before and says the woman is much better than she has been, for she once did not know enough to wear her clothes. But she is bad enough even yet. We had prayer together there. The people have not been interested in the chapel before, but so many of the people out here when they meet with something they need help for turn to us as a last resort.[12]

Nanchowting, January 28, 1922

Last week we had a very heavy snow fall the first of the week. Before it scarcely was through snowing a man came in who was sent by the famine relief committee. Mr. Draffin had to go with him and was gone five days. There were some places in the district where they have not had a harvest for five years. But those places are small and most of the men can find work and the women beg. But very likely some relief work should be undertaken at once. Then, not many hours later the evangelist came in to see Mrs. Draffin. One of the church members at an out-station over fifteen miles from here had been put in prison unjustly. Mrs. Draffin told him he could do as he liked about going. So off he went and he got the man out of prison. All he did was to send his card into the yamen [government office], and even though there was nothing written on it but his name that was enough. The man who was sent to that out-station to keep the rice from going through is taking bribes, and he tried to make that church member a sort of scapegoat. The man was getting eighty dollars a month to keep the rice in Hunan, and here he has been letting people send it out if they pay him what he wanted. The church member has a shop on the border and is a rice dealer. He may have disobeyed the law but there is no evidence of it. However it is quite a different matter whether rice is sold out in small quantities or whether it is shipped out by the boat load. The worst of it is, that official has moved into our chapel there and was gambling and doing worse things there. He is a church member too, but there is not much doubt about it that he will not be when you read this letter, or an official either.

Today is Chinese New Years Day. Firecrackers could be heard all night. Today we are spending most of the time receiving guests. Shops are closed for a couple of weeks while everyone has a good time feasting, and the heathen go through a lot of idolatrous proceedings. Last night we counted the lights on a good many graves. These are built to keep the spirits warm. Clean paper is now put on front doors, and new idols are set in place. We need to pray now especially for the new Christians that they may not fall back and replace their idols.

Nanchowting, March 23, 1922

The written part of my second examination has been done. This has taken three full half days. With this over the required work for the first two years will be done. The hard work was worthwhile since it is preparation to make the gospel known to many who have never heard of the love of our Lord Jesus.

At the conference we attended recently the matter of foot binding came up. The (Chinese) evangelists waxed eloquent about it, and the oldest man in the group, a man more than seventy, had the most to say against it. One of the best arguments he used was that a girl with bound feet could not study. The suggestion was made that the church perform no marriage ceremony for a girl unless she lets out her feet. Hereafter a man or woman in the church will be disciplined for binding a daughter's feet.

Nanchowting, April 26, 1922

This has been a week of study, but I did go to a feast, spent an afternoon teaching a young church member, and gave a short talk at a women's meeting. Even a few minutes talk was not an easy thing, but one does have to make a beginning. A young girl came to me a couple of times to have her eyes washed with boric acid. Besides using such treatment, I do believe in divine healing. We do have some remarkable answers to prayer. The church members seem to have much sense about such things. They all agree that if there is idolatry going on in the home, it is useless to pray. The Chinese helpers told me later that in the place where I helped care for a baby that later died, incense was being burned.

Perhaps you have read a little about the anti-Christian movement among the students here in China. They are enjoying themselves letting off steam, but perhaps it will not last long. Perhaps it will open the eyes of people at home a bit that the so-called student movement in China is not so friendly to we foreigners after all. Also that America's use of the Boxer indemnity money was not altogether so commendable. And talk about the patriotism of the Chinese—I have not seen any of it except in display. Japan is not nearly so bad an enemy to China as she herself. It is enough to make your blood boil to see how little their own officials care for the rights or welfare of the people.[13]

Tomorrow morning we expect to start for Changteh by native boat. All the others going are Chinese, and I have been telling them we will start right after breakfast. The Draffins are looking on with amusement probably thinking I can not get them started before eleven. Perhaps not. You know I am devoid of that thing they call "American hustle".

Nanchowting, May 13, 1922

We went and got back from our trip to Changteh safe and sound. Some of the foreigners in Changteh thought it a little rash for one who has been in China no longer than I to take a trip by native boat a hundred miles and back with no one but Chinese. We were on the trip each way four days, but I would have been no more afraid at home. We are always safe no matter where we are where the Lord chooses to "keep his angels encamped round about us".

The Chinese laughed about how Tao chiao-shih got up every night to chase bed bugs. Each night going I found at least five, one night fifteen. When we came back, there were not as many, but we had fleas which were even worse.

Nanchowting, May 25, 1922

For my next examination I must study from Romans to Hebrews, most of Genesis, and some other things. Do not pity me, for I would rather study than eat. Especially I enjoy studying the Bible.

After women's meeting today Mrs. Draffin and I went out calling on the sick. We visited three homes. At each someone was sick, but at one there were four sick. They look to us so when they are ill. If you could see the way most of them live, you would not wonder that so many are ill and die; rather, you would wonder that any of them live. It would be so much easier to keep away from them than to go among them and love them as we should. Their houses are not merely dirty. They are filthy. The streets just smelled awful today.

Changteh, July 10, 1922

I am back in Changteh again and will be going on to Teh-Shan for the rest of the summer. That is a small place about five miles from here. Miss Chaffee has gone with the Draffins to Kuling for the summer. Although she has better health than last year, she still is not strong.

The last day before leaving Nanchowting I made a few calls all by myself. I do not know what the Chinese think of my doing this, but they tell me to my face that they are not worthy of having Tao chiao-shih come to see them all by herself. I am so thankful for having the language as well as I do and the love of the people in so short a time.

I could not make you see things as they are here even though I wrote a thousand letters. The open shops on the street are different. There are gold shops, silver shops, brass shops, silk and other kinds of cloth shops, food shops, tea shops, shoe shops where both foreign and Chinese shoes are sold, shops where rice and other kinds of grain are sold besides peas and beans. The silk or gold shops are closed, have windows in front and have large brass signs. Some of the little open shops most certainly are shabby and dirty. The meat hangs in the front exposed to anything that comes along until someone puts it on the stove to cook it. They never wrap it up but put a stick through it and carry it by that or put it in an open basket. No street scene would be complete without some lousy wolflike dogs and some miserable beggars and a blind man playing a crude instrument, a remote ancestor of the fiddle. It is surprising to see some things you can buy and some things not to be bought. Stockings, buttons, needles, pins, safety pins, thread, thimbles, you can not buy. But you can find vacuum or thermos bottles, one burner oil stoves, and lots of enameled things. Besides there are many things in silk, linen, embroidered silk, silver and brass ornaments, and baskets that would be hard to find at home.

Teh Shan, July 26, 1922

From this hill we can see several pagodas. The tallest is seven stories. Each story would be about ten feet high. There are some large temples and some tombs of China's great men. There is also a large stone bridge built simply of great slabs of granite. We can see Changteh from here as it is only about five miles away. And you should see the little boats down on the river. There are so many shapes and sizes of them; nearly all are either sailing or row boats. But a few launches go by each day. More beautiful than any of the built things are the green covered hillls, the large river with its changing shades of color, the trees along the bank and the mountains in the distance. I really wish you could see this place. But there are so many things I have seen in China that I am glad you can never see.

The two young men Miss Danford has with her are helping me fine. Each is supposed to help an hour a day. She helps them more than that with their English. Nearly all the government schools teach it to them, and I suppose we will just have to use that for bait at times. Most of the really educated young people in China speak more or less English. A great part of the instruction in colleges and middle schools is done in English. Most of the business people out here only employ servants who can speak English. They charge at least three or four times as much as those who cannot speak English, and they so frequently take advantage by accepting commissions and charging their employers more than they should for what they buy. It costs a business person a great deal more to live in China than one of us missionaries who have had to buckle down and learn to speak the language. Not that I speak it either, but I can generally make one of the servants understand what is wanted if they want to understand.

Teh Shan, August 5, 1922

We are having a lot of rain, perhaps too much, as it is nearing time to harvest the rice. When rice is both the bread and the potatoes to these people, we like to see them have their crops of rice. There are quite a lot of famine refugees around here. Some famine relief work has been done but some have died of hunger. Some come to Changteh from such distant places they are nearly dead before they get here. Miss Danford whom I am staying with saw a woman dying of starvation in one of the doorways. When she went back past the next day the woman was dead. That day she gave out tickets to four starving women and two children to go to a place where they were giving out food. In Changteh we see so many women carrying wood and other heavy loads. I never saw them doing coolie work in Changteh—no doubt all the women we see carrying things in Changteh now are from the famine.

Teh Shan, August 19, 1922

Most of last week I spent in bed. I had malaria, a sun headache, and some other complaints. The doctor was called from Changteh. He couldn't get a boat, so he walked up. The medicine he gave helped right away. I now feel fine except I don't feel like making any effort. I've been careful to wear a hat and keep away from mosquitoes, but keeping well in China is difficult.

Changteh, September 28, 1922

There is fighting between here and Yochow which is keeping some of our mail from moving. Miss Chaffee has been wondering if any of the mail held up was for us. Things in Changteh are near normal.

The last two weeks while the Bible woman has been ill I have led the women's meetings. At home a number of women might hear, and that would be the end of it. Here we can multiply the group because most of those who come, pass on what they get.

We have been to afternoon prayer meeting. The man who led had fixed the organ this morning by blowing through all the reeds. It is a good thing he did because he had plenty of wind left as it was.

Changteh, October 27, 1922

Yesterday I was over at the Presbyterian mission all day. That does not happen very often, though. We were invited to dinner where the Chinese evangelist over there is staying. He speaks English and eats foreign food. He uses such a lot of scripture and never seems to refer to the Chinese classics, a thing they do so often. The evangelist himself is a young man from the most unlikely place to think of finding an evangelist. He comes from the wealthy official and educated class of Chinese. That class of men are usually too proud to acknowledge their need for a Savior. But the girl he married had been in a mission school, and was there converted. She not only prayed but asked others to pray, and what is impossible with men but not with God happened.

The Draffins hope to sail for the States on December 2nd, going by way of Vancouver. She has been away from her home ten years, met her husband in China, and now has three little children.

Changteh, November 11, 1922

Early Thursday Miss Chaffee, the Bible woman, and I started to an outstation, and we did not get back until about dark Saturday. In the evenings we opened up the street chapel, and both evenings it was crowded. Friday evening there must have been over two hundred there. Few stayed for the whole meeting for which you can not blame them because it lasted a couple of hours. Most Chinese do not have good terminal facilities.

On Saturday we went to a place across the river where a small preaching place has opened. About thirty or more women gathered for the impromptu meeting where the evangelist, the Bible woman, and "yours truly" spoke. After that we went to the grave of the inquirer who had opened this chapel. People came running from all directions through the fields until about seventy had gathered. We sang a hymn and held another service. We can only pray that some heart may have been touched.

Changteh, January 27, 1923

Our evangelist from Nanchow was here last week. Miss Chaffee had to send for him on account of some money matters that she did not understand clearly. She probably does not know the situation any better now that she has seen him. She has had to write to Shanghai. The trouble is that there is not money enough to pay the people that are supposed to be employed. The books show where all the money went that came in. So you see the problem was to know how the money was to be stretched, or in other words it is a question of how to make ends meet. We perhaps all have that kind of problem. They want to employ six evangelists at sixty dollars each, a gate keeper to look after the chapel in the main place and his wife to help with women's work, and a boy to help with the boat when they go out. In all it means nearly five hundred dollars a year for a district that includes hundreds of thousands of people. But some may have to be discharged because of lack of funds. The Chinese themselves do quite a bit of voluntary work. And they pay for the oil for their lamps and something toward the upkeep of their chapels and incidentals. One thing that happened to cause the problem is that one hundred dollars a year given formerly has been withdrawn.

Changteh, February 16, 1923

My third examination was finished last week. Now there is only one more to take. Sunday my Junior Missionary Certificate arrived. This is given for passing the required examinations and proving oneself a missionary during the first two years. Until now I have been known as a probationer. When we are out five years, we are counted as senior missionaries.

This is Chinese New Year's Day. About thirty came to the watch night service last night to see their old year out and the New Year in. For the first time in China I spoke for a few minutes to both men and women. Now that the ice is broken it will not be the last time.

Yesterday we had the Bannan baby here most of the day. Mr. Bannan came by in the afternoon. The baby is doing fine. She can talk both Chinese and English. It is remarkable how soon children learn whether to speak English or Chinese. The Bannan baby is not quite two years old, and she knows when to speak each language.

Changteh, March 8, 1923

Of course we did go to the out-station. That only took us three days, but we had a good time there. One school girl came and invited us to go to her home. She came to the meeting crying. It seems they wanted her to get married instead of going back to school. She is only sixteen and she lacks only a few months of finishing grammar school. We went and the girl's mother listened to the Bible woman preach. She also asked us to come back again. When we came back I just mentioned the fact we had been there to the head of the school where the girl goes. She then told me that girl was the finest she had in school, and also that she was not expecting her back but the night before she got word she was coming. She said the girl was attending the inquirer's class until compelled to stop by her father. She added she had work for the girl to do as pupil teacher if the parents would consent, but she had no way of reaching them. The teacher then urged me to take the Bible woman and go to the girl's home every time we go to the out-station.

Changteh, March 16, 1923

The wife of the evangelist tells me about the people being afraid to drink her tea for fear of eating the foreign religion. I told her I wished they were that much afraid of using tobacco.

On Saturday morning while at the out-station the people did not come to the meeting as the Bible woman had asked them to, so she suggested that the two of us go to a certain place. No back yard at home would look anywhere nearly as bad, but she told them she was going to preach. There is no way to stop her when she gets started, but I wondered what she would do. She started by telling the people that we had spent a lot of money to come from Changteh (perhaps a dollar, but that was a lot in her eyes) and that we came for nothing else than to preach the true doctrine. Then she told them what it cost them for the false religions when we did not charge them anything. Then she said, "You will not come to the church to hear us, so we are going to have a meeting right here". She then told them to sweep the yard and bring out some benches. Two slouchy looking women who heard this order paid no attention. One was changing a child's garments which contained a generous share of "live stock". Someone else heard, and in a very short time the yard was swept, and the benches were arranged in a circle. We hung up a hymn poster on the dirty outside wall of the house. This hymn has a well liked Chinese tune.While we were singing, about fifty people gathered and listened to a half hour of preaching. After the meeting we talked with those who stayed and gave them another invitation to come to church. Never before had I been a party to going out in the highways and byways to compel the people to come in.

Changteh, April 12, 1923

In the children's meeting yesterday we were talking about Moses and how the Lord looked after the Israelites while they went through the wilderness. I asked the children what the people did for shoes. They spoke right up three or four at once saying they wore straw sandals. When the Chinese go on a trip they are very apt to put on straw sandals and save their shoes which are mostly made of cloth until they get to their destination.

Changteh, May 14, 1923

As soon as we got to the out-station this time we were told about the woman for whom we had prayed on our last visit. She had promised us that if we prayed for her, she would have the household idols taken down and burned. This has been done, and the woman is well again after our prayer for healing. When we went to see her, we found her very happy. She had learned two verses of scripture and about two pages of catechism and was anxious to hear more.

There are just about enough of the Sunday School cards you sent left to last until we go away for the summer if we do not give each child one every Sunday. Last Sunday there were twenty five children who came. The picture rolls came recently. Those I use most for meetings, I will have mounted on Chinese paper and fixed like scrolls. Some of them are precious and will be used many times. Some are hung in the school room and in the guest room. A few will be given to children who learn a number of verses, but no child would be given more than one big picture in a year. They are all much appreciated.

Hankow, June 28, 1923

Our trip to the out-station was not altogether satisfactory. Miss Chaffee went with me and came back the second day. She had to be back to get ready and take the women's meeting. The day after she left Wednesday nearly eighty women came and listened well. Among them were ten flower girls we had invited the day before. You may not know what a flower girl is, but a flower girl or a singing girl is a bad woman. Some of these were not more than twelve and were sold into that kind of life.

We are in Hankow now. It only took us two days to get here. The foreign concession looks good with its real streets and a few more marks of civilization. They even have automobiles here. Tomorrow we are going by train to Kikungshan.[14]

The Draffins wrote that their date for sailing to Australia is in August. They will stay about a year there around Mr. Draffin's home.

Kikungshan, July 9, 1923

Miss DeJong with the Bannan baby, Miss Chaffee, and I had a compartment second class on the train coming up here. The last night in Hankow was too hot to sleep. As we went up the grade the weather was changing. At the station we put on raincoats for warmth. That night I slept under a double blanket and my steamer rug and was really not warm enough. After the train ride we came up the hill by sedan chair. In the houses belonging to the CIM here there is room for forty people. Right now there are thirteen of us here, nine of whom were at the Bible Institute in Los Angeles together. The hills here are velvety green. The terraced rice fields look like stair steps covered with beautiful carpet. Here and there one can see silver threads of streams. It is good to be away from the smells, sights, and sounds of the valley as well as from the heat that seems to press one down.

Kikungshan, August 8, 1923

Everything is going the same as usual. We go for a walk nearly every day. There generally are some meetings going on. We do not get all of them, of course. Mr. Hunter has arrived from Los Angeles to speak to us. How good it does seem to see him and hear what is going on in Los Angeles.

This is a great place to spend money. For one thing I had some dental work done. Two fillings had come out of my teeth in the spring. I thought I should have those fixed without waiting for a toothache. I suppose I should have been thankful that the charge was about fourteen dollars Mexican (seven dollars in gold) as it had been a full two years since my teeth were looked after.

Except for malaria which I get once in a while I usually keep fairly well. The altitude at Changteh is about one hundred twenty feet, low, damp, and hot. By coming away I have been free of malaria this summer. My junior certificate would not have been given me if I did not have fairly good health. Miss Chaffee still does not have hers for that reason.

This week I have been studying a text book used in Chinese fifth grades, with a Chinese teacher. This book has a great deal of what is called Wenli in it. Up to now nearly everything has been Mandarin which is what people talk. Wenli is the old literary style. I hope to study more than is required in order to be able to teach more of the Bible than the first foundation principles.[15]

Do not worry about what you read in the papers about bandits. The safest place for us is where the Lord wants us. I know of only one foreigner in the hands of the bandits now. He is an old Italian Roman Catholic priest. I do hope that the foreign concessions are maintained and not put in the hands of the Chinese. There could be quite a story told of dishonesty and corruption in Chinese politics. One of their proverbs says it, "The little fish eat bugs, and the big fish eat little fish".

We have had a few picnics up here. Every Wednesday night is a musical evening. We have sessions on methods of work and many prayer meetings. Yesterday we had a day of prayer for all on the hill.

Up here there are heavy fogs. When the sun comes out, everything must be aired and dried. This included clothes, bedding, books, shoes, and insides of suitcases. The verandas are thus beautifully decorated with so much on display. Anyway the fog is refreshingly cool. Today I am wearing a woolen dress for comfort.

Hankow, August 30, 1923

Coming back the walk down the hill from Kikungshan to the station took me an hour. The train was on time, and we arrived in Hankow at nine thirty in the evening. We came on to the mission house by ricksha. When we arrived here, we were given ice cream and ice water. That ice cream tasted very good. It had been two years since my last chance to have any, and it was such a sweltering hot evening that anything cold helped.

Changteh, September 14, 1923

Miss Chaffee and I have been back nearly two weeks. Miss DeJong and little Phyllis Bannan made the trip with us. The trip from Hankow took three days. The boat, which should have started at noon, was underway at six o'clock. By the time we were really out of sight of Hankow, it was dark. Two hundred people were on a boat that holds one hundred thirty comfortably. About sixty men got off in a small boat to be picked up later before we went through customs at Yochow. That was another delay in the heat, but little things like that do not count in China. The second night there was quite a row because the captain intended to anchor for the night. After a lengthy and loud discussion in which the captain was threatened with a beating, the decision was made to start when the moon rose. Our group was discussed in the argument too. We foreigners were accused of taking up more than our share of room (which was not true).

We arrived after dark on Sunday. Mr Bannan was there to meet us. We had to wait to get our baggage to shore by small boat. Then we got rickshas to carry our things to the compound. We had brought springs for our beds and groceries for six months including milk and potatoes.

Now for some plain, unvarnished facts. I am going to tell the whole tale so you need not imagine things are worse than they are. Tuesday morning we were awakened long before daylight by the sound of shots. These continued until about eight o'clock. We started the day as usual having breakfast at seven thirty. Then Miss Chaffee and I were just starting our morning prayers when the only male foreigner inside the city came to see us to find out if we were frightened. He explained what was going on as best he could and then went to see the two young women over at the other mission. We went on with our own prayers then went to Chinese prayers. Some of those attending were somewhat scared.

When the evangelist called on me to pray, he asked me to pray that the Lord pity China. We did not change our morning plans except, because the gates were closed, we did not go on cleaning house. The water supply was low because we get all our water from the river outside the wall. At about nine thirty before I had started out with the Bible woman, the Chinese evangelists came. They had decided that all we foreigners in the city were to stay together in the Holiness Mission. So we stayed there nearly all of three days and four nights.

In the nights we heard much fighting, but it was like Chinese fighting generally is, more noise than injury. About twenty were killed in battle. Twenty more of the enemy found in the city were beheaded. A number were wounded. After this the soldiers who were to protect the city made up their minds they could not keep off those from outside. They left, and the others came in. These new soldiers look pretty tough, and they are regular thieves. Everyone thinks they will be gone soon. There is much work I ought to do in the country this fall. The city now seems more open than usual to the preaching of the gospel.[16]

Tseo ch'i, October 12, 1923

This is the second day here at the out-station. We came part way by sedan chair and part way in a small boat. The launches are not running now because they are being used to transport soldiers. About twenty women came to the meeting today. The gospel means a lot to some people here. The Chinese men working here are very faithful. One looks after the chapel, and the other sells the books, mostly gospels and other portions of scriptures. So much more individual work is needed to have intelligent believers who will not be pulled back into the old life. The workers are too few for this place of eight thousand people with more villages around.

Learning to read is so important to new Christians. Teaching is at least half of my ministry. One woman I have been helping has been studying Matthew about four months and has reached the sixteenth chapter. I generally teach her, and she gets along splendidly in spite of the fact that her dialect is very different from that at Changteh. Many times I have seen her bow in prayer to ask the Lord to help her understand. When she gets something clear, she will say, "Praise the Lord!" She is one who will never keep all these lessons to herself. One woman I am teaching told about how their water buffalo had been stolen. A water buffalo means more to them than a horse would to us. She told how the Lord had helped them find the animal in answer to their prayer.

Tseo ch'i, October 22, 1923

Those who have become really interested since we came here would make a strange group. Among them was the "flower girl" who sat beside the Bible woman and seemed to drink in every word. There was a certain sweetness about her in spite of the marks of sin. She made one think of a tired child. There was an old grandmother of eighty-one who continually wept over the recent loss of her only son. There was a very young widow who asked if she could marry again if she believed the gospel. To these could be added more young and old, including two children I taught to sing Acts 4:12 as a chorus. The woman who put away her idols last spring is getting on well. She told us she has never had any desire to smoke again since she heard the gospel.[17]

Changteh, November 7, 1923

Last week I went with our Bible woman, the colporteur, a church member, and an inquirer from the out-station and spent five days farther out in the country. We stayed five days in the home of a man who not only fed us but spent most of his time those days helping us. The rice and the vegetable were so well cooked that I really could enjoy eating there in that Chinese home.[18]

We could have done more, but the Bible woman is not much good at walking. Next to the gospel message the thing the Bible woman talked about most there was foot binding. Here in Changteh I never see a child and see few young girls with bound feet. But out there we saw girls eleven or twelve years of age with feet bound to only half of the normal size. As the Bible woman said to me, "Tao Chiao-shih, your feet were never bound. You just do not know how much girls suffer when it is done."

We preached at several places. At the first place no foreign woman had visited before. We visited many homes and went to two market towns where every fifth day people come to town to buy and sell. Of course, we went to preach on market day to reach as many people as possible.[19]

I especially enjoyed the scenery in the country. The hills were covered with green growing things from big, old trees to little shrubs. The tea trees were in flower with an abundance of waxy white blooms. Leaves which had turned color and holly berries gave touches of bright red.

Our host in the country owns a little farm and half interest in a pottery. The clay in the area is a pretty red color. Wood for firing the kiln comes from the hillside. On the little farm most of the things they need are raised. They had their own rice and firewood. They get their oil from a kind of acorn or the nutlike seed of the tea plant. They raise vegetables, chickens, and pigs. As the Bible woman expressed it, "Best of all, their hearts were empty and ready to listen to the gospel".

Changteh, November 13, 1923

A few things have been sent home for your Christmas. The wooden toys are not so much to play with as to look at. The carved figure of the man in the boat is not a good reproduction of the way of rowing boats in this area. The man plowing is much better. The plows are made of wood except for the metal point. With the rice fields flooded the man plowing would wade all day in the mud. The best of the three figures is the man on the plank hulling rice. The cup-like thing as well as the hammer-like thing on the plank are made of stone. The man works the plank up and down like a teeter board until the rice is hulled.

The little red shoes I am sending are too small for a little tot, but are actually shoes for a bride. The bride who might wear such shoes would be carried by sedan chair escorted with musicians blowing and beating drums to her mother-in-law's house. There she would be on display for a day with all her possessions shown off. But the main thing would be to show that her feet were small enough to wear such shoes.

Since my last letter this city has changed hands again. Most of one day the noise was like a rather lively Fourth of July celebration. The soldiers in the city grabbed what they could of their own and other people's things and left in a hurry. This time we stayed in our own place. The soldiers set fire to some buildings about three blocks from here. Just as they did so, there was downpour of rain to put the fire out. Soldiers may plan things, but the Lord has the power.

Changteh, December 22, 1923

This Christmas there will be seven or eight baptisms here. Two of the women I have helped in the reading of the catechism and the gospel of Matthew. One of the men is the one with whom we stayed on our visit to the country. Another is the inquirer who went with us. At one time he was driven from home for his belief, but after months he was invited back when his father saw he was bound to go on "eating the foreign religion."

My Christmas package has come. Thank you for the many lovely things in it. You will think I am the limit when I say I had had my heart set on getting some raisins. When I get home, I am going to eat pounds of raisins and almonds, quarts of olives, and dozens of oranges. Yet the things I miss don't really count in the joys of being a missionary.

Changteh, February 22,1924

We have been to the out-station again. For such trips we must pack as for a year away at home. We must not only take clothes but bedding, food, and books, pictures, and hymn sheets for the meetings. We must have some simple remedies along such as castor oil, quinine, and soda.

At the out-station there is a room in a house for our use. This reminds me of a barn room. It contains a cane bottom bed, a table, and some chairs. While there we go out calling in the morning and then in the afternoon hold a meeting. The best plan seems to be for me to speak first and then the Bible woman. She can straighten out anything I have not made clear.

Last week we went to a feast in the home of one of our Christians. She made the feast to invite some heathen women we would not otherwise get a chance to preach to. One of the young women there had read the books of Confucius. Hardly one woman in a thousand has done that. Now along with the other guests at the feast she has heard the gospel preached.

Mr. Bannan started to go to Shanghai this week. Miss Kurtz who he expects to marry was to have started from Australia two weeks ago. They expect to be married in about three weeks.

Changteh, May 18, 1924

A note came from the Christian Missionary Alliance group asking me to take the evening prayer meeting with the school girls. About forty were present the evening I spoke. I wish you could have heard those girls pray and heard what they prayed for. My own message was on the prayer of Elisha that his servant's eyes might be opened. Now I have been asked to speak to all the girls in the school. While it does take some time to prepare to do things like that, it is so very worthwhile. My work seems scarcely begun.

There was a meeting of Presbytery in Changteh last week. While we were not a part of this, we were invited over for a social evening. We had a lap supper followed by singing and speaking. The next day some of them came over for the prayer meeting at our mission. We had two of the group as guests for supper one evening, and one stayed overnight.

I wish we could divide up some of our rain with you. Just now we can not get meat of any kind. In order to please the idols and induce them to make it stop raining, no animals are being killed for food. This will continue until the rains stop. We are playing we are vegetarians for a while.[20]

On boat to Hankow, June 19, 1924

We had a very good time in the country where I was the last time I wrote. We planned to stay a week and were there ten days. Some of the new Christians become very dear to us until I do not like to go away and leave them. One old woman was exhorting me not to go away this summer. She said it is not very hot now, and if it does get hot said she would come and fan me. At the out-station some are so new in the faith. Paul must have felt it keenly leaving new converts as he "Committed them to the Lord in Whom they had believed" and went on.

While there we had meetings nearly every day. Three times over twenty women came, and we had other opportunities besides. Those who came those three times were brought in by the other inquirers. Because the Bible woman was sick we did not get to go out much. One day two simple old country women came in. One of them, when asked why they came, said "we have heard people say that you could tell how a person's soul can be be saved and came in to ask about it". The Bible woman then preached to them a long time. In fact we both talked with them and at the end prayed with them.

This letter may look like hen scratches. When the boat is moving, it is like sitting in a rocking chair or worse, for we do not know which way we will jiggle next. Although it would have suited me better to have waited a couple of weeks before starting. Miss Chaffee and I are on our way to Kuling. Mr. Bannan reserved a cabin on the boat for us and then wrote us about it. He still seems to want to look after us. Miss Chaffee is about "played out," so she needed to get away.

Kuling, July 7, 1924

The walks up here I do enjoy, but I feel already like going back to Changteh or somewhere else to get to work. The place is beautiful. There is much green growth. Most of the houses are built of gray stone. Some have roofs painted green; others are black or red. In the summer there are well over thousand people in the village here, in the winter perhaps two hundred. There are two boarding schools, one for American and the other for English children. There are also two hospitals. One has special arrangements for tuberculosis patients. Tuberculosis is a common disease in China.

The peddlers here can be a nuisance. There must be well over twenty around every day. They may sell lace and embroidery, beads, trinkets such as candle sticks and bells, baskets of all sorts, and fruit. In addition there are many tailors and shoemakers. Most of them speak a little English which they like to air; however, one should be able to talk prices with them in Chinese.

Kuling, July 22, 1924

We are having such a good time. What a few years ago would have bothered me seems very different now. At first it is not easy getting along with people of other nationalities. The English especially have ways so different from ours. Most of the people in the house where I am staying are English; however, I am in a room with two Finnish ladies. One was a high school teacher before coming to China, and the other is almost equally as well educated. Either can speak six to eight languages. In the room next to ours is a son of Hudson Taylor, the founder of the mission. There is much one can learn from all of these people.

Last week we had the great treat in having the chance to hear Dr. Evans for a number of lectures. I had heard him in Los Angeles. Before he came I had talked a lot about how good he was. After he spoke, those in the house said I had not been mistaken.

"Old Mr. Cheng selling Gospels."

A tailor has finished completely turning my winter coat inside out. New button holes were made with the old holes mended. There was also a hole burnt in the cuff. Since it came back, I can not find this place because it was mended so well. The charge was a little over two dollars, but it looks like a new coat.

My papers came back from the examiner last week. This time the mark was 91%, not a high mark, of course, but I will never shine in language work. At any rate the required work on the language is done even though I feel that only a beginning has been made. Now that I do not have to study I seem to enjoy it all the more.

By the end of next year I may be called a senior missionary. That sounds old and dignified does it not? Yet to think of all it means my heart indeed says,"Not worthy." We may choose other callings, but this one calls us. Our hearts, hands, and feet are not clean enough to choose it for ourselves. Our strength is worse than useless. It is all His love, His strength, and His holiness, yes, and His wisdom.

Kuling, August 2, 1924

We are still up here on the mountain and will be for another three weeks. This week has been the Kuling Conference. The Modernists have had full sway from beginning to end, so I have considered their conference a good place to stay away from. Mr. Strothers the Secretary of the Christian Endeavor Society for China and many others are thinking of making a protest. There may be need of doing something more than to protest. We can not listen to the things that we have been hearing this week. Less has been said in private than in public. The main speaker said that evolution was as much an established fact as any fact in the universe, and that the third chapter of Genesis had better be rewritten. We of the CIM do not naturally think very much of such a man. The Bible Union no doubt will have something to say about the matter next week.[21]

Kuling, August 22, 1924

A big disappointment has come this week. Miss Chaffee for health reasons is not coming with me when I go back to Changteh, and there is some doubt of her being able to return at all. Whether the Draffins will stay with me or whether someone else will be sent has not been made plain. This is one of the "all things" of Romans 8:28. Miss Chaffee's trouble has something to do with her stomach. She is quite weak and just now must spend most of her time in bed.

Dr. McInnis who was here in Kuling some weeks ago is here again. This time his lectures are in English. I like to hear him just as well when he speaks to the Chinese because I hear how the things he has to say should be said in Chinese. I do not envy an interpreter's job. There are so many things that are hard to translate exactly. Abstract terms when referring to anything as simple as a plan, a compromise, or reconcile are real problems. There are things that have meaning to us that have no meaning to them such as love between husband and wife and many things relating to the home. But the Bible itself they understand often better than we do.

This summer I have been studying with my Chinese Bible, but we do not study all the time. It is a treat to hear some of the remarkably good things they have here. This week I heard one very good concert sung by more than fifty people with some solos and duets. This was Spohr's "Last Judgment."

Changteh, September 4, 1924

Here I am back in Changteh sitting as near under my own vine and fig tree as I may get to do in China. At least, I am having my own way for a few days. I am trying to clean house and do several other things at once. The cook and the woman we call in by the day are doing very well, so some things begin to look like someone lives here.

Miss Chaffee felt my coming away without her very keenly, but there was no other way. It may be that she will never be back here. As a matter of fact, she may have to leave China due to her failing health. She has had such a hard time out here. She had been in China less than two months when the man she was engaged to marry died. A blow like that would be all the harder out here. Then she has had such a struggle with poor health.

It might be interesting to count the different ways of traveling in coming back from Kuling. This included steamer, launch, and rowboat as well as automobile, ricksha, and sedan chair besides walking. Up until the last mile returning I had company. There were nineteen of us as far as Hankow. We spent about thirty hours there. I was able to buy food there for the rest of the trip. I also bought a broom, a scrubbing brush, a flour sifter, a mixing spoon, and some school books.

Hankow is sometimes called the Chicago of China, for in several ways the two cities are alike. Anyway Hankow is an important center. From Hankow on there were three of us foreigners on the launch. There was a Norwegian woman who got off a day before we reached here. The other was a Presbyterian doctor. The launch traveled slowly due to engine trouble. Like last year they had far too many people on board and took some of them off before going through customs and picked them up later. Of course, it is dangerous to overload, but what do they care if they get the money without being caught?

A peculiar thing happened on the launch. One of the porters said something rude to me and was in other ways disrespectful, and a Chinese gentleman slapped him for it. If the Presbyterian doctor had done anything, everyone on board would have said it was a foreigner against the Chinese. The strange part is that a Chinese will hardly stand up for a woman who belongs to him much less a stranger. The gentleman did not speak to me at all, which was showing as much respect as possible.

When I got back coming through the city gate, I was asked for my passport for the first time in China, but I did not have it handy. They wanted to have my card or else look through my things. The matter ended by my writing my name on a card both in English and in Chinese characters. Then they were satisfied.

Changteh, October 30, 1924

I am still alone but seem to be getting used to it. This suits me fairly well except it costs me more to live alone. Just now it does not seem right for me to play the coward and leave. We are always most safe in the place where the Lord directs us to be. There are rumors of fighting. Soldiers are heading toward here from the south and from the north. In case of trouble though even the Chinese consider our compounds the safest place to be. One of our newest Christians is the wife of an officer of the northern army. She is very much troubled these days.

One morning this week the cook asked me if I would give some medicine to a sick child. The Bible woman went with me to see this child. The child looked like it might be having convulsions and was much too sick for me to help. The parents refused to take the child to the hospital as I advised and it died later that afternoon. I wonder sometimes that any of their children live; as a matter of fact, not more than one out of three or four reaches the age of ten. One day I asked the woman who washes for me about her children. One child she knows is living. One she took to an orphan asylum, and she does not know what became of it. One child died at age seventeen and another at seven. The rest of her ten died at age three or under.

Chu-tsi-k'eo, November 12, 1924

After waiting so long this fall to get back to Nanchow, I did not stay very long after getting there, just from Tuesday evening until Saturday morning. Mrs. Draffin has a nice baby boy now three months old that I had not seen before. He cries very little. As to size and looks he is about average. There are also two new Chinese babies on the compound,

The newer Bible woman at Nanchow has gone to Changsha to see a doctor. The other Bible woman is busy with her new baby, so this time I came to the out-station without a Bible woman. The evangelist's wife has gone out on the street to call the women in. We have had six meetings with an average attendance of twenty. This is my first attempt at holding meetings without another leader. With the use of pictures the women seem to have understood. We have sold four hundred gospels and over fifty tracts. Besides we have preached on the streets and have given away hundreds of tracts. In all it has been a splendid opportunity.

One meets with plenty of problems. The first night we were here bandits came dressed as soldiers—in fact they probably were defeated ones. They spent the night going through the place demanding money from every shop. They got some thousands of dollars. The people across the way gave them a hundred dollars. They left in the morning just before daylight. They did not come to the chapel. A few days later when we were on the street someone said we had come out to get the people to give us money as these soldiers had.[22]

There was a fairly good crop most places around here this year, but there are still a lot of beggars. Some have come quite a distance. Today I met a woman from above Changteh who only had a shelter over her head of a few straw mats . So many people lack proper food and clothing while others have such plenty. Some have to work so much beyond their strength and others spend their days and nights gambling. This is truly one of the dark places of the earth and so is a habitation of cruelty. Ma-jong keeps so many of the Chinese out of the church because they get so interested in it they have no time to hear the gospel. They also keep slave girls waiting on them all hours of the night and treat them so cruelly. How I hate the sight of the game. Men in China not only gamble away their homes but their wives and children as well. How one does long to see more of His abounding grace in this land where sin abounds.

It is not especially late, but I seem to be tired just the same. After trying to think and talk in another language most of the day, it sometimes gets the best of one. But it is good to be permitted to do it. Very likely there are many whose hair has grown white in the service of the Lord at home who have never had the privilege of preaching to so many who have never heard the gospel before.

Changteh, November 12, 1924

Last week I sent the Bible woman to the out-station. I wanted to go with her the worst kind of way and tried to arrange to go but without success. The old evangelist told me that I ought to stay here and attend to my work at this place. Then when he saw I could not go, he said, "Praise the Lord" and proceeded to give me some fatherly advice. He said, "You know it has been over nineteen hundred years since the Lord came to earth, and all of His work can not be done in a day". It may be that the orient has as much to teach us on being patient as we have to teach them about promptness.

The thing the older women advise me on is wearing more clothes. One day one of the women was with me when I started out calling, and she begged me to put on another wrap. I finally did so to please her. Several days later I had to advise her about something, and she took it at once. The situation was that her room was above an opium smoking den. This had troubled me. Wednesday at women's meeting she had a story to tell of trouble with her landlord. Then I told her that perhaps it was not the Lord's will that she live in that place. Right away she started looking and has found another place to live. It is hard to be tactful, wise, and loving as one should be with these people. The hardest of all are the weak little stunted lambs that always must be hand fed and never seem to grow. We know it is the Lord's command to feed them as well as the sheep.

The gate-keeper has a daughter almost two years old and a granddaughter by his first wife a little older. Some old dolls had been thrown out in the trash, and the gate-keeper asked for one for each of the girls. At first the children were afraid as could be of them. But today I saw the younger one with a doll tied on her back. The two girls are so cute running around holding each other's hands.

Every word we hear from Kuling tells that Miss Chaffee is improving. We still have not heard whether she can come back here. One of the missionaries here in the city thought I should fumigate the room Miss Chaffee occupied here. I finally told the cook to buy sulphur to do it. His question was, "If you burn that sulphur in her room, will that make her better?" He then told me that the Chinese burn sulphur in front of the idols to keep the plague away.

The book seller was here yesterday. While his work is only to sell gospels, he wanted Bibles, New Testaments, and song books. Each church member buys his own song book and brings it with him to church. Some say that the number of Bibles we sell and the attendance at prayer meetings are the best indications of the state of the work. If so, we are doing well.

This morning I had a talk with a Chinese woman of my own age. I believe I have written a bit about her before. Now she was telling me a little about herself. She told of having been married at the age of fifteen and having 5 children all of whom died. In her early twenties she became a widow, and she is now married the second time. Her present husband is a soldier of about the same rank as the Bible centurion. She had heard the gospel as a child, but it had meant nothing to her until the Bible woman and I met her one day last winter and the word became real to her.

Changteh, November 20, 1924

This afternoon I am itching for a good walk, but I dare not go out on the street alone because of the many soldiers in the city. The city has changed hands again. There was a division of opinion among the northern soldiers here in the city whether to resist the southern soldiers when they came or to join them. Only a small portion decided to resist, and they did their fighting about twenty miles away. The others made arrangements with the officials in the city that they would leave without looting if given several thousand dollars. The amount was paid, so they left making way for those coming. I have no idea how much they may have to pay this group to leave peaceably.

Sunday evening after I had gone to bed another missionary with his cook and two soldiers came to get me. My bed felt good, and I did not care to go, but he said his wife would worry if I did not go to their place. I had to get up, get dressed, and change my bed for the night. I slept there two nights but came back here during the day. I had work to do.

The husband of one of our church members was an officer of the group that resisted. Ever since they decided to fight,the wife has been on my mind and heart because she has been so troubled. She stayed awake all last Saturday night waiting for her husband to return. When he came, he was alone. He had had some of his wife's relatives and his oldest son in the hundred soldiers in his command. All were killed or wounded. Sunday morning though they both came to church together. She wept when she told the Bible woman the story. Monday morning when we went to call, we found she had fled. I have no idea where.

Changteh, December 1, 1924

There must have been over a hundred at church yesterday. After the church service the men go home. The Bible woman starts the women all together while I get the children started in the school room. The children's meeting I have had to turn over to the Chinese this fall. After the children have begun, we divide the women. I take the church members, and the Bible woman takes the inquirers and the outsiders.

We have a story about a ham in our mission. One time a group from home came to visit the mission work. At the first station where they stopped a ham was cured for the occasion. All the Chinese brought extra things for the visitors. The ham was then sent along with the baggage as they went from station to station along the way. When the group returned to England, they told about the luxury among the missionaries that they had ham and eggs for breakfast every day. Most of the people who come to visit get just about such a distorted view of things in some way or other.

The political condition remains most uncertain these days. For us there is not much to fear as our "treasure is in the heavens", but I am afraid the poor people are going to suffer much this winter. I know this city has had an opportunity to hear and believe the gospel if any city has had and has oh so largely rejected it, but one does not like to see the judgement fall. When General Feng was here he used almost every possible way of making the gospel known, for he not only preached it and lived it himself but saw to having tracts distributed and having others preach. He also had his soldiers march the streets singing Christian songs and hymns. We can only pray the Lord to look down in mercy upon this place. The trouble here is the people are so busy about the things of this life that they have no time or though for anything beyond.[23]

The soldier's wife I wrote about has returned. She says she left due to her husband's soldiers more then the enemy. They would have annoyed her to borrow money. She also thought they would come to the church where they know she goes and would have bothered me. I am so glad to know that she is safe. She told that the last night she was hiding she prayed the Lord to protect her while she was away from home and those she loves. After falling asleep she dreamed someone told her to get under his wing, and she would be protected. I told the Bible woman later to read her the ninety-first Psalm the next time she comes if I am not here to do it.

Changteh, December 17, 1924

Last week was especially full. The young man who had graduated from Bible school died. His mother, a widow, had put him through school at her own expense making that her service for the Lord. She now regrets most that he did not have time to work for the Lord. We visited and tried the best we could to give her comfort. A family of German missionaries were through here and visited for several days. The man is a doctor, and they had four little children including a baby four months old. It would have been easier for one to entertain them had there not been a funeral on hand and then Mr. Draffin arriving with so much that had to be talked over.

Mr. Draffin visited the out-station and found things in fairly good condition there. It was my week to entertain the foreign prayer meeting. The cook did most of the work preparing the tea, and Mr. Draffin led the meeting. Mr. Draffin is such a talker. It takes a long time to go over the books and talk things over with him. He left Saturday morning without doing or taking care of any of the repairs on the compound that I had hoped he would do.

Changteh, December 29, 1924

My thoughts were more than ever with you at home on my fifth Christmas in China. I had been invited out, but I was kept so busy that by the time I could leave, it was too late. It was just a bit lonesome not seeing another person who spoke my mother tongue all day. There are, of course, many days for me like that, but it was a bit harder on Christmas. But after all we are not alone. I remember one miserable night I spent lately when such a thing as sleep was impossible. The thought came into my mind: what if I should get sick here with no one to care for me? As soon as it got light enough, I looked up to a motto hung on the wall years ago, "Lo, I am with you always even unto the end of the world."

The church was beautifully decorated, and we had what the Chinese thought was a good program Christmas morning. The school children sang "While Shepherds Watched Their Flocks by Night" and recited the first twenty verses of the second chapter of Luke. They had made two large pictures pasting white paper on black, one representing the shepherds and one the visit of the wise men. The evangelist preached and a few testified. A free will offering was taken which amounted to $7.50. That is not a great deal, but it may take a man three days or a woman seven days to earn a dollar. After the program there was tea for the grown up people. The children were given packages of peanuts, cakes, and booklets instead of refreshments.

A package of picture rolls and cards came last week. We can't get too many of these since the children like them so much. Often we have no better way of reaching the adults than through the children. Recently I visited the home of a little girl in the first class at school. Her father poured tea for us, a mark of great respect. He mentioned that this little girl had been reciting verses she had learned in school.

The city is as full as it can be with soldiers just now. I was told that they have agreed to leave if given a hundred and fifty thousand dollars. They are really bandits with all their ways of getting money from the people here.

Changteh, January 13,1925

Letters have come about Christmas parcels on the way. I am still looking for them to come. Mail is unusually slow this year. Parcels almost never get lost coming this far nor is there much duty to pay.

The Chinese government is about to pass a law that all schools that teach the scriptures or have any religious exercises will be classed as second rate. Pupils from second rate schools must enter a lower grade when entering a first rate school. In Changteh we will have our schools classed as second rate rather than give up anything in the way of Bible instruction. On the whole, mission schools are immeasurably higher grade than government schools. This is just some of the devil's work. He is getting in a lot of practice here in China.[24]

Any day now I expect Mr. Draffin to come. I have a list of at least ten things, some with subdivisions, about which I must consult him. At least two persons should be hired and perhaps one fired. I wonder though if we missionaries who were called out of darkness into His marvelous light are not altogether too much occupied with machinery and not enough in Him. We certainly never get to the place where the enemy has no means of attacking us.

Nanchow, March 26, 1925

If the weather were clear, we would be on the way to another out-station today. We have six out-stations and are responsible for work in many towns and villages besides. Also there is a school which needs some of our time. Mrs. Draffin is busy most of the time with her home and family, so she thinks they need another young woman worker. Even if one comes, she would be of little help the first year. It takes such a long time to learn the language, and some of us think it takes longer still to learn what not to say. Young missionaries can cause more trouble by the things they say than what they do not say. The Chinese after all are so different from what we are, and it is easy to say the wrong thing or say it in the wrong way.

Over in the country, so to speak, we see and hear less yet we still know that political affairs are almost as bad as they can get even if our little corner happens to be peaceful at present. The people here have had good crops and are fairly prosperous. They never can tell though when the fighting may be coming our way. It suits me just as well though to have the soldiers stay away from this part of the country. It is a blessing for China that Sun Yat-sen is dead It would be a good thing if some more would die. Sun Yat-sen had a lot of Bolshevist ideas in his head and was far from being a wise leader in consequence. It is remarkable what a grip some of these teachings are getting here in China.[25]

Nanchow, April 6, 1925

Our visit to the out-station this time gave us some great opportunities. The attendance at meetings was better than usual, and the attention was good. Women came one by one or in groups of from two to a dozen, some from a distance. Very few had heard the gospel before. We gave away ever so many tracts, and within two days sold about a hundred thirty gospels. The old evangelist was saying that he could remember when gospels could not be given away. One day there we went out in the country a couple of miles farther where the peach trees were in bloom, and the country was really beautiful. About forty women came to the meeting there. Sometimes women come after the meetings are over. Time doesn't mean much. Even those who have clocks may have them an hour slow because they have no better way to set them than by the sun.

The evangelist out there has been in the work for more than thirty years. He has some tales to tell of the opening of the work in this province. He knew some of the very first missionaries. Some of them truly sowed in tears. One man worked here many years until the hardships he endured caused his death but never found a permanent dwelling place being driven from place to place. Another when far inland had his bedding and everything except his clothes he was wearing stolen. Other stories are worse still. That evangelist's wife is a real help to him; in fact, I never saw another Chinese woman who could keep sweet under more trying circumstances. She looks after having the chapel clean and the lamps burning and serves tea to the guests. She helped by going out on the streets and to the country with us. The women love and respect her. Some of the Chinese Christians get no help from their wives. This is not too strange when the matches were settled for them in infancy with less fore-thought being taken than if purchasing a horse or a cow. This woman was a widow and he a widower, so they settled the matter between themselves.

Getting back to a clean, soft bed seemed good. Still I am going out again just as soon as possible.

Nanchow, May 11, 1925

At a different out-station last week, the evangelist there took us to visit at his mother-in-law's home. This evangelist's wife is an earnest Christian who has often preached to her mother. The mother likes to hear the word and is not as fond of her idols as she once was. She has refrained from eating meat for twenty eight years. Now she says she can not eat meat because her "heart" will not stand it. In China I never know when they say the word for heart whether they mean heart or stomach. When one has a heartache, should I give a dose of soda or words of comfort? Anyway at the mother-in-law's home we had a meeting with about twenty in attendance.[26]

On one part of the trip we were traveling in a boat so small that the evangelist and a coolie had to walk. The current and wind were against us, so it took the boat four hours to go six miles. The evangelist went ahead, and he and a teacher of the school with two of his pupils were out to meet us. They took us to the school where we were served tea. We sold twenty gospels there and twenty more when we got back to shore. We crossed the river in the boat, but all the way we could hear calls to come back and sell more gospels.

In the name Nanchowting the ting means a governing town in a division that would contain one or more townships. These divisions have now been done away with, and recently the post office has dropped that syllable; however, either Nanchow or Nanchowting may be used on a letter.

Nanchow, May 25, 1925

This place does not lack for noise from daylight to dark. One day last week there were fifty workmen here, but that was too many. Most days there are around twenty. The house for the Chinese workers to live in is up to the top of the first story. Today workmen are laying the joists for the upstairs floor. The house will have ten rooms. The old church is now only a shell, as only the framework and roof are left. The new church is planned to hold five hundred people.

There has been a little trouble here recently with a Chinese religious society who speak with tongues and call themselves the "true Jesus denomination." Their leaders from the beginning have mostly been those who have been cut off from the church role because of deep sin. Of course the trouble is not especially serious as nothing outside the church can very greatly harm it. But what is inside can cause any amount of trouble. They say after saying "hallelujah" a certain amount of times the Holy Spirit comes, and then they can heal any disease or cast out devils. Of course this appeals to both our carnal nature and to the untaught Christians. As to the "hallelujah," I tell our Christians that means "Praise the Lord" and it is taking His name in vain if we say that without meaning it in our hearts. They make a great point that they have no foreign missionary to manage them. Of course the Chinese cannot see the necessity of church discipline, especially if they are the ones concerned. One of the characteristics of this religious society is that they go down to the river and baptize themselves in the name of "Jesus." They have lots of noise and outward show and that is what the Chinese like. This is not the first Chinese religious society formed, but the others have had their day as they had trouble over the question of money and who would be leader. If it were not for pride and the love of money these sects would have never been formed, and churches can never thrive on such. There was one place where the work did very well for a long time but was neglected too much. There most of the people who once came here have gone over to this false sect. In this case it was the lack of teaching on the part of those who should be at it.[27]

Kikungshan, July 5,1925

We have had some rather exciting times the last two weeks. The students have been stirring things up. Of course, they say they are against Japan and England, but the deeper we look into it, the more we see that it is both anti-foreign and anti-Christian as well as Bolshevistic, and therefore against the law. While they have done us no personal harm, they are stirring up the people, so one can not tell how soon some might do something rash. During the parade past our chapel at Nanchow, the students called out, "We do not want the gospel hall," also "We do not want the teaching of Jesus". Fortunately the governor of the province of Hunan had taken a very firm stand, so the local officials dared not let the students injure us personally. Before the parade the officials sent around two from the police, and the military sent two soldiers. That did not keep them from calling out, "Kill Mr. Draffin," "Kill the foreigner," or "Kill the evangelist." They did not call out about Mrs. Draffin or me, not so much that we are women but because we are Americans. Mrs. Draffin prefers to keep her American citizenship even though she did marry a Britisher. Nothing did happen to us, but the sound of those voices seemed as though it came right out of the pit. On the streets goods in three shops were smashed because the businesses opened that day. A lamp in the bend of the station wall was destroyed, but it actually belonged to our neighbors.

On our way from Nanchow we went to Changteh where we spent two days. The chance to talk and pray with the Bible woman and others there was enjoyed. Reports there as far as spiritual things are concerned were good. Materially though there is real want. Lack of rains is a factor as well as looting and high taxes needed in part to pay off the military. I gave the Bible woman some money to use for the very poorest people. One church woman who had been making a living for herself and two children was sick in bed. The money I gave her would little more than pay for her medicine.

We got away from Changteh without much trouble. We waited until it was about dark and then slipped out the quietest way. The Presbyterians were not so fortunate. Two of them were prevented from coming because the students wouldn't let the coolies carry their things. Two helpers were beaten, and those who got on the launch, made it with much difficulty. Those of us on the launch had things thrown at us but none hit us. Mr. Draffin directed the Chinese who helped us board to take a long roundabout way back to shore to avoid the crowd. Our Chinese servants and the Chinese Christians sometimes get the cruelty instead of us.

The brightest spot on our trip happened where the launch stopped the first evening out at a place where Biola bands had worked. A sharp looking boy standing in the boat we stopped by asked me, "Are you a missionary?" Perhaps my faith is altogether too small, for I was unprepared for his next remark made so earnestly, "I also believe in Jesus". An elderly woman standing beside him also claimed to be a Christian. I could not help telling her that we do not divide Chinese and foreigners when we believe in Jesus. In Him we are all brothers and sisters.

Getting here to Kikungshan was a difficult trip all the way. When we stopped at Changsha, some of the men went on shore and reported our troubles to the British and American consuls.

Kikungshan,July 22,1925

The real facts about what is going on in China are not especially encouraging. General Feng Yu-hsiang, the Christian (?) general of China, seems to have gone out of his mind and is suggesting the strangest things. General Feng was considered by some to be the hope of China, but now it seems that Satan is using him to bring reproach upon the name of the Lord. I know that Americans love to pat themselves on the back because of their return of the Boxer indemnity, but in the light of present facts it is almost impossible not to question the wisdom of it. Many of the students who studied abroad under this fund are the most bitter.[28]

We are enjoying many things here on the hill in spite of what is going on around us. There have been six or seven of us women here in this house. I have part of a glassed-in veranda. The house is a block up the hill from the house where we eat. Most of the missionaries I know best have gone to Kuling this summer. Miss Chaffee is still there.

One of the treats here this summer is a series of lectures by Russell Howder from England. His lectures are difficult to follow because he says so much in a few words.

Kikungshan, August 4, 1925

We have not had especially encouraging word from Nanchow. The evangelist Mr. Draffin depends on the most has been arrested. In view of the corruption of Chinese courts and the bribery of wicked men this is very bad news indeed. The evangelist if he is in the wrong is no more wrong than all the others in that district. The charge against him is that he acted as the spokesman in buying a piece of property on which the former owner did not have a clear title. In buying it these men did get a proper deed, but while everything is clear now, some who have had to be cut off the church role because of their sin are using this as an opportunity to get back at the church. The church members realizing the seriousness of the situation had a special prayer meeting for him the first night. This evangelist spent quite a lot of time helping me with the language. He has a wife and child.

The enemies of the truth are having many lies circulated about us this summer. Among them are that many Chinese are being killed in foreign countries and that we are paid agents of our government sent over here to make way for taking their country. Many of our Christians even believe this latter lie. How little do they realize that we are often "hated of all men for His name sake." Of course, many out in the country still think we take out people's hearts and eyes to make medicine. It is against the law to circulate such lies, but who cares for laws here in China these days.[29]

Nanchow, December 26, 1925

Yesterday at the chapel there was really too much going on. Due to scarcety of food in other places, the usual Christmas feast was just a tea with cakes, peanuts, and melon seeds. The church was well decorated with large characters on the walls with paper flowers all around them. The children had made paper chains.

The evangelist who went to jail and had to pay such a large fine last summer has been quite discouraged since. Another evangelist preached yesterday. There were eight baptisms at the service, and this was followed by communion. The large crowd included some officials and some of the poorest.

Christmas night those who were baptized gave testimonies. An especially interesting testimony was given by a former Taoist priest. He had come in contact with a gospel hall where he listened again and again. He learned the Lord's prayer and began to feel its power and protection. Finally he came to understand and believe.

Today the Bible woman tried to get out of going out with me even though it was the regular time to go. Of course, she did not talk with me but sent someone else. That is the Chinese way of doing things. Another example of this was when the evangelist wanted an advance on his wages so he could buy a coffin. He sent the cook to ask me about it. Fortunately, the money I had on hand was about gone. After I stated this fact, he thought it best to go elsewhere for the funds. Both buying coffins in advance and borrowing money are again Chinese characteristics. Interest sometimes is as high as ten percent a month making it an abominable custom. I always speak out against this practice when it comes up.

As to my address, one may write to me at Changteh or Nanchow. They are only a hundred miles apart. The Chinese at either place declare I belong to them, and sometimes I think the foreigners are worse. One feels very unworthy of the love and confidence the Chinese come to have.

Nanchow, January 19, 1926

One incident here should serve as a warning to any Christian worker in any land. I asked each woman as they came in if they had heard the gospel before to feel around where to begin or for the Bible woman to begin. Most had never heard before. Finally one came in who had heard. I said "Did you like to hear it?" Then I said "Did you believe the doctrine?" Both answers were in the affirmative. Now I said "That is very good—you say you believe, but what do you believe the Lord Jesus came down here on earth to do?" After briefly telling of His death on the cross for us, I said "Now do you think he is still in the tomb?" She knew almost nothing of this either, so I told of His rising to be our Mediator. This last the Chinese can understand very well because they are so accustomed to having a middle person for everything. But there are no doubt many who call themselves Christians who are no more intelligent about it than this ignorant Chinese woman.[30]

News just came today that the mission has granted my senior certificate and so have recognized me as a Senior missionary. As one gets older such things mean less. The greatest joy we get in receiving our crowns will be to cast them down before Him.

Nanchow, February 15,1926

They are having a feast this afternoon and I am just fed up with such things and will not go. One side of the matter is that if we attend their feasts, it makes it hard afterwards to rebuke them for their misdeeds that they so often do. Also some of their feasts have back of them just about as good a meaning as the feast Esther gave for Haman. Their wretched system of giving and expecting a return, feasting and expecting an invitation makes one often wonder just how to maintain the proper relation toward it. Sometimes I think of refusing to ever go to a feast again except for special occasions.

Although it was muddy, over a hundred people were out to church yesterday. The evangelist spoke of being a new creature in Jesus. Of course, this being the beginning of their New Year he had many illustrations to bring out the points. His wife had the women's meeting, but while her message was good, I have heard her do better. Her subject was the Sunday School lesson on "Jesus the Good Shepherd". Their acquaintance with sheep is so slight that the Chinese are not good on preaching such things nor do they understand it very well. Furthermore they are so cruel to animals that they can not understand anyone loving them. However on the whole I think they get a better meaning of the text than we do.

The cook put pepper in the porridge this morning. He thought it would be good that way.

Nanchow, March 3, 1926

The time for the dedication of the new church has been put back two weeks. This was partly because it is hard to get the work done in time and partly because it is hard to get some one to come to speak. According to the present plans I will have charge of some meetings for women. It may be possible to have some prayer and solid Bible study. Someone else may have control in the church, but the one who can take the woman aside one by one to pray with them and listen to them talk of their needs has something vastly more precious—their hearts.

The two hundred soldiers in this place left this week bag and baggage. I do not suppose the poor coolies who had to carry their things even got thanked for it. Of course the soldiers just catch the men out anywhere, tie them together, and at the point of a gun demand them to carry. In one case in a mountainous district forty such men were seized, and on the way the soldiers actually killed about ten for no other offense than that their strength gave out so they could carry no further. This is the kind of thing I do not suppose you read in the newspapers at home. The best Chinese acknowledge China is in an awful state of affairs. Those who believe Confucius' teachings are good enough for the Chinese ought to have to come to the interior of China and live a while under Chinese law.

A place quite a distance from here has just been rented for a street chapel and school. This makes another place from which to work and reach people. I am sorry that it is not nearer the main street, but it is very close to where the boats land. In the summer this should be an advantage,

Nanchow, March 17, 1926

We have been busy advertising the meetings in connection with the dedication of the new church. About ten men are still on the work. There are two men putting tar on the floor. Two painters are painting benches. The others are putting in partitions and doors and repairing the best of the old benches.

Last Friday many students marched around Nanchow and past here with such cries as, "Kill the Christians" and "Hit at the religion of Christ." Of course, it was not wholly anti-Christian, for they also called out away with certain prominent officials of China such as Chang Tso-lin and T'ang Sheng-chih. T'ang is the leader in the south of China where Bolshevism has taken hold and conditions are very bad.[31]

After the parade of students was past, the old woman who often goes out with me and I started out in the direction from which they came distributing tracts and selling gospels. We sold about thirty yet that afternoon. We have sold nearly two hundred since the parade, working three days. "We must do the works of Him who sent us while it is day. The night cometh when no man can work." We often are called names and are spoken against when on the street. In a way the opposition is better then indifference. We have had a great deal of free advertising because many now want to know what we really do teach.

Nanchow, April 9, 1926

The eight days of meetings connected with the dedication of the new church are now over. They were very busy and happy days. In all there were more than thirty Christians from the country and out-stations who came for all or part of the time. Those who came were to bring their own bedding, pay their way to come and half enough for their food. The Chinese here understood that they were to manage the entertainment, and this was done with scarcely a hitch. There were a number of meetings each day, and in between the Christians went out on the streets to preach, to sell books, and to invite people to come to the meetings. Most of the meetings were led by the Chinese, but I had a Bible class each afternoon for the women. At the closing service on Sunday morning there were about two hundred people in the new church. Many new people were reached by the meetings. Besides, the Christian women became more determined to do more work to reach outsiders.

We have a new Bible woman. She is a widow only twenty five years of age. She has had a year of hospital training and did the preparatory work for Bible college. Being an evangelist's daughter she has had some practical training. She is interested, but best of all she seems to love the women.

Shihshow, Hupeh and Nanchow, April 17, 1926

I am beginning this letter up here in Hupeh but expect to go back to one of the out-stations in Hunan before going all the way back to Nanchow.

On the whole our visit here has been rather disappointing. Some of the out-stations need a revival so much. Shihshow needs it as badly as any do. They do have a good evangelist and some good church members but it has grown very little for many years. In fact I am afraid the old church members have died faster than new ones have been added. The women seem almost impossible to reach. Most all of them are unwilling to come to meetings even from the homes where the men are Christians. We got a better reception in a Buddhist nunnery than in most of these homes. We went almost daily to that place and in the end two of them came to see us. We believe that even yet there may be those from that nunnery who will come to believe the gospel. One of the nuns had sore eyes. We went back to take some medicine, and the old Bible woman washed her eyes with boric acid.

To get to the out-station we must take a boat or walk. An automobile would be of no use. The paths are so narrow that in many places when walking one must stand still to let others go by. The Bible woman thought she could walk most of the way, but as one of the evangelists put it, "Her faith is big, but, alas, her feet are small." They were kept bound ten years from age four to fourteen, so her feet are little more than half the size they should be.

As we walked nearly all of the way back from the out-station, two men were hired to carry our things. One had been taking opium, so he was very slow and had to hire someone else to bring his load part way. For the first time on this trip I saw the opium poppy growing. Formerly it was not grown in this district but evidently some intend to introduce it now. Opium smoking is so much more frequent here now than when I first came to the district. From the door of the chapel in Kuangtang out-station we saw those who were preparing the opium.[32]

Nanchow, May 24, 1926

My last trip to the country was too much of a good thing. We came back on Thursday afternoon, and I went to bed and stayed there until after breakfast Saturday. I compelled myself to do what was necessary on the trip, but we did come home a day early. My temperature on arrival back was one hundred three degrees. My trouble was a combination of a bad cold and malaria. Malarial headaches last longer than regular headaches. They stay with you all your waking hours until you get enough quinine to stop them. That may take several days.

Nanchow, June 9, 1926

When we got to the out-station last week, we were afraid we couldn't stay because there were so many soldiers around. There are hundreds of them stationed there at present, and the first day they were a bit rude. But after that they kept their place very well. I gave the evangelist some tracts and asked him to give these out to the soldiers and preach to them as though they had come to hear the gospel instead of to see me, the foreign woman. Assuming that their motive was right served more than one purpose. Some of the soldiers did come to some the meetings, and I also met the wives of two or three. Many shops are closed because soldiers are occupying them, and it was thought best for me not to go on the street. I think this is the first time I ever went to an out-station where I did not go out on the street to help invite the women in.

This last spring there has been difficulty about getting some supplies. We have run out of both tea and coffee, a fact which does not bother me any. More important we had almost run out of scripture portions to sell. When the American Bible Society asked to report on the supply they sent here last fall, I had five left out of twelve hundred. I added that I could use twice as many. They sent two thousand five hundred at once. So now we have a good supply. Of course, these are to be sold.

Hankow, June 28, 1926

There was much to do before we came away. I tried to see each church member the week before leaving because in the summer everything is in the hands of the Chinese. They have the tracts and books and must know the prices of those to be sold. Someone must have a supply of castor oil, quinine, boric acid, salve, and other medicines which may be needed. This does not exhaust the things to be given out or attended to. Besides one must pack as for a camping trip.

Coming away from Nanchow we didn't get started until ten in the morning. We always have to wait for Mr. Draffin. The Draffin family, the cook, and I went the first thirty or forty miles in two row boats. The cook helped us put things on the launch before going back. One would have needed to work for a day with tons of buckets of water, soap, and scouring powder to have cleaned up our cabin on the launch. Later I told the captain this, also that his boat was almost alive. The first two nights Mrs. Draffin and I slept outside the cabin, and Mr. Draffin stayed by the "happy hunting ground" as he called it, for he said he killed about fifty bed bugs each night besides using kerosene to combat them. The first night was too noisy for sleep. The second night I managed to keep dry from the rain by keeping an oil sheet over me. The third night was the climax, and what made us so provoked was that had not the captain wasted so much time scrapping with people on shore, we could have arrived that night instead of the next morning. The third night the oil sheet was not big enough to keep off the rain, and when I raised up to drain off the water, it all went into my bed. I had to jump out and go into the cabin. At first I sat on a berth leaning my arms on a table, but the horrid bugs bit my arms, and there was a leak where I was sitting. Then for two or three hours I stood because there was no dry place to sit. Even then several bugs climbed up into my shoes. The children were also having to stand up for some time. Vernon Draffin, to keep himself awake, began singing "Jesus Loves Me" in Chinese. This greatly impressed the Chinese, and was the only relief of that night.

Sunday morning we landed here in Hankow. Instead of going to church I went to sleep after breakfast and didn't wake up until dinner time. Today, Monday, we have been shopping. I bought quite a good umbrella which is for me much more satisfactory than a hat. I had to dry and repack my bedding. Now we will have a night on a train with a hill to climb and we'll then be in Kikungshan for a couple of months.

Kikungshan, July 10, 1926

There are now nearly forty missionaries of the CIM here for the summer. This includes three doctors and three nurses, so we should keep well. There are quite a number of the German and Swedish members of CIM also some from other missions. I like especially well those of the Christian and Missionary Alliance. They are the most like the CIM. Their chief points of difference are that they immerse always (the CIM does also in the greater number of stations), they are nearly all Americans (the CIM was started in England, the C&MA in America), they have a home branch, and do take up collections. On the other hand they do not have a guaranteed salary, they go into the most interior places in China, and their work is almost wholly evangelistic. In these latter points they are like the CIM, so they call the CIM their sister mission and use our course of study of the language and the same Chinese song book. They are both a smaller and newer mission than ours so they are often glad to copy.

After not hearing a sermon in English for a long time, it is a treat to hear some of the speakers here this summer. Some of the preaching makes one want to go straight back to work more earnestly than ever.

This summer I am trying to finish going over the parts of the Old Testament in my Chinese Bible that I have never read before in Chinese. In doing this I can average five or six chapters an hour. I am also practicing Chinese writing. This is my chance of the year not only to go to meetings and mix with other missionaries, but to study.

Kikungshan,July 24,1926

Another two weeks have gone by so swiftly. Up here we go to meetings, walks, study, and sleep and eat. That does sound lazy I know but one does get so tired down on the plain. It is not so much that one is too tired to work. It is just that one's head just feels uncomfortable so much of the time. And the Chinese, much as we may love them generally, with their sin and dirt just do get on one's nerves.

This summer there has been both fighting and floods. In Changteh the Presbyterian compound had water up to the clothes line with four feet of water in their rooms down stairs. The CIM compound there is on higher ground and so was unharmed. The floods have washed out a lot of crops, so a lot of people are starving. The soldiers have taken nearly all of the rest of the rice. The Chinese used to store up rice for a year ahead in case of famine. But now because so much land is used for opium, what is raised each year is scarcely enough. Added to this are the high taxes that many people on the farms are required to pay two or three years ahead. Then the wretched soldiers are always destroying so much. Truly China is in a terrible state of affairs. If these Chinese soldiers should all sink out of existence in one night, China would be better off than she is. They would be no protection against a foreign power for they would run if they saw them coming. Their only use is to bother the people to get money for the officials and a lot of them lead a dog's life doing it.

It has rained nearly all the week. We do hope and pray it will clear up soon as sunshine is needed before the harvest. We cannot like the Chinese look complacently on and say "they are sinners" as much as to say they deserve to go hungry. When suffering comes their own way, they say it was because of the sins of a previous existence. This of course is false and that they are sinners is also, yet it is usually the innocent that have to suffer. Things are divided up so unequally. The Chinese accept so many evils as a matter of course that they could easily do away with if they tried.

Kikungshan, September 16, 1926

If I should be in China next summer and have my own way, I will stay right at the station. In August we began to hear that we could not get back to Hunan Province because boats going through were being fired on. We were packed to leave on September 7. On that day those wanting to go north went down to catch the train at five o'clock in the morning. They waited all day without seeing anything but troop trains, so all came back here. Since then we are just going on with our knitting.

We also had word that day that Hanyang where the arsenal is had been taken by the southerners or "Reds." Day before yesterday some say they began to hear guns. Evidently the southerners have been coming right on north ever since last Tuesday when they must have taken Hankow. We heard and saw smoke from the guns yesterday afternoon. Last night the northerners gave up and ran. Today the southerners are in charge of this place. We hope in a very few days the road will be clear and we can leave. A general by the name of Chin has his home on the hill. Because he delayed so long about leaving it, it was impossible to get enough coolies to carry everything. It is said that over sixty boxes of clothing, etc. were left behind. Before the other soldiers arrived people began to come in and help themselves. When the soldiers came in they destroyed everything they could not sell immediately. Of course General Chin's wife and family fearing danger had fled to the foreign concession some weeks ago. General Chin has almost a palace. It is not only large but he has copied foreign houses to the point of having bathrooms with both hot and cold running water. It is by far the nicest and largest house on the hill. It is fortunate it is there, for having something so much better than the missionary houses to go to, the soldiers probably will not desire to do so.[33]

Yesterday a letter came from Mrs. Draffin enclosing a picture of the four children. Ruth, the oldest, was holding the new baby. The other children looked very proud of their new brother. The family has spent the summer in Shanghai. Ruth and Vera have both gone up to Chefoo to be in school. From now until Christmas the Draffins will have just the little boys with them. I am keeping most of my things packed up so we can get away quickly when the trains commence to run. No doubt many went to France during the war and never came as near the real fighting as we did. To those of us who have faith in Almighty God our hearts are still in perfect peace.[34]

Hankow, September 27, 1926

At last we are away from Kikungshan which is a nice enough place during July and August. But an enforced stay is never particularly enjoyed. Today we went to the wedding of two doctors. There are only about twenty doctors for over eleven hundred CIM missionaries. Most missions aim to have a doctor for every mission station but we cannot have this. Of course our mission lays less emphasis on institutional work and more on direct evangelism.

We finally got away from Kikungshan all right. A business woman and two or three missionaries went to see the Chinese officer on the hill. The former went alone. She generally dresses with skirts up to her knees and without stockings besides having her hair bobbed. She says the officer's men treated her like a coolie. Now no Chinese woman unless she were the poorest of beggars would ever appear with so few clothes with arms and legs exposed—besides, it is not good custom for a woman to go to see a man. But that kind of woman is not apt to be reasonable. The missionaries had been in China long and knew Chinese custom and went as gentlemen and were treated as such. The officer promised to procure a special train for them and did so. This made the business woman very mad that the missionaries got what they wanted and she did not. She said she would be willing to put out a hundred dollars to outdo the missionaries, also that she was going to write up the affair. In the end she did bribe the station master to let part of the train go off before it was supposed to with business people in it when it was really provided for the missionaries. The officer who provided for this train is a Christian and so may have been just a bit partial towards the missionaries. However, do you wonder that the missionaries and business people have little to do with each other? We ought to do what we can to win them, but on the other hand we come out here principally for work with the Chinese. If we have too much to do with the business people, the Chinese would think we countenance all their misdeeds.

One of the girls I knew at Biola was here when I arrived. She has just come down from Szechwan, having been ordered to come because of the troubles up there. The Wanhsien affair was pretty bad. It looks as though matters have gotten very bad. Leagues of Nations and Peace Conferences may have some very nice things said about them, but when such combinations will all sit still rather than offend another nation and allow outrages such as Turkey slaughtering the Armenians, we have little to hope much will be done about China unless the value of her trade justifies them in doing so. China seems determined to see how far she can go like a naughty spoilt child. And there is not much likelihood of things getting better until she has had a lesson, but the question is who is to apply it. For the good of China herself if not for the outside world it should be done promptly, justly and thoroughly. If not, she together with Russia are likely to become a menace to the whole world.[35]

At present Wuchang across the river and Hanyang right next to Hankow are at war. The first night we were here there was quite a lot of firing, but at present they are trying to starve out Wuchang. A general from outside has sent word to them to hold on and he will eventually bring help. Many of the poor people are starving inside and there is no way to take in supplies. An American launch was sent across to carry relief to the missionaries, but even though it had a flag it was fired on from the inside. So you see how little China cares for the flowery flag or the country for which it stands.

This letter had better stop without writing anything more of wars and rumors of wars. My own patience, if I ever had any, is worn almost threadbare. It has gotten to this: we go tomorrow to catch yesterday's train and next week to catch last month's boat. I have knitted a pair of bloomers while waiting besides doing a number of other things.

Changteh, October 15, 1926

After many delays we are again in Hunan Province. The boat we traveled on to Changsha had been commandeered by the military to come to Hankow. Then their idea was to take on passengers to make it pay in going back to Changsha. But those in the military had another plan and made them carry soldiers and ammunition coming back. They made all the Chinese passengers get off, and had a great discussion during the night about whether or not they would allow we missionaries to continue our journey. The one man who stood up for us against the others was called a demon. The Naumans, the missionary couple with me, either did not hear or did not understand this conversation, and I did not tell them about it. When we had been on the boat twenty-four hours and had not started, Mr. Nauman was going to get off because it was too crowded. I finally persuaded him much against his better judgment to stay with the boat. In the end we started forty five hours after boarding the boat. We got on the boat Wednesday afternoon, started Friday afternoon, and got to Changsha Sunday evening. I visited some people I knew who were working in Changsha and stayed at the German CIM home. We left Changsha Tuesday before noon and arrived in Changteh early Thursday morning

Sunday on the boat I had quite a long conversation with a Buddhist nun. She had read through most of the Bible, and I think she is convinced that it is true but that she does not wish to give up the standing she now has in her present religion. She asked quite a lot of questions, among them "Where do our souls come from?" When I started asking her questions about her own religion, she went off into such deep language, I did not understand and I suppose most of those who heard her did not either. It was not intended to satisfy or explain matters but to mystify and impress people with her superior wisdom. How much we can praise the Lord for the simple gospel of the grace of God. This nun had travelled a lot here in China and although twenty-eight looked like she was forty. A religion like Buddhism can never bring peace to the soul.[36]

Changteh, October 28, 1926

Today finds me in the midst of packing to go to Nanchow. I've never traveled with as many pieces of baggage, and there is no bird cage nor cat among them, but most of the things belong to someone else. It would have suited me much better to have started today, but I left getting the boat to the Bible woman's husband. It is quite a trip, so he may go at least part way with me.

Word came today that the Draffins have reached Nanchow, but we were here a week before their return. It has been good to be here a while with the Naumans. I seem to be a bone of contention between here and Nanchow, but it would be far worse not to be wanted at either place. I feel that my short stay here has been worthwhile. Some here have backslid if one could say they ever slid forward, but some are as earnest as ever before. One thing I did see to while here was to get an old woman to go to the hospital for care for her badly infected foot. She says it was the Lord's grace that Tao Chiao-shih came back, for if she had not, she would have soon been going to heaven. She thinks it is a treat to be in a hospital where there are morning prayers every day.

Hankow, November 29, 1926

Were it not for the Lord and His keeping power prospects would be black this night. Mrs. Draffin was thinking in the days after the riot how the Lord opened a way through the Red Sea and that He could open a way through Tongting Lake. Fortunately we took this way even though usually it is anything but safe due to bandits, but we could not very well get through the fighting to come down the Yangtze.

There is not much prospect of our seeing the things we left in the house in Nanchow again. I have been praying that the Lord will either reconcile me to their loss or preserve them for me. Every once in a while I think of some little thing I want that is gone. There were tracts, gospels, books, and a few medicines, and groceries I should have liked to have either put in the hands of those who could use them or in a safe place, but I was at an out-station unable to help. Mrs. Draffin was packing the suitcase with my things just as the guards were withdrawn, so her selection of my things was not the best. My winter coat was so heavy she decided to leave it behind.

The Lord has a purpose in all this: He gave and He is worthy to receive our all. It will help in the future to comfort others having had my own goods spoiled. Some of the Chinese Christians lost even more heavily. There was no personal violence to any one of us, and all our Christians remained loyal.

You may wonder why we left in such a. hurry. It is just that there is no controlling a mob. Also we implicate every Chinese helper, servant, or any Christian who tries to help protect us.

I joined the Draffins in an out-station about fifteen miles from Nanchow. From there we went cross country twenty miles, more than half of which I walked. The two evangelists who will have the responsibility of the work, went this distance with us. One of the questions one of the evangelists asked me while we were alone was, "Are you coming back again?" Of course, my reply was in the affirmative.[37]

We got passage on a boat loaded with pigs, duck eggs, and coppers. It took two days to get across to Chieng-ling-chi. Upon landing, some foreigners who had heard of our trouble asked what they could do. When Mr. Draffin spoke of our not having seen any bread for a week, we were brought a loaf of bread and some cookies. No boat arrived so we could travel on that day. The commissioner of customs was a Portuguese and his wife French, but they entertained us in their luxurious home that night. The next day we took passage on another native boat. We did not part with our cook until this point. He surely had done all he could for us, working the boat, transfering baggage, or anything else. A twenty two hour trip on the boat brought us to Hankow.

One could hardly understand our relief on getting here. I had spent five nights in a house in more than three weeks. Other than bread Mrs. Draffin had saved enough food for the trip, and I had some things too. Between us we had two little one burner stoves to use for cooking. We all had enough bedding. All along the way we either had our own Christians, or the Lord raised up someone when we needed help.

Hankow, December 2, 1926

It may be that my letters in the past have painted things too black, but in view of the trend of affairs it is very hard not to do it. This much is certain—the government in these parts is compelling all laborers to form themselves into unions. The police have been instructed not to interfere with the unions destroying property. All laborers who work for foreigners are liable to a heavy tax for the privilege of doing so. Yesterday some one in moving from one concession to another had to pay the union a greater sum than the coolies actually received.[38]

In the matter of schools, all have been ordered to close if the children are required to study the Bible or attend morning prayers. They are also supposed to have the children worship the picture of Sun Yat-sen. Of course this will eventually mean the closing of all mission schools unless these rules are done away with or evaded. I heard just yesterday about the closing of one mission school.

"Draffin family, January 1927."

Hankow, December 13, 1926

We keep hearing of the troubles others are having, and we have reason to be thankful we got out as well as we did. Where some of the helpers or servants became disloyal the missionaries fared much worse. Disloyalty at a time like that would hurt more than the loss of things. This is quite a changing household. Hardly two days in succession do we have the same crowd. Two young ladies are here because their station has been looted and the house where one lived was burned. Others are delayed for one reason or another. Not many are going back to their work just now. I feel sorry for the new workers especially. One does not know which is harder, to hear voices all about one and not understand, or to understand and know some of the awful things being said.

I have been trying since I came here to write a letter in Chinese characters. It is quite a job. One could write several in English with less effort. Anyway my first letter in Chinese characters was sent away this week. We get encouraging news from Nanchow. The Chinese Christians are still meeting for worship. They are using the street chapel which was rented. The evangelist wrote that there were fourteen at a recent prayer meeting. The chief theme of their prayers seems to have been that the Lord will soon open the way for our return. Fourteen is no great number until one realizes the ridicule and persecution each one attending faces.

We hear that the official has put a proclamation outside the Nanchow house that the windows—only temporary slats nailed across—are not to be tampered with or things taken out on fear of punishment. But we hear things are being stolen, so it is not likely anything will be left in the house when any of us go back. One of the favorite tricks of the new regime seems to be to drive the missionaries out, steal everything in the house and then leave it in an indescribably filthy condition. Then they wonder why America will not recognize their government! It is very hard to understand why if they do not want imperialism, why they should oppose we American missionaries.

Kiangsi, December 22, 1926

Today finds me on another boat, a large river boat with its destination Shanghai. My main reason for going is to be that much nearer home. Since I am cut off from my work, I might as well go home and come back to the work fresh when the way opens. The headquarters for the China Inland Mission is in Shanghai. This property, as well as so many others I have visited in China, belongs to the mission, so I can stay rent free. Board is given to missionaries at cost. For the trip I paid a little over ten dollars native fare. Foreign fare would be at least fifty dollars.

Shanghai, December 30, 1926

Christmas began with carols, a thing the English go in for more than we do. "Noel" is a favorite. Then we looked at our presents. The Draffins had given me five dollars, and I had several packages and cards. In the morning I went to a church service. Then a special dinner was served of chicken, cold ham, cauliflower, plum pudding, mince pie, fruit, nuts, and candy.

After all the years of missionary work in China, only one person in a thousand is a Christian. Bolshevism in now gaining a headway among them. They refused to believe the truth and now believe a lie.

Shanghai, January 6, 1927

This is the only letter you are likely to have from me written in China this year. You probably will have to wait for me two weeks after you get it as the Taiyo Maru is rather a slow boat.

[Hazel was met in San Francisco by a number of newspaper reporters as well as some members of her family. She refused to talk with the reporters. From February 1927 to February 1929 Hazel was home on furlough. Her time was spent partially at Strathmore, California and partially in Los Angeles where she studied a course given for medical missionaries at her alma mater, the Bible Institute of Los Angeles. During the summer of 1928 she and her mother traveled to Minnesota to visit relatives. Hazel went on to visit China Inland Mission headquarters in Philadelphia, Washington, D.C., and other places in the east.]

S.S. Taiyo Maru, February 26, 1929

This is the third day the sea has been so rough that racks were needed on the tables. The deck is too wet to walk around much, and even reading is difficult.

On board we missionaries study and read Chinese. My turn has come twice to lead morning prayers.

S.S. Taiyo Maru, March 8, 1929

We were more than twenty four hours late running into Yokohoma. The storm was not severe but lasted a long time. We missed Kyoto due to snow and bad weather, but we had a ricksha ride through Tokyo. One day we had a fine view of Fujiyama. Yesterday afternoon we went through the Inland Sea. Mountains on both sides stick right up out of the water. Where the slopes are the least bit gradual, they are terraced. One is always impressed by the way the land of Japan is utilized.

Shanghai, March 22, 1929

Finding notation of Chinese music has been impossible for me. I am sending two Chinese posters to be used at church. The characters on one are Matthew 28:20. In both posters the Lord is represented as having Chinese features.[39]

Nanchow, May 15, 1929

We have been back here five days which have been full of renewing old acquaintances. The people seem more friendly than ever before. The Christians seem especially glad to see us. They are very sympathetic with us and seem to feel our losses as much as we do. The bond between us is very real.

Today a great many government students have been on the compound looking around. Their minds have been badly poisoned with much of the teaching they have received. They were not too friendly, but I gave out tracts as they left. They were most interested in the phonograph I brought back from America. There is no need to tell anyone to be quiet while that is going.

I was in Hankow three weeks. Mr. Draffin met me and got us passage on a Japanese boat which left us at a small place seventy miles from here. Mr. Draffin arranged for two boats to come farther. We had to pay about two fares each because we had so much baggage. Among the Christians who came down to meet the boat was the old man who helped me so much in the country the last week I was there. He is now nearly eighty. When he was seventy he had a stroke. He made a vow that if the Lord would give him ten more years, he would spend them preaching.

Nanchow, June 13, 1929

Day before yesterday was the fifth day of the fifth month. The people hang green bows in front of the houses in honor of the occasion and go through many idolatrous customs. As far as possible they have feasts and new clothes. One special dish of the season is the steamed glutinous rice done up in leaves into a conelike shape. Since the belief is that anyone who does not eat one of these during the holiday will surely be ill, we are supplied with some of this treat.[40]

The evangelist here thought we should take advantage of the holiday and had asked the church members to help him have a service in the afternoon. Shops were closed, but there were many people in from the country. When the time came, only one old church member was about. The chapel was opened, and I took out my phonograph and set it going. In fifteen or twenty minutes there was a crowd. Nearly two hundred people were here during part of the hour and a half of the meeting, some staying clear through. They listened very well too. We are hoping next time the church members will enter more heartily into inviting the people in and also looking after people after they come. The phonograph often does good service in getting a group together when the workers want to sell books or preach.

Last week we had a boy come with an abcess just below the eye lashes of the lower lid. He was only here twice after it opened, but he did not come back again so we do not know how well it is healed. The young woman who came to us with her ear canal swollen shut was a more discouraging case. The treatment we used was to syringe out the canal with saline and put in hot oil. She says what we did helped her ear but we are not entirely satisfied. If we had a better speculum and more skill, we might have saved her a lot of pain.

Kuling, July 4, 1929

I had thought it would not be necessary to come away this summer, but here I am. Mrs. Draffin complained about the heat and maintained that little Keith could not stay in Nanchow during the summer. She minds the heat more because she is too stout and also because she does not know what heat is. I admit though there were a number of nights I slept without a sheet over me.

We came by a fast launch to Changsha. From there we had second class compartments on a train to Wuchang, across the river from Hankow. We took the ferry across and spent the weekend there. An overnight trip on a river steamer got us to Kiukiang. Then we came by motor to the foot of the hill then up the hill by chairs. Mrs. Draffin's chair bearers made a fuss about needing two more bearers, but as soon as the four men I had hired were out of sight of the hiring area, they readjusted the poles, and one went back. The three left claimed the one man was sick, but, of course, it was just a scheme for three men to get the pay of four. If foreigners managed things, a motor road to the top of this hill would be considered a necessity.

Kuling, July 19, 1929

Since coming up here I have read a book on psychology and one of Ralph Connor's books in English and a book used as a reader in eighth or ninth grade in Chinese. I did go out once for afternoon tea, and perhaps I should have spent more time getting acquainted. But you know books are always more interesting to me than people. Books are more instructive and do not tell the same thing over and over. Besides one has to dress up to see people. With books one can read them any time and put one's whole attention on them. In talking with folks one has to keep up part of the conversation and not say anything more dull or dumb than what other people say. Of course, I know this is rather a one-sided argument because we are supposed to give rather then receive.

There are some beautiful walks one can take around here. From one spot one can look out on the lake, from another one can see the Yangtze. Some times there are special cloud effects to add to the interest and beauty. There are some big trees, some peculiar rock formations, and old Chinese temples. Temples usually are more attractive in pictures than actually seeing them. In pictures the dirt is not as conspicuous, and the idols are not as hideous.

There is a peculiar something about most idols that almost makes one shudder, and many look terrible enough indeed to be the habitation of demons. The awful bondage the people about us are in because of their fear of them no doubt has something to do with our feeling about them. I would much rather see a mouse or snake than many idols I have seen. It is a great reminder to us of how much we have to be thankful for that we have never been so in bondage to gods made by men.[41]

Much has been done in past years to improve the roads and property here at Kuling. But as the Chinese gradually get control of things, the roads are not in as good repair. The Chinese are buying the property up here to a great extent and probably it will not be many years before they confiscate the rest. It is interesting to see though that there is one hotel being built by Chinese for Christians of their country. They are to have rules against smoking, drinking, gambling, and late hours. Board is to be cheaper there than in the ordinary hotels.

I have been offered some work in a hospital for a time. I would refuse it if it were not for the experience to be gained. Of course if I make anything on it that should be turned over to the mission. The experience may be worth something, although a half day for a month is not much. In the hospital there is not a lot of regular work to be done. None of the patients are dangerously sick. We are not supposed to answer the bells from the rooms. The boys are expected to do that, and if anything is wanted that either they or the amah (Chinese woman servant) cannot do they call us. We keep track of pulse, respiration, and temperatures of the patients, look after giving their medicines, and keep an eye on whether they eat. We must keep care of sheets, pillow cases, and towels. Between other jobs we mend. The doctor sometimes calls us for help; for instance, today I held a baby while the doctor clipped a bit of skin under the tongue. The child was tongue tied, and that is all that was necessary to keep the child from talking as though he had mush in his mouth all his life.

Kuling, August 12, 1929

An average of more than six hours a day at the hospital and a little study fill up my time. Most of the patients are not seriously ill. There is a trained nurse on duty when I am learning to do some of the hypodermic injections. I am rather afraid of giving them even though I know I must learn how. The doctor sometimes asks me to help with something like opening a boil or taking an Xray, and one morning he sent me off by myself to give an injection.

We have not decided on the time to leave the hill. The little Draffin boy needs a slight operation, so we will stop in Changsha a few days for that. In normal times I would go the rest of the way by myself; however, this time Mr. Draffin intends to leave Mr. Mason, the young worker, by himself while he comes to Changsha to meet us. Mr. Mason has been in China almost a year, but he is the kind of man who gets afraid in a thunder shower or needs help to move a piece of furniture in his room. He is just five feet one and a half inches tall, and in many respects makes me think he should have been a girl.

Shihshow, Hupeh, September 30, 1929

This letter is being written from our most northern out-station which is about thirty-five miles from Nanchow. It is in another province, and the people are quite different. One of the evangelists once told me that if I wanted to know what China was like thirty or forty years ago to look at Shihshow. One still finds little girls here with bound feet. Although there is less of that seen now than the first time I came, much of it is still done. The women too stay in more. You would see very few women on the street. It is rather difficult to work here as the women are afraid of us. I have been advised not to go on the street to invite women to come to meetings but to only go to homes of church members. The postmaster was here this morning to invite me to come to his home and possibly to try his English. He was once an evangelist but gave it up because the salary was not sufficient. As postmaster he gets four times as much.

On our return trip from Kuling, we were nine days in Changsha. While there I visited a school for blind girls run by one of our associate missionaries. Forty girls are enrolled. There were some cute little girls there. This teacher has in the past trained other teachers for the blind. She seems to know what she is doing because the girls were busy and interested. They do beautiful knitting or spend a lot of time making books for themselves and others.

The trip by launch from Changsha to Nanchow took an extra day because there were over fourteen thousand silver dollars on board. So they were afraid to cross the lake at night for fear of brigands. Some of the lake is shallow enough for high reeds to grow, which makes a great hiding place for brigands. So the launch anchored during the night. We arrived early Friday afternoon.

Saturday in Nanchow I went out to see a few of the people. Then I had to see to getting furniture for the Bible woman's room and for the guest room.

Then I got ready to come away. My things to take out with me were scattered all over the house, so packing medicines and things took some time. We started out Thursday for the out-station. That was our first clear day after reaching Nanchow, and it has been clear since.

Nanchow, October 14, 1929

My birthday was spent going from one out-station to another on my way back to Nanchow. The Draffins seemed determined to celebrate even though late. They gave me a very pretty tray and had some extra fixings for dinner the Sunday after my birthday.

We did not get as much done on our trip as we had hoped. Shihshow has been the most difficult of our out-stations, and the people seemed more indifferent than ever. The evangelist who has been working there fifteen years, has not had any converts, but one can see that the testimony he has given is counting. We went to see the Buddhist nun who had about decided to leave the place the time we were there before. She seemed very glad to see us. It may be hard for her to break away but if she is really sincere in wanting to believe the gospel she must do it. We went to see one young man who had been chosen as a leader by the communists during the uprising. Although he had been a church member, he had succeeded in getting money from the church for the communists. Then he was afraid to ask the evangelist to conduct the funeral service for his mother and had a regular heathen service with the spirit tablet, incantations of the Taoist priest, and all the fixings. Just before I was there he had been very ill and delirious from fever and sent for the evangelist. When I heard of the invitation, I suggested that I go too. There was rain four days to keep us from going. When we did go, we walked nearly three miles through mud. When he found out who I was, he wanted the spirit tablet burned. His wife and the evangelist kindled a fire outside and burned it at once. They also threw some scrolls onto the fire. I do not know what was wrong about the scrolls, but, no doubt, they knew. Then we went in and had prayer with the man, and he wept over his sins. Fortunately, he is well on the road to recovery.

The last day before my return the evangelist and I walked well over ten miles stopping to talk to people by the way. To pack, the curtains and mosquito net had to come down, the bedding has to go in the oil sheet, and the bed has a special cover. Cooking utensils, food, and medicines go in a galvanized iron box which will keep out rats. We went by a small boat out to the river. There we got on a larger boat. We could easily tell that the boat man and his wife had come from a distance because of their dress. They had quite a tale to tell of their having been burned out and forced to leave home by the communists. They came away with very few of their possessions. The boat they had had for use in high water. They were hard working people and fortunately young enough to make a fresh start.

The evangelist at Meitienhu came with us when we came back. On the way he asked us to stop for the birthday feast of a child a year old at the home of a church member. The baby was already engaged to a baby now ten months old. One wishes they would cease making engagements for little children.

We still see many children with bound feet at our northern out-stations. On the way on a boat I was sitting where I could see only the face of a girl about ten years old. I remarked to the Bible woman, "That girl has bound feet." The Bible woman looked at me and asked how I knew, but she had to admit it was true. One can almost always tell because it is imprinted on the face.

Nanchow, October 29, 1929

We have just spent eleven days at an out-station where we should have spent that many months. The widow of a former evangelist has promised to do what she could for the women until we can come again. She seemed so glad to see us and told the Bible woman that she would rather see us than her closest relatives. One girl told us that our message just begins to have a flavor when we go away. But we have so many out-stations besides the work at Nanchow to do, so we must go on.

The wife of one of the evangelists has just come back from her mother's home. She brought me a chicken and the cotton filling for a comforter. She had not been back at Nanchow since before my furlough.

She helped me with the language my second year in China. Now that her children are older she can help us out some.

Nanchow, November 16, 1929

The house here is very quiet now. Mr. and Mrs. Draffin, Keith, Mr. Mason, and the cook are gone for a few days. Mr. Mason has been living here the last few months. There is a girl in Scotland with whom he keeps up a regular correspondence. She expects to come to China too.

Thursday afternoon we got back from a trip where we spent ten nights in five different houses. While out we attended a wedding . To get there I walked what seemed like three miles through the rain. The mud was much like that at home. In order not to slip I put on straw sandals such as coolies wear over my rubbers. The Bible woman could not walk that far anyway so had to wait to have a chair sent for her. She weighs very little over eighty pounds, but the evangelists say that when it comes to transportation, she is reckoned with the bedding and the baggage.

One evening I heard the Chinese having a good laugh. One of the evangelists was giving a demonstration of how the Bible woman and I cross ditches. He was making the motions of the way I lift her across. This seems to be an abundant source of mirth in spite of my threat to let them help her.

We spent three days at one place at the time of the wedding and had meetings twice a day. The last evening they called on me to speak. I had never been where the people seemed to appreciate us more. Several want to be baptized. There is no place there to hold meetings other than homes. On Sunday we had benches arranged under a matting.

While at one of the homes they asked for some popcorn to be used for seed, and they would like other varieties of seeds too. This is the first time I have been asked for anything of this kind. I hope some can be sent to me.

I have been treating three patients. The one I dread most is a year old baby who has erysipelas. Fortunately it is on only one leg and is extending toward the foot. The whole family was ill at the time of the father's death about three months ago, and the child was neglected.

Nanchow, December 9, 1929

The most important thing we have done recently was to have a month of study for women and girls. The evangelist's widow from the out-station came. With her she brought a girl about thirteen years old who has been most cruelly treated by her step-mother. Also from an out-station came the new bride whose wedding I attended and her husband's sister. The bride has much encouragement because her husband and his people are Christians. The sister-in-law has it hard because she would not worship idols as her mother-in-law wishes.

Mrs. Feng, the Bible woman, is teaching two classes each day. One is from a book of simple Bible verses which the class memorizes. The other is a more advanced study of Matthew. Mrs. Chin, the wife of one of the evangelists, is teaching the catechism. My daily class is on Old Testament history. It is rather advanced. I also have two classes on story telling where I am trying to get the girls to tell Bible stories and a class on simple hygiene. Mrs. Draffin is teaching hymn singing. We have two hours a week on handwork. Not more than a third of the women who come care for the handwork. We are not sorry about this because the aim is Bible study. The Chinese workers are really enthusiastic about this study, and have done some good work on it.

"Feng Hwei-min as evangelist."

Today we were called out at noon to deal with a case of attempted suicide. The woman had taken face powder. We gave her mustard water to get rid of the poison, but I am afraid she had absorbed some of it, and, no doubt, it contained arsenic. A man is coming in later today to have his eyes treated. We have reason to be glad that the child with erysipelas has recovered.

Mr. Draffin is away to meet the children coming home for the Christmas holidays. He had just returned from Changteh where he had conducted a funeral and started out within two days for Changsha.

At midnight after a busy Christmas day we were called next door where the woman had taken opium. This family tried to look after our things while we were gone. Mrs. Draffin gave her a solution of permangate of potash. She stayed with her an hour, and I stayed on another two hours. I should have felt better during that time if I had had a hypodermic needle with the proper medicine on hand. Anyway the woman and her husband were most appreciative of what we did.

Nanchow, December 27, 1929

The three Draffin children help keep things lively here. We have Keith here all the time, of course, but with the other three he is noisier than ever, but with them here he has not been so tempted to wander off to the Chinese quarters.

Nanchow, January 30, 1930

Right now I would give all the tea in China for a good walk. But there is not much chance to work out because the roads are like mush. There have been at least patches of snow on the ground since the middle of December. The cold hasn't bothered me with the warm clothes I brought back.

The girl with the burned leg that I was trying to treat died. Someone suggested to me that the real cause of her death was the smoke she breathed in when she was burned. It was a Chinese who reminded me of this. Her leg steadily improved from the first, but I had my doubts about things and made the father promise that should she die, he was not to blame me. Poor little girl—if only she had proper food even after she began being brought here, her life might have been spared.

Only two or three days later another girl began to come to have her feet attended to. She had chilblains which have swelled and burst. One ulcer is half the size of my hand, and there are several smaller ones. Her feet are not healing very fast yet there is some improvement. Her feet were bound which makes matters worse. Her shoes and stockings are only the cast offs which had belonged to others. She is a strong healthy girl of about sixteen so I have reason to hope this case will not terminate fatally.

The first copy of the Ladies Home Journal has not yet come. All the mail has been held up. The popcorn is great. I do not enjoy giving any of it away for seed. The people may go on with their anti-foreign propaganda, and yet still get hold of everything possible that is foreign.

Nanchow, February 12, 1930

One of the girls who was baptized at Christmas time says she objects to being married to an outside man as her parents are likely to arrange. She wants to go to Bible school to prepare to do definite Christian work. This would mean some expense, but this can be settled. She has been faithful and quick in doing her work, and now makes her living by knitting, crocheting, and other handwork.

The man whose eyes I treated has been coming to church regularly. The girl with chilblains needs my attention yet nearly every day.

Today I gave a girl some hair pins to pin on a switch. During the troubles her hair had been bobbed. Now she is to be married out in the country. She knows she must have hair when she goes there, otherwise they will think she is a bad girl.

Tomorrow four Chinese expect to go with me to a town four or five miles from here. Sometimes we take the phonograph to help draw a crowd, but where we hope to go tomorrow we will have all the crowds we can handle without any such help.

Nanchow, March 25, 1930

The Draffins and Mr. Mason have been away nearly two weeks now, and when alone the work fills a lot of my time. Some days there have been as many as nine patients or even ten. Yesterday the daughter-in-law of one of our church members was very ill. Her husband and other members of the family thought she was going to die. I gave the usual treatment for round worms, and today she is better. There is a young child with bronchitis I am trying to treat, and among other things today, I opened a sty on the inside of an eyelid. A boy who spends most of his time looking after a horse has been coming in every day to have a foot dressed. A Chinese doctor tried to treat him without success, so he sent him to me. Even I poulticed the foot a couple of days before getting up courage to pierce the thick skin with a knife. Now since the sore has drained, the foot is much better. One of our out-station church members has quite a name as a Chinese doctor. A young man from there came here last week who had been going to him for a sore hand. It was swollen badly when I began treating it, and some of those on the compound thought I was a bit bold in undertaking the case. Six days later he went home almost completely cured. Some of the Chinese put me up against the Chinese doctor, saying I can beat him. The Chinese workers will not listen to my giving up the medical work. One of the evangelists said, "Leave the work of visiting the church members and working to reach outsiders to us. You work with patients." The last few months, with so much time spent on physical needs, have been just as productive in spiritual results as any time I have served. The Chinese workers are bringing in outsiders, and some days they sell as many as a hundred and fifty gospels.

If someone could get some bichloride of mercury for me, I would appreciate it. Such poisons are hard for me to get. I wish Unguentine were less expensive. It is simply out of the question for me to buy it. If we used it, we would be even more than now kept going by patients.

Everyone thinks it was fortunate that I came back from the northern out-stations when I did. There has been trouble with communists there since then. They came to our chapel at one place and commanded the evangelist's wife to bring out the Bibles and hymn books. She got them out and then they asked her to burn them. She refused, saying they were God's books. They replied, "We even burn idols". "Yes," she said, "It is all right to burn idols because men made them, but these books came from God and so we must not burn them." "Alright," they said, "we will go and burn idols." They left then saying nothing more. The out-stations to the north are apparently now adequately protected against communists, but they must have had a bad time of it for a while.

Nanchow, April 24, 1930

Seems as though just when I start a job, I am called out to the dispensary. Then it may take me a long time to read up on the case and diagnose it. This week in the few days since coming back from the out-station two cases have come to me which need minor operations. That would not be so bad if there were some one in Nanchow capable of performing a minor operation, but there is no one.

Since this letter was started Easter is over. Only two were baptized—an old blind man and a young girl of about thirteen. The girl's grandfather, father, two uncles and an aunt have been or are church members. Her uncle who died was the first one of the family to become a Christian. The old blind man's wife and son have been church members some years. His wife learned to read the catechism by describing the characters to him and he would tell her what they were. Two women were examined for baptism but one of the men on the church committee objected to their baptism. If the things he charges them with are true, it is right that they should wait. Years ago the church committee would not have said anything about these matters as they did not want to offend anyone.

We are expecting another man to come here to work sometime later in the spring. He is an American from North Carolina. He has his master's degree and another one besides. We wonder how he will get along with Mr. Mason, our pocket edition of Scotland who came last year. Mr. Mason was fearfully spoiled before coming to China, and his hat still is not big enough for him.

Nanchow, May 15, 1930

My "practice" seems to increase. Today was my record so far with sixteen patients in all. Had Mr. Mason been here, he would have attended to some of them, but he has gone to meet the new man who is coming. Now that the Bible woman is away the work is even harder. I do not know many Chinese medical terms, and those I do know are not what they use. For instance, a tooth that is decayed they always say was eaten by worms, and they speak about fire when we would say fever or poison. Besides, when they talk about their heart, usually they mean their stomachs. We are treating an old man who had a carbuncle and it spread before we began doing anything for him. Even after handling the case nearly three weeks I am not any too sure about matters, although he says he is much better. Because of the seriousness of the case we tried to persuade him to go elsewhere. But he said he had no money to go elsewhere, and if the time had come for him to die he could not blame us. It is true we do not generally have so many people come to me as today, but sometimes their ailments are more serious and take more time.

Sometimes I wish people would be as ready to tell what was done for their souls as they are to tell what was done for their bodies. Yet after all this does result in a larger church attendance. Last Sunday we had the largest attendance since we came back here. About one hundred and fifty were present, and more than half were women. In addition the bell was back at the church for the first time since the trouble. A bell that makes a reasonable amount of sound is a great help to us here. So many people do not have clocks. As one church member said today, she had too much to do to come too early, and is ashamed of being late,

Our Bible woman has become a grandmother. In China the custom is that for a mother's first baby her mother must furnish the clothes. The grandmother should not be seen preparing the things.

Nanchow, May 30, 1930

Yesterday a man came in who said he had been bitten by a mad dog. I told this at dinner table and they began giving all kinds of warnings about not letting the man bite me, undertaking the case, etc. They almost wanted to throw something at me when I told them where he was bitten—on the trousers. It seems the Chinese believe that the bite of a mad dog even on the clothing will cause hydrophobia. We told him to scald and sun his clothes and try to get the dog killed lest he harm others. The evangelist told the man he would guarantee that if he believed the gospel, no harm would come to him from the bite. But the evangelist's wife told me I should have given the man a dose of medicine, if nothing more a dose of castor oil. It is often easier to paint on some iodine, for instance, than to explain matters, and they believing so firmly in counter-irritants, just because it does burn think it is wonderful medicine.

Changsha, June 26, 1930

This letter is being started on the way to Changsha. We have started out to go away for the summer, but so far it is a case of not knowing where I am going but being on my way. The British Consul has declared Kuling and Kikungshan unsafe. The Draffins are on their way to Chefoo, but there is no reason why I should go there.

Since my last letter there has been quite a military movement in our province. Some say forty thousand soldiers passed through Nanchow within ten days. They merely passed through, causing no great amount of trouble. Some did start to occupy our chapel but had been there only a few hours and were still eating their first meal they prepared there when they got word from headquarters to move on. It did not take them long to get away. The soldiers made a bridge across the river with small row boats and kept it there for about a week. These soldiers were fairly orderly, and they paid for most of what they ate and used. The prices of everything eatable went up, but we minded ever more not getting any mail for two weeks. The greatest inconvenience to me was not having medicines I had ordered.

The medicines you sent were certainly appreciated. A few of my patients can afford to pay something. Four chickens and a good many eggs were given me within the two weeks before I left. One chicken was brought the day before we left for something to eat on the trip.

Shanghai, July 2, 1930

We had a good trip here. From Nanchow to Changsha took three days. That is good time to make a hundred and fifty miles when one has to depend on the wind and man power. Ordinarily there is a launch which makes the trip in a day, but due to troop movements these launches were elsewhere. We found a Japanese boat leaving about two or three o'clock Sunday morning, but nearly everyone boarded on Saturday evening. We arrived in Hankow Sunday evening about eight o'clock. Then we caught a boat leaving for Shanghai within an hour. Travel on this side of Hankow is not like being in China. On this side meals are served decently and in order. On the other side it was more like camping. What cooking we did was done on my one burner stove.

Shanghai, July 23, 1930

Many have asked where I am going to get away from the heat, but I am not going anywhere that will make a lot of extra expense. This is somewhat cooler than Nanchow.

Three days after we left Nanchow bandits or communists came with the intention of inviting Mr. Mason and Mr. Moore, our new worker, to join them. The two young men were warned by loud banging on the front gate. They put on Chinese clothes, slipped out the back gate, and went through the rice fields where they were met by several church members. From there they went to an out-station where they stayed a few days. The bandits looted the town. They took with them the Roman Catholic priest, a man from Spain whom I have never met, some of our neighbors, and a few well to do people. They frightened the Bible woman so much that she fled. Things at the station were scattered about, and some things were taken. In regard to our own things we will not know until we return, but I was informed that some of my medicine and instruments are missing. My phonograph was taken, but a church member saw it on the street and brought it back. The officials telegraphed Changsha, and withing twenty four hours thousands of soldiers had arrived to clear out the bandits.

The Draffins went from here to Chefoo by boat. Their boat crashed into a cargo boat carrying coal so that it sank within a few minutes. No lives were lost though. Mr. and Mrs. Draffin and Keith are all in need of medical attention.

Shanghai, August 11, 1930

One wonders what you see in the papers this summer about Hunan. They have had plenty of excitement there. If when the governor left the capital nearly two months ago he had stayed out things might have been all right, but he went back in again and since has let the communists in. He has always seemed to be a good official but has almost made a fool of himself this time. At any rate he has seemed to put an end for the time being to the foolish discussion about giving up extraterritoriality. I guess for once some Chinese are ashamed of themselves for they do not seem to be publishing it to the world that American, British, and Japanese gunboats helped put the communists out of Changsha. They did not succeed in doing this before the consulates and most of the mission property there were wrecked. The communists used the Bible school there for their headquarters, so those buildings fared better. The Chinese government headquarters was burned.[42]

You may wonder why the taking of Changsha should so greatly concern me. Mr. Mason and Mr. Moore had become alarmed over the various rumors that had come to their ears. So, gallant young men that they are, they determined to save the Draffin's and my things as well as their own. Mr. Moore packed about everything of mine, and Mr. Mason took all the things to Changsha. Mrs. Draffin had told them to put things a few in a place around in the homes of church members in such a situation, but I do not know what possessed them. The things were left at the Liebenzell Mission (the German associate branch of the CIM). Their buildings were unharmed in the 1927 troubles, but this time everything in them has been looted and even the brick walls thrown down.

As for my own things, I brought most of my clothes along except those for winter. In my trunk which I brought to Shanghai I brought besides clothes some photographs, a few books, kodak, some sheets, towels, and pillow cases. I brought some blankets and a pillow in my bed bundle and a basket of just such things one would need when going camping. My winter clothes must be replaced and I have started knitting to that end already. The phonograph and many books are gone, also my notes and everything else needed for medical work.

Most woolen things are cheaper here than there, but outing flannel is much more expensive. I ought not to ask for anything, but a dozen yards of outing flannel would come in handy.

Shanghai, September 2, 1930

One realizes that things after all do not count for much. A fresh reminder of that came last week with news of the death by violence of one of our native fellow workers. The letter said the Mr. Chang Loh-han had been killed by brigands but they probably also had very strong communistic tendencies. The evangelist who wrote the letter is in great enough danger himself to perceive that he could not tell the whole truth. Loh-han is the Chinese romanization for John, the name he took at baptism. Mr. Chang did have some property it is true, which may have had something to do with his death. But very likely his very faithfulness in his work as evangelist counted against him. He had worked as an evangelist between fifteen and twenty years. I do not know how many years before that he had been a Christian. It was Mr. Chang's wife who persuaded the communists not to burn the Bibles and hymn books, and they went away saying they would burn idols. They could find plenty to burn in Shihshow.

We will miss Mr. Chang terribly for he worked hard there at Shihshow. It is an extremely difficult place. It is easy to get a large group of unsaved men to hear the gospel, but on the street there are not many Christians. So Mr. Chang took many trips many miles into the country. He believed strongly in doing pastoral work. He said it was like kindling a fire to boil water—if you do not fan the fire to get the water to boiling, the water will make people sick (in our part of China all drinking water must be boiled). He did his best to look after the number of country Christians, and thousands must have heard him preach the gospel. So far as I know, only one church member helped his wife bury him. They buried him the day of his death, so the others perhaps did not know about it or may have been afraid to do anything in too open a way.

Shanghai, September 28, 1930

All "the powers that be" are agreed on one thing, and that is for the present I am not to go back to Hunan. There are some parts of China considered much safer, so they are asking me to go to one of the Baptist stations of our mission in Anhwei with three practically new workers. Two have been studying the language a year but have never been in a station in the interior. The other has been there a few months. Miss Knight is a very small girl from Massachusetts. At present she has a pain in her side and is having X-rays taken. I think I am going to like her, for she seems like a girl who will wear well. Miss Hinckley who has already been there a few months is English. We have shared the same room about a month here in Shanghai so we have begun to get acquainted. She is a very good mixer and I am sure the other girls will like her. The third girl I have not met but I have met her parents both in China and in California. Miss Elliott herself was born in China. Her mother is a doctor and she herself has a degree. In these days it is no small undertaking to be at least twenty miles away from any other foreigners with three other girls all in their 'twenties. Of course they only expect me to go to Shucheng, Anhwei for a few months or possibly a year because, being a Baptist station, they cannot send me there permanently.[43]

From what I hear the evangelist there is a hindrance rather than a help to the work. But on the whole they have a fine work there, better than Nanchow or Changteh as it should be because it is older. There are no out-stations. More of the managing of things is in the hands of the Chinese, and so far they have not been ready to do that. The last missionary there broke down partly because of the way the evangelist acted. He is anti-British but thinks America is all right. Even so, here is where I need to watch my P's and Q's.

Someone has turned over to me more books than I had before, but the supply lacks medical books or those for reference. There is no dictionary or concordance among them. It rather bothers me to have to use dishes, table linen, kitchen utensils, and such which belong to the other girls, but that can not be helped.

Mr. Draffin is in Shanghai, and will go back to Hunan just as soon as he can get passage on a boat. Since the British Consul forbids women and children to go back to Hunan at present, Mrs. Draffin may just as well stay near the children at Chefoo.

CHAPTER TWO

Reassignment to Anhui: The Middle Years, 1930-1937

Anking, October 28, 1930

A man had to leave his wife and four tiny children to come one hundred twenty miles here to escort us to Shucheng. Our station is eighty miles from here, and fortunately it is on the way to his. These distances would not be so much to go in a car, but when one must go in a chair or on "old Shank's mare," that is the difference.

This Anking compound is where the new young men of our mission come to study the language. So far there are only twelve here. Week before last five came from North America, and last week seven came from England. This week three more will come. The work here is about twice as old as that at Nanchow. The people here do contribute more money than those there, but the church attendance is less than a third as large.

Our baggage increases rather than diminishes here. We are getting a galvanized iron tub made to use as a bathtub. We also buy potatoes and onions here. To get to Shucheng all these things go eighty miles by wheelbarrow. We would think the men much underpaid. Yet with things sent by train or truck, and ourselves too for that matter, it would be much cheaper. It is said that in some places in China transportation costs are the highest anywhere in the world. Margaret Elliott and Eva Knight have been spending the waiting time here studying. I finished a sweater today. It is brown as is the coat I had made in Shanghai. I also had two wool dresses made and two house dresses.

Shucheng, November 25, 1930

We have been here now ten days getting acquainted and putting the house in order. Margaret and Eva are both fine girls. They don't like being confined on the compound, and perhaps they mind that all the Chinese come to me about anything. The language is enough different to be a handicap to me here.

We waited four weeks in Anking for Mr. H. Costerus to come to escort us here. We made the eighty mile trip in three and a half days. We rode in bearer chairs the distance we did not walk. I walked nearly half of the way. A folding bed and a tub were tied on my chair. Six wheel barrows and four other men were needed to get our things here. About half of what one man carried was food for the trip. Another man carried two suit cases and two rolls of bedding. A third man carried the bedding for the other two. The wheel barrows brought our trunks, four cases of milk, over a hundred pounds of potatoes, twenty five pounds of onions, the same amount of prunes, butter, and other food. Mr. Costerus will come later with Miss Doris Hinckley.

"A hard place on the road here. This is the way all freight comes the last eighty miles to Shucheng."

We came over some pretty hills coming here. The first day I counted eight varieties of wild flowers. Many of the leaves on the trees had turned red or gold, so it was really beautiful. We also saw some holly and lots of stones. One village where we stayed was paved with red stones.

News from Nanchow is bad. Mr. Draffin arrived there but was out for a few days when the place was looted again. When he went back and found everything was gone, he started out for Hankow to get clothes and other things.

Shucheng, January 4, 1931

The package of books and the money came this week. I am very glad to get the books particularly. Thank you.

Just before Christmas Margaret took her second section examination.

The other girls expect to take another examination soon, so they are studying much of the time. This week we are having rain and snow which keeps us in, so that I may get time to do some studying myself.

We have been hiring a man the last two weeks to work on the grounds. He has cut down most of the mulberry trees and has spaded up part of the ground. The girls want a tennis court in part of the yard. We want part of the bamboo grove cut down. The bamboo could be used for rooms for the gardener and a place for goats.

The most important event of the week was having the evangelist move off the compound. He never hurt himself at his church work. Perhaps now that he is gone the church members will do more.

Shucheng, January 26, 1931

What worries me lately more than anything else is a message from Nanchow last week. The evangelist did not not write very much, but what he did write was significant. He merely said the church was having trouble. All one can do is pray, and not just that His children be kept from harm and danger much as we would like them to be spared. In the eleventh chapter of Hebrews there is a list of those who were delivered from special trial, and then there is a list of those who were not delivered "of whom the world is not worthy". Among my acquaintances there were four last year who won the martyr's crown.

Shucheng, February 19, 1931

Anyone would enjoy looking at things outside today. The snow is almost two feet deep. The people here say they have not had as much for forty years. With very little wind the snow stays where it fell. The houses are not built to stand such a weight of snow. There have been deaths from houses collapsing. In over three weeks we have not been able to go out visiting, and few have come in.

Shucheng, March 15, 1931

Here in Shucheng I do very little doctoring; in fact, I have not yet been able to afford a good supply of medicines. Sometimes the most necessary thing to do is to use one's wits. A few weeks ago the cook and his wife came in to say that their daughter had a terrible heart attack. Having been in China a few days I have very little trust in the average person's knowledge of anatomy. I mixed up a strong dose of peppermint tea. I slopped a lot of it on the way as the street was horrid, and I stepped in snow water above my ankles. Anyway the peppermint touched the spot immediately. The cook now wants a bottle of it. He said last year he had called in someone who gave a hypodermic injection with poorer results. Eva Knight saw me going and drew a picture of the cook's wife and me going down the street as a cartoon in her diary. She made the spoon I left in the cup about a third as big as me.

"Eva Knight, one of my fellow workers."

Shucheng, March 30, 1931

At present we have three men at work on the wall. In a couple of days we have to have a mason mend the holes in the brick wall. It has been mostly children who have picked out bricks one by one until there are holes in two places large enough for a person to crawl through. We are also having a new door put in. The cook and his family live near this door, and it will save them much walking. The cook's little grand daughter has been out in her future mother-in-law's home. She was brought back from there with both her face and stomach swollen, the latter hard. We had someone give her castor oil yesterday, but this evening I gave her salts. Perhaps she has worms—about half of the children do seem to have worms.

Shucheng, March 31, 1931

This afternoon we went out to a couple of homes. At one place there is a young man probably dying with tuberculosis. It does not seem possible for him to live out many more days. One marvels at the faith of these people, for they still believe the Lord will heal him. His brothers went clear to Nanking, at least a hundred and fifty miles away, and with the help of two others carried him home. The foreign doctor in Nanking told them they would never get him home, and it is now a month and a half since he returned.

Today the cook's little granddaughter was buried. He feels simply terrible about it and well he may. Someone said today he did not mind it so much when his only little grandson died. This time the hard part of it is that he feels she died of neglect. We think it was beri beri. Had I had my notes taken at Bible Institute or a suitable medical book, I might have found out in time what to do to save the child's life. It was only by chance I discovered what it was.

The child was dying before the cook confessed to me that in the mother-in-law's home where she had been living she had not been properly clothed or fed. This morning he sobbed as he tried to tell me it was his wife's fault, not his. We hope this will be a good lesson to our Christians not to let the future mother-in-laws of their daughters bring them up. This darling girl was just four or five years old. The coffin was only a rough box. Two of the deacons and a few of the relatives were the only ones besides those in the compound who came to the funeral.[1]

Shucheng, April 28, 1931

We have not had things going too smoothly the last few weeks. The former evangelist wrote to the central committee of the province saying something about this church being independent, that is, having nothing to do with the CIM. I was pretty certain that it had not been put before the church and did not think it even expressed the desires of the deacons. After inquiring of one deacon I found he knew nothing about it. Another deacon said he knew Mr. Hsiao the former evangelist had written about that time. But Mr. Hsiao was supposed to write a sort of apology for his own wrong doing. Instead of that he has gotten himself and the church in deeper. Up to now everything has been referred to him and he has always had his own way. But the deacons are going to have to oppose him or get in trouble with "the powers that be" of the mission.

"The leading deacon and his family.
Three of the girls are daughters-in-law."

A nice little message was brought me from one of the deacons yesterday to the effect that I came here to preach the gospel, not to heal the sick. Instead of wholly taking this to heart, I sent back word that we preach the gospel with our hands as well as our mouths, and even our Lord sometimes healed the sick. The case in point is that his little daughter has been ill with bronchitis for over a month. They live in dark stuffy rooms and do not know how to look after her. Unless she gets some extra good care and that soon there is not much hope of her recovery. She vomits the coarse kind of food they give her, and her heart is fearfully weak and respiration terribly high. I feel sure we could do something for her if we started giving her milk. He may bring her to us yet, for it is almost the only hope of saving her life. Still he can not bring himself to bother us.

A wife of another church member has really become insane. We saw her last week. She asked me if she would not get better if we let her come to the mission compound. Perhaps I showed a lack of faith to say I did not know. Years of undernourishment and overwork have brought on her condition in addition to her having been mentally weak in the first place. Her mother-in-law had killed two daughters-in-law before she got this one. One of them was killed with a blow from a stick of firewood.

Shucheng, May 10, 1931

After discussing the matter with the other girls, we got permission of the deacon with the sick daughter to bring her here to take care of her; however, the permission wasn't granted until the choice was lose her or let us try to help. The first few days there was too much anxiety for me to enjoy it, for I had to take the responsiblity for her medicine, diet, and all. The first night her respiration was both so fast and noisy I dared not sleep. I had visions of her dying during the night and my not having a chance to send word to her folks until morning. They live in the country, and the city gates are closed at night. We can praise the Lord she is now out of danger and can soon go home. The Chinese hate the idea of using cow's milk, but humanly speaking this was the only way this child's life could be saved.

Mr. and Mrs. Costerus, who serve at the CIM station nearest to us, are to start on their furlough next month. We have not yet met Mrs. Costerus and the children. Word has come that Mrs. Draffin is on her way home to Pennsylvania. She took Keith with her but left the other children in Chefoo. Mr. Draffin may already be back in Hunan with Mr. Mason.

Shucheng, June 4, 1931

There are so many things everyone takes for granted I must attend to. Yesterday morning at five o'clock I was awakened by a crazy woman. I put on my clothes and went down and escorted her off the compound. She usually calls me mama and will do just as I tell her to do. Everyone else is afraid of her. Later on in the morning she did a lot of damage to our front gate. She was using a long spike. I was afraid she might hurt somebody with it, so I walked up and asked her for it. There must have been thirty people gathered about to watch the excitement. She meekly gave me the spike which I asked someone to return to her husband.

We have been having men working on the little house for the gardener. Each job takes a different man. A mason was needed to build the kitchen stove. Two men have been sorting the straw to thatch the roof. None of the Chinese know how to advise me about the upstairs veranda on our house. It looks as though it is near collapse. When it comes to mud walls, thatched roofs, problems with help, and such things the deacons can help me. But they don't know about verandas. I surely wish Father or someone like him could be around here for a while.

Since my last letter I spent ten days at our new out-station. Doris was with me a week then went home, and Eva came with the new Bible woman. Margaret was ill so couldn't help. A Shucheng church member and her son were with us the entire time. This station is about nine miles out. We have rented a house there, and we spent some time buying things for the place. We spoke to scores of people individually or in small groups. Most of the people came out of curiosity to see us rather than to hear the gospel although very few had heard before. A few professed to believe in Christ.

"Mr. and Mrs. Costerus."

We are interested in the family who live in back of the compound. The mother-in-law there has put four baby daughters to death. The daughter-in-law was sold first as a very young child. She passed through a number of homes being sold each time. One place kept her and she became the wife of one of the sons. That husband died, and she was sold again to the home where she now is. She now has one little girl about three years old. We gave this child a black oilcloth cat which she carries around nearly all day and sleeps with at night. We talked to the mother about becoming a Christian, but she is not yet ready to face the persecution. She has been friendly with us by bringing us flowers and lending us things. The morning our stove failed to work she brought us hot water.

Shucheng, July 19, 1931

Last winter the snow was the most in forty years. This summer is the worst flood in eighteen years. There has been a great loss of houses, crops, grain stored in houses, clothes, and furniture. Many of the houses are built of mud, the walls being tamped down with a weight. A mold is used which is raised as the walls go up. When a flood comes, the walls dissolve, and the houses collapse. Those who can afford it, and this includes the deacons and most of our church members, have a framework of timbers put up with beams resting on timbers. Most of these stood.

The four of us proposed giving some money to help the most needy; however, the deacons do not want to have the responsibility for such a fund. They propose that instead we keep good supply of quinine for those who need it.

We are sorry the girl we had hoped to have for Bible woman is turning the job down. She does not want to go out calling with us or do that kind of work. Anything else she is willing to do without pay.

Shucheng, August 3, 1931

There has been a second flood not as bad as the first, but it spread out more. Three of our deacons have lost most of their crops. Of course, they can still plant a crop of buckwheat or vegetables, so we are not facing real famine conditions. We hear that there was some damage done to the house we had rented at the out-station.

During the second flood there were several extra people on the compound. One of the most recently baptized church members brought not only his family but also most of his worldly goods. Besides their own five children, the wives of two brothers and another girl came. Their house had been washed down, their food spoiled, and everything they had was wet. They stayed here nearly a week, and we provided the rice for them. You should have seen the way those children ate the first meal here, for they hadn't had a properly cooked meal for days. All of them thought it was great to have a dry place to sleep.

Doris has been helping me with the medical work. One of the most difficult cases recently has been a little girl badly burned on chest and abdomen and one hand. Her hand was so much worse than other parts, we used Unguentine on it and cheaper ointments on the rest. Now the hand is much nearer healed. Doris says it makes her ill to think we don't have enough Unguentine to use on all burns.

Shucheng, August 17,1931

The child with the bad burn got all right again. Her grandmother takes a real interest in coming to church. The child's mother died some years ago, and her father ran off to be a soldier. She just has an older brother and her grandparents.

The young woman who was chosen by the deacons is extremely foolish if she continues to turn down the job of Bible woman. One cannot help feeling sorry for anyone who really turns their back on the Lord's work—they have to suffer so for doing it. I long to go to her and plead with her once more, but that must not be just because of a bit of pride. She is losing such a terrible lot of blessing.

There is some talk of employing a young man for colporteur. Before his conversion two years ago he was rather wild. The country deacons have not yet seen sufficient proof of his conversion to be willing to have him taken on. Of course in this case, seeing he would be employed by a Bible society, I could go over their heads, for he certainly can sell gospels. If he really is not suitable it is better for me to know it before he is employed. On the other hand the young man should give the deacons reasonable proof that he has been converted.

We like our new language teacher very much, but he nearly despairs of ever getting me to change my dialect. He will not have it though that I am not staying here. When I become attached to this place so it will be like leaving home, and I get some freedom in using the dialect, it will probably be time for me to move on. There does seem to be growing a certain attachment between the Chinese people and myself, and this is no one sided affair either. It is like the Lord to so often give tokens of His goodness.

Shucheng, September 16, 1931

Last Sunday I spent at the out-station again. It was the first Sunday any of us have been there since June. The colporteur who stays there wants someone to go up there every Sunday. Perhaps that can be arranged when Doris and Margaret return from Shanghai. In the meantime Eva and I will try to get there every other Sunday. Of course I would like to see the church members take more interest in that place, but how many Christians at home will take a nine mile walk and back to preach somewhere?

Shucheng, September 22, 1931

The Lord knows why so often he has given me a real man-sized job with often less than the strength one should have to do it properly. Twice during the last week I should have opened abscesses and failed to do so because of not having the courage to do it. One was on a child's head where I knew it could do no harm to any important nerve or blood vessel. But my hand was not steady that morning for some reason. I lent my knife to the child's grandfather who is one of the deacons. The parents could not afford to pay a so-called doctor several dollars for doing it. Yesterday it was an abscess on a woman's hand I failed to open.

"Shucheng Chapel."

Yesterday I was called in to look after a girl whose very bad whooping cough had apparently become complicated by pneumonia. She had become delirious before I went. Anyway this morning while she was still very weak, her fever was down a lot and also her pulse rate. It seems a Chinese doctor had prescribed for her, but she would not take the medicine. The girl's mother and another woman had been wailing before I arrived as they had not expected the girl to live through the night. They had about decided to send for me when the girl in her delirium suggested it. She was wanting something to eat this morning. It meant so much to the mother to have her better that she has promised to make me a pair of shoes. This year I have had four pair of Chinese shoes given to me and these promised. Leather shoes are frightfully expensive, so I don't wear them as much now. But one can't wear Chinese shoes when the ground is damp.

Shucheng, October 8, 1931

Among the problems of the last few weeks was the wife of one of the deacons. She is about my age and has seven children, the oldest of whom is away from home. She also has two daughters–in-law to be who live at their home most of the time. According to Chinese standards or that of common sense she ought to spend most of her time at home. But someone with more zeal than sense talked her into thinking she ought to come to the compound and act as a voluntary Bible woman. Her husband came and asked me not to let his wife take any meetings, and gave as his reason that she is not smart enough to do it. After becoming better acquainted with her I am inclined to think he is right. I am glad she has decided to go home to stay there. One other problem is the wife of a military officer who comes in nearly every day. She heard the gospel before coming to Shucheng. Last night she bought a Bible and she is beginning to read it. She told me then that she is very fond of smoking cigarettes. And she said, "You say if I become a Christian I will have to give them up." She asked what she was to do about the matter. We will find out later whether she is sincere or not when we see what she does about the cigarettes.

The little grandson of the cook seems to have scurvy, and it is so hard to think of anything for it that we can get hold of and that the child can digest. The goats are going dry. Our tomato plants aren't doing much. The last lettuce we planted did not come up. We are out of potatoes and can not buy lemons. Carrots and oranges won't be on the market for another month. Perhaps I should give him calcium lactate. He has been ill for some time, and his mother feeds him almost nothing but rice.

I have written about a woman who was out of her mind. She is much better now but she is feeling terribly sorry for herself. When she did not know what she was doing, her husband took the money she had saved while raising silkworms and by other means. It was as much as a laboring man would earn in two or three months or more here. It is not easy for a thing like this to be straightened out. The only thing one can do is to sympathize with her.

Shucheng, October 13, 1931

We went out to the country yesterday. We sold eighty-four gospels. Our teacher preached to people who listened very well. When we were entertained for dinner, Eva was the last one through although she ate the least. It takes time to learn the use of chop sticks.

I am learning to be almost like the Chinese; that is, express in my last two sentences what I want. I would like a pair of shoes and a pair of rubbers. In a place like this one just has to bother someone to buy things. The shoes should be durable and fit well enough for the ten mile walks I must sometimes take.

Shucheng, October 29, 1931

One would not think of my having much to do, yet by the time the week is over there will have been five meetings led, every one requiring some study. People are getting so they understand me better here. Not every day do I get an uninterrupted half hour for study. Coughs, malaria, sore eyes need attention most days if it's not the cook, house woman, gate-keeper, or gardener who want my attention. This whole bunch is rather careful to do nothing unless I tell them to do it. The woman would never sweep down cobwebs unless told to do it each time.

Most of the deacons are steady farmers without much nonsense about them. They have families which they bring to church. They take their turns leading prayer meetings and church services or appoint someone else to do it. For real earnestness and zeal they would average up very well with most deacons in home churches.

Our personal teacher has gone to Wuhu to escort Doris and Margaret home. At least this is home for the present. They have been gone two months.

I mentioned the child who had scurvy. If only I could have gotten the right food for him! The very day he died I noticed the first Mandarin oranges of the season on the street.

Shucheng, November 27, 1931

Around here as soon as the rain is over, the roads are fairly good. At our out-station the soil is gummy much like at home. The natives have rain shoes made with pegs in the bottoms. When these get well loaded, they each weigh pounds. It seems as though one is walking in glue. I tried a pair meant to fit a bigger foot then mine. "Tell it not in Gath," but they were men's shoes. This caused plenty of amusement. We had been staying in two or three days before trying these. A foot and the shoe did part company once. Eva saw this, and again my picture was subject of a cartoon in her diary.

Shucheng, December 26, 1931

Nearly a week ago we had a letter from the Consul advising us to leave. Things seem quite peaceful here in Shucheng. We decided to ask for advice, so each of us wrote a letter. Mine was to the mission nearest to us on the south. The missionaries there wrote back that they were packed ready to leave, but they are not sure whether they will go. The other letters have not as yet been answered. If we have to leave, you will probably hear before you get this letter.

The adopted daughter of one of our deacons is away at school. She got it into her head the same as thousands of other students have, that she is going to fight the Japanese. Her folks have written to have her come home. If it were not for so many students like her, the situation might be less dangerous.[2]

There are several cases of bronchitis about, and there is some whooping cough. At last, I have found the Chinese name for it. It translates to a hundred day's cough.

Shucheng, January 12,1932

You see we are still here and may be for some time to come. The heads of the mission do not think it necessary to move. It might be well if we had some things packed, but we have not done that.

The most exciting things for our compound in some time happened Sunday morning. Between the small hours of the morning and noon a baby and two kids were born. The parents are pleased with their baby girl because it is their fourth child and first girl. The mother and baby are getting on as well as can be expected. As to the kids, they are both nannies. The gardener stayed up all night with the goat. Eva has just been out to take a picture of the kids. They really are cute.

We have been having wonderful weather. Just now though it is not wise to do too much visiting as people are preparing for Chinese New Year. That will not be for another three weeks, but there is a lot to do to get ready. We have our own way of preparing by buying tracts, posters, etc. to prepare for a week of special meetings. We ought to take every advantage of people taking such a holiday. Shops are usually closed and people take the time to go around visiting.

Today I was called to quite a well-to-do home where the only little boy has some liver affliction. Two Chinese doctors have already been called in and failed. If he is not better, tomorrow I shall suggest calling in someone else. The Chinese often tell me that it would be no difficult matter for me to make a living here in China by means of medical work. I would not object to it from the standpoint of the amount of work it would be. There seems to be no less graft among Chinese doctors than in other lines of work. They charge enormous fees considering the small amount of training they have.

Shucheng, January 16, 1932

Yesterday I spent the forenoon studying, the afternoon in bed, and in the evening I had to write a letter to one of "the powers that be" of the mission.

The missionaries in our next mission station are away, and I was informed that soldiers have taken some of their goods.

That day one of the girls also wanted help on an arithmetic problem. Eva and Margaret thought they would help her with it. But after nearly half the afternoon was over, they brought it to me. It took me fifteen or twenty minutes to do it. Margaret had some mathematics in college and she sees through it now, of course. But Eva does not see through it yet. She went to school more than I did too.

"Mission house on Shucheng compound."

Shucheng, January 27, 1932

We are staying in most of the time this week and next. I suppose I ought to study but instead am looking up a lot of texts where the clue only is given in Chinese and the book. It takes hours to find a dozen or so in Psalms. Sometimes the translation is not very literal, which makes it worse. There was one passage that is only "thousands" in English. In Chinese it was "ten thousand thousands." But sometime I may get familiar with my Chinese Bible yet. It is not easy to learn a lot of names like Melchezidek and Mephibosheth in another language. It almost seems as though I always knew them in English. Of course it is the same sound as near as possible, but my idea does not always agree with that of those who translated the Bible. Names of medicines and diseases are another place where I have not yet attained. I suppose these take a while to learn in any language.

The colporteur who has been at our out-station is being let out until such time as the missionary he has been working under returns. He was not selling enough gospels to suit the Bible society. One time when I suggested his getting out more on his job, he said he would do so if the Lord led him to. I may be fearfully lacking in spirituality, but it looks to me as though when one is accepting the pay of an organization, one is to do the thing one is employed to do or resign.

Shucheng, February 10, 1932

We had another deacon's meeting this week. The most important thing discussed was about having some week night meetings in the country. The people can not come in the city gates at night. They plan to have a prayer meeting in one home and a Bible study at another on different evenings so some can attend both.

There is money now on the books for a new well. I can not see the point of having one done. No one seems to use the well water for cooking or drinking but uses water carried from the river. The objection to the well is that it is too near the city drain, but no well in China seems to be any great distance from something of the sort. Since we had the well cleaned, the water seems to be all right, and we would not drink any water without boiling it.

You, no doubt, hear a lot about the trouble with Japan. You may know more about it than we do. The Chinese newspaper office where most of the papers that came to Shucheng were printed has been burned. We get little news.

Shucheng, February 25, 1932

We hear in a roundabout way that China is on the winning side of the fight, but one who knows the Chinese is suspicious. We do know that orders came out to finish the automobile road through Shucheng in a hurry. The official is afraid that he will lose his head if this is not done by the first of next month. Each head official of the county the road runs through is responsible for his own county. It is said that the road is an urgent matter because the governor of the province wants a good road on which to flee should the Japanese come up the river and take the capital. We should be able to reach Anking inside half a day when the road is finished. From there it takes two days to reach Shanghai.

We spent several days at the out-station at Taochen even though it was cold with rain and snow. Most women stayed at home due to the cold, but we got out visiting about every day. The teacher had about a hundred men out to listen to him on two different evenings. Some men were staying near working on the road. They came from miles around, so this was a good chance to come in touch with them. We sold well over two hundred fifty gospels and gave out tracts.

One of my callers this morning was an old woman with a face long enough to eat butter out of a churn. She wanted some salts and some money. After getting the salts from the dispensary, I took a round about way to the kitchen to ask the cook if the woman were really in need. He generally thinks people should not be given money, but this time he advised giving her some which I did.

We have had another letter from the Consul. The heads of the mission know this part of China very well, and they have not advised us to leave yet. We will try to be careful. With three younger workers with me, for whom I would be responsible, I am not keen about taking risks.

Shucheng, March 11, 1932

The new automobile road has not yet been used for cars. There will probably be a big commotion when the first one does appear. Not more than one person in ten around here has ever seen one. Trees have been planted along the new road. We are not altogether sure the bridges were built strong enough. That it is better to be safe than sorry has not occurred to many.

Margaret and Eva got started off to the out-station today. Doris felt terrible to have them go off without her. Doris has been quite ill. She is still pale and needs to just lounge around a few more days. While Doris was sick, we sent for a foreign trained doctor, but he knew very little more about what's wrong than I did. She probably had influenza, but a red place on her face made me think it might be erysipelas.

Shucheng, March 29, 1932

The man with the bad sore on his back, which I began looking after over two months ago, now comes for attention every two or three days. From a sore fully as big as one's hand it has healed until it is about as large as my little finger. Best of all, both he and his mother have definitely decided to believe the gospel. To be sure I did change the dressings, but the healing of the sore was the Lord's work, and even more so His work, the changing of the man's attitude toward Him.

Shucheng, April 27, 1932

There is one experience one often hears other missionaries relate that I began thinking would never happen to me. That is to find a baby girl parked at our door step. She is a lovely baby to have been accorded such treatment. Of course, the only thing we could do was to take her in. I think her age is around two months. Her big eyes were wide open when we first saw her. That was the only attractive thing about her. She was dressed in rags, most of them too dirty for mop rags. Usually in this part of China if they do not want a child they do away with it right after it is born. But the mother of this child although she had other girls intended to keep it at first. But recently when brigands in their district were so bad they had to flee. It was then that she tried everywhere she went for two to three days to find someone to take her baby. The baby is really not badly nourished but was terribly sore from not being kept clean. The sores have healed much faster than we thought they would. Much of our time this week has been spent in getting the baby some clothes. We have also employed a wet nurse for her, as goat's milk did not agree with her. We did not think the mission would like our being tied down to a child. We will at the most not put in more than a dollar a piece for her clothes now. The Chinese think she is being provided for wonderfully well. For the present the four of us will share in the expense of her upkeep. She is so cute and smiles so when we play with her. We have not yet decided on a name. Our teacher suggests "Loved Precious" and I suppose that will be the name.

Since we took in the baby girl, one couple thought because we did so much for a girl surely we would be even more pleased with a boy and came offering theirs. Of course, there had to be a flat refusal which they could not understand. If we let it be known that we welcome such presents, we might be presented with enough children to fill an orphanage within a week.

Shucheng, May 13, 1932

If I wrote all I hear, it would fill a long letter. The girls with me get rather excited at times. Truthfully, some things do get on one's nerves. They should not though. When we act as ambassadors of the King of Kings, we do not depart when the first rumor comes. So many rumors have no basis in fact. We may go to our out-station in a few days and there await developments. People are accustomed to seeing us go there. One never wants to give the impression he is fleeing unless absolutely necessary.

An airplane flew around Shucheng this morning three or more times. This is frightening to the people. This is the second time this has happened this spring.

Margaret and Doris are away just now. They have gone to a place about thirty five miles from here where Margaret and her sister are to work later.

We are sending them word to stay where they are a few more days. We are also sending bread, cookies, cake, and a few other things as well as some gospels and tracts. I understand they are depressed by the whole aspect of things there. I have told them that the church in Shucheng is better than the average one in China. That is not saying a lot though.

"Street scene in Shucheng."

Shucheng, May 16, 1932

Things are much better. No doubt we will send for Margaret and Doris to come back soon.

The baby is growing fast. We have found out more about her. She was less than a month old when we found her. From most points of view she should be taken to an orphanage, but we will keep her for her first year.

On my last trip to the out-station I took the cook along. While I was gone, Eva had a dreadful time trying to make biscuits. Her mother brought her up without teaching her to do anything in the kitchen. She is not lazy though and wants to learn, but I could make a batch of biscuits while she looks for a recipe. We had run out of yeast, so any bread had to be made with baking powder.

At the out-station we did sell more than two hundred gospels, but there was so much rain that we did not have many come to meetings. One man who heard the gospel for the first time since we began going there a year ago has now learned to read his Bible and is almost ready for baptism.

Just now there are many refugees at the out-station. Some say two thousand have come. The deacon who went to take the Sunday service yesterday preached until he was hoarse. Some more should go to take advantage of so many people with leisure. Usually we find that people in trouble will listen.

We met three refugees Saturday at the home of a deacon. One boy with them had typhus fever, the first case I have seen to know what it was. The father kowtowed to me thinking that necessary in order to have me give the child some medicine. They had almost given up hope. I assured them that there was hope yet and gave the boy some medicine. He was somewhat better the next morning. What happened next I do not know, for they all left. The housing situation is serious, and rents have gone up. One family of refugees is being allowed to live on the compound. A few of the refugees are Christians. One of the refugees brought us a bunch of orchids one day. These were green with red spots. They were very lovely.

Shucheng, June 11, 1932

Week before last was spent at the out-station. Eva went with me as well as our gate-keeper's wife, our personal teacher, and his sister. From the point of view of interest it was the best trip we have had.

Doris and Margaret had been ill while we were away and had some difficulty keeping out the soldiers. To top it all they had a telegram from Shanghai saying that if in the opinion of the Chinese workers we ought to leave, we should go to Anking. They were inclined to want to leave at once, even before my return. My coming back and having a quiet discussion with the deacons has delayed their chariot. What we did do was send off four wheel barrows of our things. Since two of us, Eva and I, do go away for the summer, and Margaret is to move, we thought we might as well send some things to where it is supposed to be more safe. If it really gets dangerous enough so that we must leave, there is just not time to stop to look after our goods. There are two reasons as well as the other light given me why I think it best to wait a while before leaving. One is that if we run away every time we hear a rumor, we contradict the statements we make about the Lord being our protection. Second, if we leave when there are so many soldiers about, the house is almost certain to be used by them so that we would have a terrible job getting it clean again. The director of our mission wrote that he was sure I would do the right thing. I wish I were sure. Where one's decision affects three younger workers, one simply must have the wisdom that is from above.

About forty miles to the west of us is a hot bed of communists and bandits. The first lot of soldiers who went to fight them simply surrendered their guns. That, of course, made bad matters worse. Now tens of thousands of soldiers have gone to wipe out the place like Old Testament doings, but that may not be an easy task.[3]

Our teacher is doing fairly well. He often says he is called to do definite Christian work. The deacons have decided to have him take a Sunday service once a month. At home the persecution one might receive on taking a stand to be a Christian would end with a few sneers and irritating remarks, but it may mean more than that here. The other day he said that the young fellows all know where he stands, and if there is any trouble, he would have to leave.

Kuling, July 18, 1932

The decision for Eva and me to come here for the summer was made by me. Things are not very dull when Eva is around. From Shucheng to Anking took us three days. In the afternoon when we came in sight of Anking, Eva said, "I wish we had another day on the way." She never fusses about being tired or such things. She weighs only ninety eight pounds and is an inch or two under five feet tall, so she can get away with acting like a child. Some of the time she likes this, but sometimes she says, "I am thirty, and it is time people quit treating me like a child."

This morning I consulted a nurse about Doris. I was advised that it was my duty as senior missionary to see that she gets to a doctor or to let those in authority in the mission know her symptoms. If I had not taken that year of study at Biola while on furlough, it might not have occurred to me that she needs a doctor. She is English, and there is much she won't tell me.

Until coming here there has not been much opportunity to wear the things sent me for Christmas. Now they are appreciated. One has to dress up occasionally here.

We have gone on a number of walks up here. At least, I do not have too much to carry. This summer I weigh just under one hundred twenty pounds. My loss is not from being ill or from not eating enough. It is just China. Hunan would have been worse than Anhwei, but I'd love to go back to Hunan.

Kuling, August 17, 1932

I hope to get back to our station very soon. Our teacher promised to look after things until the first of September. Even with the best he could do, soldiers did stay in the church one night. They also broke in the house, but apparently there is nothing missing. I'd like to go back ahead of the others to find out how things are. We have attended many good meetings this summer. Music has been featured. It has taken until now for the most advanced Christian Chinese to realize the value of music in worship, but for the churches to care for music as we do would probably take another century in China. They nearly always sing translations of English songs for the special numbers, and they explain beforehand what they are singing about, for the tone of words changes the meaning completely. We understand in spite of tones, but the Chinese are not used to so using their brains. It is very easy to throw their minds out of gear.

"Myself, Doris Hinckley, Margret Elliot and Eva Knight (reading from left to light)."

Shucheng, September 9, 1932

When Eva and I arrived back at Anking, Doris, Margaret, and her sister Ruth came down to meet us with a servant. The servant was a big help because from the steamer we stepped out on a row boat, and all the baggage had to be managed. At Anking I repacked and brought with me just what I would need for three weeks or so when the others can return. They will see that the other things are brought by barrow.

Of course, the house was dirty after our being away over two months, and the soldiers having been in it made it no better. So far, in looking through things, all that I am sure is gone are some spices and extracts. The mustard tin had been left open, so that was molded.

Twice today I have seen Hsih-chan (Pearl, the baby found on the doorstep) sitting in her cradle with nothing to support her back. I notice some of the people are watching how we do things for her and copying us. For instance, the Chinese use a razor to shave their little babies' heads. They think this would be done the first month before the mother goes out. Yesterday I saw a baby two months old whose head had never been shaved. That mother told that they had bought some toilet soap to wash the baby every day. They think the fact that Pearl went through the summer without any rash or boils is wonderful.

I must wait the return of the others before I can go to the out-station. I am advised not to leave the place if I do not want it occupied by soldiers.

I hear that Mrs. Draffin does not want to come back to China. I am thinking of the statement made by Elisha, "Went not my heart after thee?" When others turn after things rather than the Lord, our hearts can feel it deeply.

Shucheng, September 22, 1932

There are usually twenty persons on the compound. These all seem to be under my care. Besides the most important thing to direct is the church with over eighty members with more interested. Attention should be given to the many villages around that we should visit. There is never a time without plenty of work to do. The cook went to the out-station Saturday and stayed over to take the Sunday service. Sunday was the first time I heard our teacher preach the Sunday service here, and he did very well.

Shucheng, October 11,1932

Glad as I am to be in China, birthdays, anniversaries, and such celebrations at home are remembered. "Home Sweet Home" though is a song we missionaries never sing. Our Lord and His cause must come first.

Margaret and Ruth Elliott have come back, but Doris Hinckley is not able to return to the work. The seven year old daughter of our baby's nurse died the same day the girls returned. The mother misses her dreadfully and has been very upset. Having our baby to care for has been a help to her, and we are now offering her the baby for her own. Old maids usually do not have great success in bringing up children, and it is much worse yet when that child is of a different race. Hsih-chan would be frightfully spoiled by the Chinese Christians if we were to keep her.

We got rid of two kids last week. Another missionary wanted them badly enough to send a man two hundred miles for them. Two of our goats were left with us by a missionary who was going home on furlough with the offer that we could keep all of the kids born. One of these goats had four kids. Now I am being called Jacob.

Some young teachers have come to ask help in learning English. The other girls object to this, so the job has fallen to my lot. For having me teach them English an hour a week, they will be required to attend church. I am not fond of doing this, but it is almost my only contact with young educated Chinese.

I am sorry to hear that my home church has no pastor now. The membership there is almost the same as the one here, and this church gets along without a pastor, and someone takes the out-station service too. The people at home may be so surfeited with good things that they are too particular. The coarsest kind of bread will satisfy the hunger of a starving man, but people at home can quarrel over cake and jam.

Shucheng, October 26, 1932

Two groups of women have been in to see the house. They were very much disappointed because I did not let them go upstairs to see everything there. The sooner we can get it through their heads that we did not come here to show what we have with us off, the better. I gave each of them a gospel and a tract to take home to have read to them. Very few if any of them can read. I never get used to the way they yell out so everyone can hear, "I do not recognize characters." No one ever seems the least bit ashamed of not being able to read.[4]

One of the very few times I have done something for an outsider lately was to attend to a scald on a child's stomach. It healed up very quickly. For this I was given thirteen goldfish. We keep them in a water kang that holds about three buckets of water. Eva wants them kept in the house. I do not object if we can find something to put them in.

Our teacher has come back from a conference. There has been a great change in his wife in recent weeks. Before she annoyed him by taking a delight in the fact that she couldn't read much. But lately she seems to be working to make up for lost time. Now she begins to give the impression that she likes to come to meetings and has begun to listen. It makes a tremendous difference to a man in China if he is in definite Christian work whether his wife is determined to help or hinder.

Mr. Draffin was in Shanghai the last I heard, probably planning to go home soon. That means I will not have a chance to go back to Hunan until next year this time, for the mission would not send me to manage alone.

Shucheng, November 9, 1932

Mr. W.J. Hanna, the superintendent of the mission's work in the province, was here in Shucheng last week. There are fifteen stations in this province In four of them the work is more flourishing than it is here, and they are older work, too. There are only two of all the stations where the work is newer. Mr. Hanna had some very nice things to say about the work, especially about the way the Chinese cooperate with us. But that is all the Lord's goodness and the wonderful missionaries who went before me. When they first asked me to come here, someone made the remark that it is one of the best stations in the province. I was not inclined to believe it then but it must be true. He spent four days here and they had two deacon's meetings while he was here, so it was a busy time for me.

As an illustration of how things go when a district superintendent comes, it was agreed to meet once a week and thoroughly revise the church register. They have met once and cut one man off from communion for a few months. The others are being given a chance to redeem themselves. They were also to form a constitution, but it is going to take a lot of tact and perseverance on my part if it is done. And yet what Mr. Hanna was trying to do was to get the Chinese to handle things themselves.

Shucheng, December 13, 1932

As I am writing this letter, two girls are sitting near having me teach them how to turn the heels in knitting socks. Fortunately, I have a good book for reference.

Margaret and Ruth left last week. Eva and I went with them a couple of miles. I had made cookies, catsup, jam, and pickles and had asked the cook to make peanut butter and fresh bread for them to take along.

Yesterday a group of us with a coolie to carry our things went out about four or five miles. We took six hundred gospels and more than a thousand tracts. We sold these along the way and came back without any left. We all enjoyed ourselves except we nearly froze our fingers. I might have taken my gloves, but the Chinese who went with us had none, so I am not sorry about not wearing mine.

Shucheng, December 29, 1932

The church paid the traveling expenses to have a Chinese lady, Miss Chiang, come for special meetings. For more than a week including Christmas day meetings were held twice each day. The attendance for these averaged around one hundred. Christmas was a rainy day, but there were about two hundred at the morning service that day. I know many were blessed from the meetings. Two young girls from the out-station attended. A year ago these girls knew nothing of the gospel. They listened carefully and copied the characters for the choruses that were sung.

Shucheng, January 14, 1933

Today has been dark and chilly with snow all afternoon. In spite of the cold there were about a hundred who came out to church this morning. About a dozen women church members, most of whom can read, came into the sitting room for Bible class. We had a fire in here so the women were in no hurry to leave. Some of them like looking up references. This form of Bible teaching is my favorite occupation, I will admit. Last Sunday I was at Luchow where the Christian Mission work. They have a hospital and a large girls' school there, but they have very few more people at church than we do. The two young women from here who are there for nurses' training help them in their well organized Sunday School. They have eight foreigners working there.

Doris, the English girl of our number, expects to go to the next station south of us sometime this week. Perhaps I ought to go instead but she wants to go. Margaret and Ruth Elliott are having their difficulties there with people throwing bricks and stones into the house. Also there are some fearful lies being circulated about them. Besides, the church members are not having anything to do with the missionaries there. That does not tell all the trouble they are having. If things do not improve soon it would seem better to go and see about it. Margaret Elliott in charge there is a fine level headed girl, and having lived in China the first years of her life is a very good missionary. But on the other hand, just the very fact of my being so much older would make the Chinese far more likely to listen to me than to her.

In Luchow I stayed several days with two women who spend most of their time teaching English in a school. I went there to have my teeth fixed. The doctor put in two fillings and tried to pull one. That was a wisdom tooth with the top all gone to pieces. The doctor worked more than an hour trying to extract the root. He was not very thrilled at the prospect of trying again, nor was I, so it was left.

"Dressed up as Wise Men for the Christmas program—fourth generation Christians."

Shucheng, January 21,1933

When Margaret and Ruth were here, they were almost daily suggesting something new in the way of Bible classes or something else. My method of getting money was wrong as were the servants and many other things. I know I am not perfect, and I was a new worker once. In most respects they were probably right. Today came an S.O.S. letter asking me to send money the quickest way. They had run out, and no one would cash a check for them. How would you interpret, "We are having our troubles, but are getting along all right?" They do have a factious church with which to deal.[5]

Mr. Costerus has been here several times. Mrs. Costerus and the children are expected before long. Mr. Costerus brought news of the missionary who is being held captive by the Reds. He had been seen in November with a Roman Catholic priest. Earlier we had heard that he had been killed. His mission was a hundred miles from here.

Shucheng, February 14, 1933

Today some men came from the officials of the city asking me to translate a letter they wished to send to the Famine Relief Commission. I put their letter in quotation marks and added some comments of my own at the end. Their letter would give the impression that people of this district were living on roots and bark. Some people may be living like that, but I have not seen it.

The other day we were in a home and saw that they were rid of their idols and incense burners. They had put up posters instead, the center one being the Ten Commandments. This was a great improvement to our minds.

We ran out of coal and cannot buy any more here. The last wood the cook bought was so damp that it is hard to keep burning. Now we are using charcoal on an open fire. This is not so good for us but is a great deal cheaper, a consideration when just Eva and I pay the bills. Our cook is often more economical than necessary, perhaps penny wise and pound foolish.

A church member cleaned up a hunch-backed beggar, and we put him to work selling gospels. He is reaching places that have not been touched in years, if ever. He is a professing Christian, of course.

From a letter that came recently I learned that the workers in Nanchow examined twenty-one candidates for baptism, and twelve were baptized at Christmas time. Seven were baptized in Changteh. This almost makes me want to go right back there, but I know this won't be possible until fall. I like Shucheng, but the difference in dialect has been a handicap. I am so thankful that wherever I have worked in this land there has been fruit. This has been gathered not because of me or my striking personality but because of Him who endured the cross.

Shucheng, February 28,1933

The last trip to the out-station was really Eva's turn, but I needed to see about renting different premises. The building we have there is outside the city wall, and there is a stream between there and town. The bridge is merely some boats with planks placed lengthwise across. At night the bridge is pulled apart and the gates closed, so only the very few who live near can come to meetings in the evening. Besides most of the older women are afraid to cross the bridge any time without someone to lead them. When it rains, crossing is worse. Unfortunately finding a place inside the city that is suitable and not too expensive is very difficult. Most of the empty places are occupied by soldiers.

Eva is planning to make a trip next week to a place where missionaries have not been in many years. I do envy her, but one of us must stay here. Four or five Chinese will go with her. They will take about two thousand gospels along to sell.

Shucheng, March 14, 1933

It was not good walking but I went to the out-station and back yesterday. That is about eighteen miles in all. Because we are expecting company I did not think it best to stay overnight. After hearing how things there were I should not have stayed in any case. The place is left with too few soldiers to defend it and there are brigands very near. Eva's visit has to be postponed for a time until things clear up.

This afternoon I was in the home of a lazy church member. He has been living mostly on rice husks the last few days. Many of these people are very poor but the really earnest Christians really have food to eat. One woman came into our out-station the other day and began by saying," It is no wonder you Christians have money to spend. You do not gamble, drink or smoke. We would have money to use too if we did not do these things." It is surprising how much money they waste on sin.

My reason for going to the out-station again this week was to look for a place to rent. What I saw this time may be suitable, but we did not talk prices. I am leaving that for the deacons to do. Just now while the soldiers are away is the time to talk about these things. All the people would rather have us in their place than soldiers as we pay rent and they do not. But when the soldiers once move into their places they are not obliged to move out, no matter what they themselves may want the building for.

Shucheng, March 16, 1933

A bus came in today. As the woman who was with me had not seen one before, she went back to see it as though it were something wonderful. The Costerus family hopes to get a bus to bring them the distance that took us four days in one day. Even then eighty miles in a day is not a record, but these rough dirt roads are horrid in places. They hope to engage a car to come to our gate. I suppose that will thrill everyone on the compound.

Shucheng, March 31, 1933

The Costerus family arrived a week ago Saturday. Since they were here less than two years ago, they have been around the world. The oldest child is away at school. The youngest of the three with them is two and a half years of age, and the oldest is not yet six. They behave better than most children.

Mr. Costerus left this morning to be gone a month, but last week he helped with some special work at the fair being held in Shucheng. Many people come from a distance which gives us some opportunities. We have spent some time there selling gospels.

One of the things I bought at the fair yesterday was a small table for the children to play with. It costs fifty cents Mexican or around fifteen or twenty cents. Someone even then told me I was taken in. I do not mind paying a few extra cents, but I do not like anyone saying I am a poor buyer. For that reason I usually have the Chinese do the buying for me. We also bought a basket to use at Easter time for about four cents Mexican. We dickered on that and wasted enough time to earn several. Some foreigners get so they really enjoy the buying sport as the Chinese do, and I may get there yet. Fixed prices would save time though.

This week again twin kids were born on the compound. We will raise these nannies for another missionary. One billy died, and one kid we butchered. All the rest of the kids are doing well.

Mrs. Costerus is a very good nurse, so she takes the responsibility of that work now. She has the medicine room open four mornings a week.

Shucheng, April 13, 1933

Today I had a call from a young government school teacher not yet out of his teens. What he wanted was to join the church. He comes from one of the most wealthy families in town. Our teacher has talked to him, and he understands very much what it all means. Very few of those who live in this town are church members. Most of the Christians come from the country.

We are getting acquainted with Mrs. Costerus and the children. The youngest child is the favorite with her bright smile for everyone. Eva's surname is Knight. The children call her Auntie Knight. Sometimes the youngest child calls me Auntie Afternoon.

Shucheng, May 10, 1933

Today someone came in to get information about the size and worth of this place, etc. I think the easiest way out is to refer them to the office in Shanghai. They have the deeds and more accounts there than here. One can think of two reasons why they seek to know these things: taxation, and also when soldiers destroy mission property, the government is asked to repay the damage. Less than two hours later a man who claimed to be a church member in another place came in wanting some money for traveling expenses. He said he was on the way back from looking for his son who had either run away as a soldier or perhaps been killed. I gave him a little money to buy food on the road to the next mission station. He was walking.

The other day I saw something terrible. It was a child burned on the back of her legs from hips to heels by some kind of acid. The elbows, back of the neck and front of the face were also deeply burned. The mother was a concubine to a man across the street. In a quarrel with the real wife, she deliberately poured boiling water on her feet. For this reason the concubine had been put away and her husband was not greatly concerned about what happened to the baby. One feels most sorry for the baby, who had suffered agonies for days.

Shucheng, May 23, 1933

Sunday six men and two women were baptized. The hunch backed beggar who sold gospels was one, and the young school teacher was another. When the latter was examined, he was asked, "Supposing you are called 'Foreign Dog' as many other Christians are called?" His only answer was, "I would forgive them."

Our teacher and Mr. Costerus went to the out-station today. The new place is not ready yet as partitions are needed. Mats will be used for this. These have been made to order and delivered to this compound, but most of the deacons are so busy harvesting seeds for vegetable oil and planting rice that they can not put up the mats now.

Shucheng, June 4, 1933

This week I had to make another trip to the out-station to see about moving things to our new building. When we get it fixed up, the new place will be quite all right. Last week some of the deacons carried the partition mats there, and they blistered their shoulders doing it. They concluded that they would not ask me for more money for doing this even though the mats were heavier than they expected. They said it was their opportunity to pay Tao Chiao-shih back for some of the things she had done for their children.

Last week our Chinese teacher took the entrance examination to go to the Bible Institute in Changsha. I looked over the paper before sending it in, and the worst mistake I saw was that in giving the names of the major prophets he left out Lamentations. We will have to wait at least another week to find out what his marks are. Unless a student is a high school graduate, the course takes three years. Although he did not finish high school, he intends to take the course in two years. This may be very difficult, but he is needed here.

Eva Knight was all ready to go to see a doctor about her ear yesterday, but there was no bus. There may not be one for several days because the weather is so unsettled. The roads are dirt only, and as soon as it rains, they are impassable.

Shucheng, June 20, 1933

A letter has come from Margaret Elliott telling of her engagement. A year and a half ago a seminary student had written proposing to her. She only accepted the offer conditionally, that is if he felt led to come to China under the CIM. Last week he sent her a cablegram that he had been accepted by this mission. He has graduated from seminary and has been ordained. If he is good enough for Margaret, he must be very fine. She is just twenty-seven and she has worked her way through both the Bible Institute and college and has worked in China nearly four years. She shines brighter by far as a missionary than most, and she sings beautifully.

Mrs. Costerus had a birthday yesterday. Mr. Costerus walked back from their station where he has been the last three weeks, arriving here late in the afternoon. That is around thirty-five miles. We had the birthday cake and other extra things for supper. Eva and I had a special lacquered sewing box made for her.

During the morning some soldiers were in who wanted to occupy the chapel. I was busy for one thing, and besides I get tired of them coming about. No elaborate argument or nice words were on my tongue's end. There was just a dumb question, "Who wants you to stay here?" They answered by telling me to get the key for the door. I calmly asked the question over again. The third time I asked, one of the soldiers said he was going off to find some other place. I thanked him for his trouble. All the other soldiers went off with him, and we saw no more of them. One of them remarked as they went off, "That foreigner talks Chinese."

Yesterday one of the callers was a church member from another province. He and his family had been fairly well-to-do, owning their farm. But they had to flee from before the communists, bringing almost nothing with them. They have four little children, but they only had with them what they could carry on a wheelbarrow. There are tens of thousands of families like them. One cannot wonder that they want to give at least one of their children away. One is glad the people at home do not have to see much that we see. It is a wonder how so many live in matsheds, pick up some chips for firing, and beg some rice. As for clothes, it is hard to tell which is clothes and which patches.

Shucheng, July 13, 1933

A young man who recently joined the church came in and we had an opportunity to talk over with him some of his plans for the future. He has been attending a modernist mission school, and we are hoping we can persuade him to go to a place that is sound. I would far rather see them attend a government school than a place that is likely to wreck their faith.

Last week I went to Anking. The first time we came from there it took us four days, but this time we went the eighty miles in one day. Mrs. Costerus with the three small children needed someone with her. We left here at eight in the morning and arrived there at five in the afternoon. There was a three hour stop at Tungcheng where the Elliott girls are. Of course, they were all tired from the jolting on the bus, even though the children did enjoy looking out the window. The boat Mrs. Costerus took from Anking was one with only native fare. She was much worried about this until I got on and recognized there one of the most prominent Chinese Christian workers. They will be on the boat two nights before reaching Shanghai. Mrs. Costerus will have the summer with all her children and will leave the six year old boy in school before she returns.

I stayed over night at Anking. In the morning there was time to make a visit on a girl from here who is in training to be a nurse. On Thursday when I arrived back at Tungcheng, the Elliotts had sent the gate-keeper to the place where the bus stops to help me with my things. Besides a suitcase I had nearly thirty pounds of potatoes which Mr. Costerus wanted for seed. Eva was at Tungcheng already to be there to help with their Daily Vacation Bible School. We had a celebration in honor of Margaret's engagement. We were together over the weekend, and Eva and I came home Monday.

Our personal teacher has been off for a few days. I think he has malaria, at least I hope it is not more serious.

Eva has been busy studying and preparing for Daily Vacation Bible School. There are enough Chinese helpers, so she will teach only handwork and singing.

We went out to see our leper Christian a couple of weeks ago. He is thinner and can no longer stand up, but he is just as earnest as ever. He loves to explain the elements of the gospel to anyone who will listen. He does not fear death but only the trouble he is likely to be before that.

Shucheng, August 17, 1933

Since my last letter the most important thing we have tried was the Daily Vacation Bible School. The weather was too hot for a good attendance, but some days there were over forty in attendance. We gave out seventeen pictures from a picture roll for those with perfect attendance. My part was a Bible class for some of the older girls who could look up references. The two young men and the two girls who helped were very faithful.

Mr. Costerus and the young man from Australia who has just come to work in the next station hoped to leave this morning, but there was no bus, Mr. Costerus has started a Sunday afternoon Bible class while he has been here. They are such keen students that it will take a good amount of time to prepare for it when I have to lead it.

Eva is taking a language examination. She has done very well so far on her studies. Eva is the kind of person who does not grow up, yet she will always be pleasant to live with. Just now our bone of contention is a scrawny, bony kitten of which she is very fond. She always wants to have a kitten around.

Shucheng, August 28, 1933

Someone at home asked Eva in one of her letters if she ever goes to the movies. Perhaps we can count ourselves fortunate that those things have not come within a hundred miles of us. The people here are enough taken up with the things they see rather than the unseen eternal things without having those other attractions added. Every year I stay in China I become less willing to discuss the things of the homeland with the people, lest they go away with their minds filled with what does not matter instead of the message we came to preach. The attitudes of the mothers of two of the young people baptized in May are quite a contrast. The young man came home last Chinese New Year time and told his mother he was a Christian. She was very favorably impressed by the splendid way he treated her. During this hot summer she has missed coming to church only the one Sunday she was away. She has her own Bible and hymn book. She has given up cigarettes of which she was very fond, and she intends to join the church this year. But a young woman is having quite another experience. She comes from a family where her father, who died some years ago, had two wives. She is the daughter of the younger woman. The wives seem to be united in their opposition to her coming to church. So they see to it that breakfast is so late on Sunday that she has to go without or be very late. That means that she generally comes to church hungry. I am afraid she has yielded too much at times. One thing they want is to get her married, but she is determined to have a say about that.

Shucheng, September 10, 1933

Yesterday morning before daylight Mr. Costerus left to meet Mrs. Costerus and the little girls, Elsie four years old and Helen nearly three. They should be here in a day or two. Our personal teacher started out with Mr. Costerus. He is on his way to Changsha to the Bible Institute and expects to be gone at least two years. When he comes back, he should be ready to be an evangelist. His going was almost like letting my right hand go. He has been with us on most of our trips the last two years to do the preaching to the men, helped keep the military out of the premises, wrote Chinese letters, ran errands, and gave us advice besides teaching us. For his own good though, he needs more training.

On our last trip to the out-station we had good crowds out for three evenings. On the second and third evenings the benches which will hold over eighty held only two thirds of those who came.

Eva hopes to join Margaret Elliott soon to stay about a week. Ruth had a hemorrhage following having her tonsils removed, so she could not return after their summer in Kuling.

A little boy who lives very near here is about six or seven years old. He has had a fever nearly three weeks which has not been diagnosed. The father had suggested obtaining some magic water from the priests for the boy to drink. The mother, who is an earnest Christian, was at her wit's end to know what to do. The child saved the situation by this remark, "I will not drink the water. Idols all are false." We are giving him some of our goat's milk every day now. He is such a splendid child one wishes there were more ways we could help.

We are expecting Mr. and Mrs. Eldon C. Whipple and their little boy soon. They were students at Biola when I was home on furlough. They will be working at a station near here.

Shucheng, September 29, 1933

The little boy who had been getting goat's milk every day is much better. His trouble was typhoid fever. His mother is a new church member, but the father works in a shop where the influence is all against believing in the Lord. The boy sided with the mother in trusting in the Lord and would not try the idolatrous performances. This makes us even more glad that he is gaining strength. He has not had fever for more than a week.

Yesterday the woman who went off her mind the first spring we were here came in. She had managed to raise a pig until it was large enough to get some money from selling it. Because she used some of this money to buy cloth for a new blouse, her mother-in-law helped her husband beat her. She appreciated having someone in whom she could confide.

Some of the Whipple's things arrived ten days ago. Their things were loaded on wheel barrows eighty miles from here. The men bringing the second lot ran out of money when still twenty five miles from here, and some of the men were not well. Yesterday two men came for cash and reckoned they would get here with the things today. A couple, who will work for the Whipples, arrived on the bus from Anking today bringing more of their things. The Whipples stopped off to visit at the station where Margaret Elliott is.

Shucheng, October 10, 1933

It may be difficult to realize that today I am forty years old. In many lines of work most of it would be done by now. As a missionary, if the Lord tarries, the best years should be yet to come. A long time is needed to get to know the people and how to talk with them. For myself, I do not covet being the missionary that makes a big noise, but the one the Lord can really use. Some of us of the common variety the Lord does seem to bless. Sometimes the Lord "takes the weak things of the world to confound the mighty."

Shucheng, November 14, 1933

Monday I returned from a place about eight miles out where I had never stayed before. We slept in a better class inn there, yet the furnishings of the room included only a flat unpainted table, two benches like sawhorses, and two roughly built beds with only straw on the slats. The girl who went with me did not take any bedding, so I had to share. Since the weather was warm for this time of year, that part was all right, but the bed was hard! Another church member came out on Sunday and helped carry our things when we came home on Monday. We came home by a round about road which meant walking about fifteen miles; in fact, in the four days there were about twenty seven miles of walking. We sold three hundred sixty gospels and gave away over a thousand tracts. We preached to a good number of people. Off up in the hills many can not read nor write, and many are afraid to accept tracts. We visited one place in the hills where the big earthenware containers used for water are fired. Some of these jars will contain a barrel or more.

When I returned, I was very disappointed to find the Whipples gone. Mr. Whipple had not expected to come so soon, for their house was not ready; however, the military was sending a car over to deliver someone here, so he took the opportunity for a ride. Mrs. Whipple wrote a kind note of apology for having left while I was away.

Shucheng, November 28, 1933

Margaret and Ruth Elliott are back here with Eva and me again. Margaret was in charge of Thanksgiving dinner, and it was very good. I did make the mince meat for the pie and pickles. The girls drew pictures of turkeys for the decorations for the table. On Thanksgiving day we heard results of the presidential election, but we were not at all thankful about that. A bundle of magazines had arrived for me that day which all of us enjoyed. Margaret,

Ruth, and Eva finished off the day, as they often do, singing trios.[6]

The Chinese baby left at our gate last spring is now eight months old. By holding onto things she can walk. Without anyone here to consult about it, I have had to figure out the formula for using goat's milk for her. Yesterday one of the mothers was comparing her baby with this one saying that her baby is not nearly as strong. Then she went on to say that goat's milk is better than mother's. The Chinese in this district do have goats, but they would let a baby starve rather than try to use it. This is partly because they do not know how to dilute it. It has been possible for us to give a practical demonstration on how to feed babies. As far as strength is concerned, Pearl is two or three months in advance of the average Chinese baby.

Shucheng, December 4, 1933

One of my most recent letters was from the young man who acted as our personal teacher and is now in Bible school in Changsha. The real point of it was that he did not think it was safe for me to go back to Hunan. He then described the latest communist raid in that province. Unfortunately those things can happen in Anhwei Province too. While he is away, I am trying to persuade his wife to learn to read. I told her if she would read through the gospel of Matthew and do some other simple reading before her husband came home, that I would give her a good Bible.

I have been making plans to make a little trip for a visit and to get some dentistry done. Then this evening one of our newest church members was in to ask me to go with her to her old home about fifteen miles from here. She says there are several out there who professed to be Christians. My dentistry and visits can wait until I can make this walking trip.

Shucheng, January 5, 1934

For the past three years our personal teacher had done most of the Christmas decorations of the church. To my surprise the decorations were more elaborate this year than ever before. Practically all the work was done by the young people. Fully three hundred people attended the church service Christmas day.

Three days after Christmas I started from Shucheng to visit the Costerus family in Liuan. A church member came along to help carry my things. We walked twenty seven miles in less than eight hours. Before daylight the next day the rain started, so an extra day was spent in a Chinese inn. Even the next day after that, the roads were so bad I had to hire a chair to take me most of the fifteen more miles. Going up one embankment the leading man fell. More than once the other man nearly fell. In the end, they would not go the last mile into the city, so I had to walk that distance. I was happy to get to the station, and the Costerus children were especially happy to have me come.

After a week in Liuan, I traveled to Luchow by bus. It took at least seven hours to go the sixty miles. About every two miles the bus stopped to fill the leaking radiator. We were passing plenty of ponds, so there was always plenty of water. A few times the bus had to be pushed out of the mud. In spite of everything I had a lovely time away. Leaving Shucheng and its problems, much as I love the place and people, is a rest. Elsie and Helen Costerus both cried when I left them. Elsie is four and Helen three.

Liuan, January 24, 1934

Last Friday evening a letter came from Mrs. Costerus saying Elsie had a sore throat and she was afraid it would be serious. Then Sunday evening I received a telegram saying that Elsie was seriously ill and asking me to come. Doris had gone to Tungcheng to spend two weeks. Sunday evening I spent packing and telling Eva how to carry on. Monday morning I started on the more than forty mile walk to get here. I arrived just after noon on Tuesday. This time there were no cries of, "Auntie Todd is here!" Those I met as I went in were too quiet. I asked the cook how Elsie was. His answer was blunt enough, "She died yesterday." Then I heard a sob as Mr. and Mrs. Costerus came to greet me. They showed me what was left of Elsie as they had laid her in the little coffin they had covered with their own hands.

The funeral was the next day. It was held all in Chinese with most of the arrangements Chinese. There was not one single real flower, not even a wreath of pansies, but the foreign trained doctor had some flowers made as much like real ones as possible and fixed them on top of the coffin. After the service twenty or more children carrying banners of greens and paper flowers went ahead. Next came the coffin carried by Christians. Next were Mr. and Mrs. Costerus and myself. Behind were more Chinese, different ones taking turns carrying three year old Helen. The Chinese had been so kind and sympathetic, but I regretted so that I was the only missionary friend to be there.

Mrs. Costerus had been very wise in her care of Elsie. As a trained nurse she had spared no effort. Elsie was a delicate and hard to manage child, the one her mother had the most trouble with, and so she is missed the more. There are two Costerus boys in school and a fifteen year old girl, a child of Mr. Costerus by his former wife.

Shucheng, February 4,1934

When I left Liuan Tuesday morning, Mrs. Costerus said she was coming with me two miles. It was not until we started that it came to me that her destination was a newly made grave. When we got there, we gathered up the evergreen branches carried there the day of the funeral and arranged them around the grave. Then the two of us had prayer together. Just as we finished, Mr. Costerus arrived with an umbrella saying he was afraid it might rain. A second time that morning he tried to urge me to stay longer. I think the weather was a lame excuse for Mr. Costerus coming out to walk home with Mrs. Costerus. But it was a tactful thing to do. I left them standing near the grave.

Since coming back to Shucheng after walking over a hundred miles in ten days, I have sat by the fire and written letters, not thinking of being in the need of exercise. I have been reading a book Revolt in the Desert by T. E. Lawrence. This is a war story, but it is not fiction. The author has a brother, Mr. Montagu R. Lawrence, who is working with our mission. Besides Mr. M. R. Lawrence, we have a nephew of Robert Browning in our mission.

Mrs. Costerus would like one of us to come to stay with her a while. The station at Tungcheng needs help too. Ruth has gone to Shanghai and may have an operation on her neck.

Liuan, February 20, 1934

Two weeks ago a telegram came from Mrs. Costerus during church service asking me to come because Helen was ill. That day we had about two hundred people in church. They were told about the telegram and joined in prayer for Helen. I got ready and started out that afternoon by bus. I think it better to put the money out even though it means going around Robin Hood's barn and past broken down Fords with rough roads all the way. I waited about three hours for the bus in Shucheng. It was seven o'clock when I reached Luchow where I stayed all night at the Christian Mission. Monday morning I went on with their doctor who had also been summoned. The weather was changing, and half way on this trip snow began falling. I got to Liuan four hours sooner than I could have by walking.

Fortunately Helen, who had a lighter case of bronchial pneumonia than Elsie had had, was on the mend; in fact, she started to improve soon after we got the telegram. Mrs. Costerus said she had remarked, "I am sure the people at Shucheng are beginning to pray for us." Part of this letter has been written in the night while watching Helen. Perhaps she will need watching another night or two. Next week I will probably be able to return to Shucheng.

Shucheng, March 4, 1934

Helen's temperature had scarcely become normal when a telegram came from the school at Chefoo saying that Christian, the second Costerus boy who is six years old, had pneumonia. Three more telegrams came while I was there each telling of improvement. Three children in the same family having pneumonia within six weeks is rather thick, especially when one did not recover, a high price to pay for being missionaries. Mrs. Costerus is a fine trained nurse and has asked me to send for her if she is ever needed.

On my return trip I again stayed with the Christian Mission folks. They talk as though it is a pleasure to have any of us stay there.

Doris Hinckley plans to spend this week at the out-station. Eva and I plan to go to another place ten miles out on Friday. While there are three of us here, we are not often together.

Shucheng, March 18, 1934

Last week I tried four times to find an inquirer who wishes to join the church, but she plays ma-jong and this church does not stand for that kind of thing. So I have to see what she is going to do about it. Of course if she is unwilling to give up the ma-jong she cannot join our church. There are not many others to be baptized this time.

There were nearly two hundred women here today. I will not say they came to listen to the sermon. More than half came came to see the foreigners and the house they live in. Of course, as to the house, they all went away disappointed because we locked the gate and kept them out. We could not let such a mob come into the house.

The last few weeks we have had such a number of groups of callers. Those from the country do not understand us very well. That may sound like quite a confession, but my talk still is mixed with Hunan dialect. Those who live in the city understand me, but many from the country do not.

Shucheng, March 26, 1934

The mission superintendent of this province was here last week. He is making some changes. Doris Hinckley and Eva Knight are going to Tungcheng next month, and Margaret and Ruth Elliott will come here. No one is too pleased with this move as far as I know, but conditions are better here than there, and Ruth's nerves won't take much more there. The Chinese do not respect the judgment of the Elliott girls due to their youth. The superintendent made it clear that I was to be in charge here.

When the superintendent left, Eva Knight went with him. A telegram had come from Liuan that Mr. Whipple had come there ill and needing medical attention. The doctor from Luchow was not available, so they were depending on the superintendent who has had some medical training. Mrs. Costerus could do the nursing, but Eva would be needed to look after the house and the two children, Helen Costerus and Elden Whipple.

Shucheng, April 23, 1934

The three day conference has been held. There was some difficulty finding an outside speaker, but a good one was found, and all went fairly well. The conference began on Friday. In the morning there was a devotional meeting followed by a Bible lesson from the outside speaker. In the afternoons there were business meetings. The finances of the church were thoroughly discussed, sometimes in not too friendly a way, but several matters were cleared. On Saturday six persons were baptized as part of the conference.

The girls were away leaving me alone for nearly two weeks. On those two Sundays there were about two hundred at church. I played the organ and in between times helped look after the people. Gradually I have learned to recognize most of the women. I try to keep track of them. My week's work is taken up with visiting those who do not keep coming and looking after the flock.

Doris Hinckley came back from the out-station Monday. Tuesday Eva Knight came back from Liuan, and not more than an hour later the Elliott sisters arrived. I surely was glad to see them all. Eva and Doris started packing almost at once, and Thursday morning most of their goods were sent off on the same rickshas used by Margaret and Ruth.

Shucheng, May 8, 1934

Doris Hinckley and Eva Knight have gone to Tungcheng. They probably will not find it so much fun for they will have such a tiny house and almost no yard. Here we are not far from the country and the compound has about three acres of land. Do you wonder we have space to keep goats and have a garden?

Last week the young man engaged to Margaret and another man were here visiting two days. They slept in a little house on the compound meant for an evangelist if we had one.

Since my last letter there has been a conference. They had quite a talk about church finances. They had so much money put out at interest years ago that is hard to collect. Most of the people who are owing have promised to pay back the principal. Some had died and their relatives agreed to pay for them. The man who was so recently killed by brigands had agreed to contribute ten dollars and interest from several years ago. Interest usually is about thirty percent a year. His son agreed to pay it, but the church say they are quite willing for him not to do so. I am glad something is being done about that money, and that the problem is being looked after.

Yesterday one of the deacons said that there was a fair at the out-station, so we must send two men to do evangelistic work during those days. Two or three years ago the deacons did not realize they had any such obligations. I may go out too with one of the women. I am not so much afraid of what will happen to a church that keeps busy.

Shucheng, May 20, 1934

Last week the leper member of our church died. He had leprosy of the anesthetic type which is numbing but not disfiguring. We had gone to see him at least twice a year at his place five miles out. Each time he wanted us to preach to the outsiders there and have prayer. He was a most earnest Christian but had not been able to attend church in years. Of the three members of our church who have died this year, two had been invalids for some time, and the other was killed by brigands.

Shucheng, June 5, 1934

Margaret and Ruth were called to Kuling at the death of their father. They could not get there in time for the funeral, but they would be with their mother. A suggestion was made that the mother come here, but as there is another daughter still in America, she will, no doubt, return to the States.

Shucheng, July 7, 1934

All last week Margaret and Ruth were in the out-station holding a Daily Vacation Bible School. We have a married couple with their daughter staying out there this summer, and the young man who has been studying at Changsha went out with Margaret and Ruth. Much interest was shown. In China we think people are sincere when they are willing to buy their own Bibles and hymn books.

It seems so good to have the man back from Changsha. He had an average grade of ninety one for this year. As yet I have not told him that when he applied at the school I had to guarantee his expenses. To have told him then would have been more folly than to break a chrysalis. It would have meant his trusting in the missionary instead of on the Lord. Some may not see the point to this, but there is one. Now we have another church member who is applying to enter a theological seminary run by the Southern Presbyterians.

Shucheng, July 26, 1934

A letter just came from Miss Smith who worked here for many years. She was very glad to hear about the interest of the people in Taochen, the out-station. She said it had been the most anti-foreign place she had ever seen. One time there was almost a riot when she was there because of the way a professing Christian's wife had beaten a slave girl. When they saw that a missionary was as indignant as they were about the way the girl had been beaten, the tide turned in her favor. The man of the house was beaten, they had to leave town, and also give up the slave girl. Not only had they beaten the girl fearfully but they had stuck slivers under her nails. When the Chinese become wrought up about the way a slave girl is treated, you can depend upon it that there is a reason for it. Usually they pay no attention to anything that is short of murder, and this case was not much short of it.

Shucheng, August 5, 1934

We are having the hottest summer in years, so we do not often leave the compound. One can not wonder that the church attendance has fallen below sixty adults twice this summer. A meeting is held at the same time for children so that the church service will not be too much of a movable feast.

In spite of the heat a Daily Vacation Bible School was begun today. Not many came. My part is to teach a Bible class for some older girls. One small boy was sent home because he had malaria. I sent quinine with him.

Taochen, August 27, 1934

We came to the Taochen out-station on Wednesday. We walked two miles of the way before sunrise to avoid the heat of the day. Buses run, but there are not enough of them to carry all the people who want to ride. There are rickshas too, but if I rode in one because it is hot, all the other women would expect to do so also. Our Changsha student, home for the summer, and his cousin are with me again.

One of my reasons for coming was to meet some of the new Christians. One whole family believed and have put away their idols. Several are learning to read so they can read their Bibles. The new Christians are coming out to the services with their Bibles and hymn books. They are not very good at singing, but they certainly make an attempt. One can get good preaching much sooner than one can get good singing in a Chinese church.

Shucheng, September 12, 1934

Our colporteur has gone with three other Christians to do some work where hundreds go to worship idols. Many of the pilgrims who go to burn incense pierce both cheeks with a chop stick and let it stay there all their way to the temple and back. They wear special skirts and caps. One man who lives at our out-station had heard just enough of the gospel before he went on this pilgrimage last year that he wasn't keen about going. This year he is an enquirer, and he made the statement that he would not worship an idol again even if he would be beheaded for not doing it. That young man is among the brightest of our out-station enquirers. His mother and his wife also profess to be Christians. He is having the skirt he wore to worship the idols dyed and made into other garments.[7]

Our young worker has gone back to Bible School in Changsha. Our other young church member who is just beginning seminary has written to me once since he arrived. He says his school is the best of its kind in China. It took me some time to convince him he should go there. The school is run by Presbyterians and has high standards.

When we go out preaching we sometimes hear people say, "How can you worship God when he is the one who has withheld the rain?" There are many answers like, "Why should you expect Him to send rain when for generations you have received so much and have bowed down and thanked idols for all favors?" Still one can not help feeling sorry for the people when calamities come.

Shucheng, September 26, 1934

Yesterday was such a horrid day. I had a long talk with one of our deacons whose daughter-in-law has committed adultery. Of course she will have to be disciplined as she is a church member. I thought at first the deacons had known she was doing it before she was baptized, but it seems they did not. We are very much disappointed in her, and she is intelligent enough to know better. So many of the girls in this district are so dumb that one is not surprised at anything they do. According to the custom of this place, her father if he finds out would be justified in killing her. That is one reason why it becomes awkward to discipline her.

Another thing that had happened was that while I was away, our house woman's husband came and spent a night on the compound. She argues that I allow the wives of two other servants to live on the compound all the time. Where her argument breaks down is that her husband is a thief, and she knows that I know it. She has made some fine promises it will not happen again, but she has promised enough times before. Very soon I intend to fire her. She is not really satisfactory in any case. For one thing, she allows her husband to bring stolen goods onto the compound. Of course that is something I must see about.

Shucheng, November 26, 1934

Week before last I spent at the out-station. An old deacon and his wife went with me, and for the last three days one of our newer Christian girls was with us. All liked the preaching of this young girl, and she was thrilled by the reception she was given. The local Christians are beginning to help with some of the preaching and in many other ways. After the services each night, which were well attended, the Christians would go to the guest room for prayers. Some tarried afterwards. One night some of the young men were telling how before their conversion they had gone on long pilgrimages to worship idols. They took with them small stools to kneel on every few steps. These stools were reckoned as idols also and they must wash their hands before touching them. That evening these men were telling how they split these stools up and burned them for kindling wood after they became Christians. One of the young men pointed to the passage in Matthew where it speaks of "burdens grievous to be borne" that had been put on them before they became Christians. No one wanted to stop singing and talking that evening. Along about mid-night one of the men started to apologize about keeping us up. The young Christian girl from Shucheng said, "Of what importance is that? Think of the times we have spent the whole night gambling!" It does one good to see the "joy of salvation" in these Christians who have so recently begun to taste it.

Shucheng, December 14, 1934

The rent of our out-station building costs about thirty dollars a year. It has been open for preaching half of the evenings of this whole year. The average attendance has been well over fifty. How I wish we had the workers to carry on such work in other centers in this county, but at present we do not have them.

We found the woman who handed in her name last time we went to the out-station going on well. She had been demon possessed but had nearly become normal. This time we met a girl of seventeen who says that she believes the gospel with all her heart. But her mother-in-law will not allow her to come to church or us to go to her home. Fortunately the girl can read, and I have given her a paper-covered Testament.

Shucheng, December 18, 1934

Margaret is very busy these days. Just now she is hemstitching sheets. The wedding is to be the end of next month. Ruth is preparing for another language examination.

This year I have gone to the out-station nine times, walking every time. Besides I have had other long walks. I believe I have walked more than three hundred miles in long walks this year, not including any short distance walking I have done. This year has been as full as there has been strength to keep up with it all.

Shucheng, January 3, 1935

The day before Christmas about a dozen of the young people worked on the decorations for the church, and nearly a hundred children and young people took part in the program Christmas day. Even though there was rain for several days before Christmas, over three hundred people came to the service. This included seven young men from the out-station for their first Christmas since becoming Christians. They stayed several days, and I gave them some lessons on the first chapter of John. They learned the song "Down in the Valley with my Saviour I Would Go" and sang it over and over. Even though their singing is mostly joyful noise, and you would not understand them, I do wish you could hear them sing and pray.

This week I am supposed to be reckoning accounts. That is a job I do not like. Perhaps I am halfway through with it. When Eva Knight was here, she used to do this for me. In fact, Eva does so many things the rest of us do not want to do. She always looked after the garden too.

No doubt you have read of the murder of Mr. and Mrs. Stam of our mission in this province. They had not thought their station was safe, so he went back without her after their baby was born in September. They had only been married the October before. Because the official assured them it would be safe, Mr. Stam went after Mrs. Stam near the end of November. Then the official failed to let them know when he withdrew the military when communists came to take the place. One wonders why the Christians were not alert enough to let them know. I think they would here, but the church here is much larger and better established. There are some details much better not written. At any rate the baby was not harmed in any way. An evangelist and his wife had a good deal to do with rescuing her. Since this has happened in this province all our missionaries south of the river have gone to Wuhu. Until something is done about those communists, it is considered best for us not to go to out-stations. We are eighty miles north of the river and perhaps they will not cross it. Margaret and Ruth knew the Stams well, and they as well as everyone else tell about what splendid young people they were.[8]

The wife of the young man in Bible school in Changsha has typhoid fever. This is the second case in that family just recently. I have been trying to urge them to get inoculated.

I must go to see what the servants are doing. They may save our hands and feet but certainly not our heads. We have discharged two women recently for taking things, and our cook may have to go for the same reason.

Shucheng, January 13, 1935

Thursday I went to see the wife of the young man studying at Changsha for the last time. She recognized me but could not speak. She had improved slightly from typhoid when she got her young sister-in-law to get her some things to eat that she should not have had. She died very early Saturday morning. Sunday morning I went out to the funeral. On the whole I think the young man's parents had done the best they could for her, but there was considerable quarreling between her in-laws and her own parents. Her folks claimed they had not had the right doctors, that her mother was not sent for in time, and the coffin was not good enough.

Shucheng, January 20, 1935

Tomorrow Margaret Elliott who has worked with me over two years is to be married in Nanking. She and Ruth have been gone from here two weeks. Ruth will come back and keep on working with me.

I am wondering how the young man studying in Changsha will take the news of the death of his wife. When he was away working several years ago among worldly folks, he got engaged to a girl he liked. When he came home, he found that an engagement had been arranged with a quite homely and stupid girl. She could work around the house and make her own clothes, though. He begged his father to let him out of marrying her, but to no avail. He even went so far as to try to persuade her to commit suicide. She died of typhoid the week before last. His father told me he was thinking of writing to tell him not to grieve too much as the girl was not worthy of him. She was not altogether true to him when he was away.

America is doing plenty of playing with fire. I remember the first impression I had of communism was that it was of Satanic origin. That was before I reached the twenties. My observations have extended since, but never have I been given any reason to think any differently. Unless the Lord comes for his own soon, many of us will suffer beyond measure because of it. My hatred of bolshevism and the way it is run grows. It is not merely having lost my goods, it is the innocent Christians they so dearly love to slaughter that makes one despise the sysytem. But one wonders if it is safe to write these things.[9]

This week I gave a worn out night gown to a famine refugee. She made three garments out of it for her children. Where they came from they were living on the bark and roots of trees. Even here they only have turnips and rice husks. The baby girl is so sweet. I give them bean curd milk for her every day because the mother does not have enough milk. They have been well-to-do as the Chinese reckon. As soon as the wheat harvest comes in May or June, they will need no more help. Yesterday I heard of a family of six who with their last money bought poison to put in their last pint of rice. Before they had a chance to eat it, they saw some brigands coming and fled. There were thirteen brigands who partook of the meal, and twelve died.

Shucheng, February 3, 1935

Ruth Elliott, the younger of the two sisters who has been working with me, came back a week ago yesterday. The older sister Margaret and her husband may be back from their honeymoon most any day. Margaret will be going to another station very soon. She has worked here with me three years altogether.

Next week it will be six years since I came back to China. In one sense of the word it becomes a little like home to us, but it is more like a boarding house. Perhaps the heavenly home will be ever so much more precious because of having had so little of home life here. After all, we are only pilgrims and strangers on the earth.

Shucheng, February 5, 1935

Yesterday was more or less of a scramble because of it being Chinese New Year time. We had groups of callers all morning. Then about noon we had a meeting. After our noon meal there was a short meeting before a group of the Christians, mostly young people, went out to hold street meetings. I stayed in, as someone needs to be here to talk with the groups who come in.

I just received a letter from the young man studying in Changsha. It was in answer to the letter I wrote to him telling him about the death of his wife. He feels the loss very deeply. They have a baby about a year and a half old.

Shucheng, March 10, 1935

The superintendent has not been around for a year. He probably will come soon. There is one prize station in this province which ranks with the best in the mission. In all there are twenty-one stations of our mission in Anhwei. Shucheng in church attendance ranks second, so they say, in this province.

There were only four baptized. We hope there will be many more next autumn. Some are waiting until the provincial conference. There are a number of inquirers who are being instructed, and some of the church members are very good at this When a church has a few members the missionary can do most of that work. A somewhat bigger church is like a big family—one has to put the older ones to work taking care of the smaller ones.

Shucheng, March 26, 1935

Mrs. Crossett, formerly Margaret Elliott, who did work here with me has gone to a station about a hundred miles from here. The man who worked there for many years was taken captive by communists, and it is thought he was murdered because he refused to tell where he put famine relief money he had on hand just before they took him. It is the place I was asked to go to as soon as I returned from furlough. Of course, the Reds searched the house thoroughly to find all the money in it. When the Crossetts went to the station and Mr. Crossett moved a trunk that had been left there, they found a sum equal to about a hundred seventy dollars underneath it. The exchange rate is different than it was then, being only about a hundred dollars then. To think that that money has been in the house nearly three years—it is no longer safe in many parts of China for a missionary to handle famine relief money.

It has been more than a year since I have been more than ten or eleven miles from this station. All of the missionaries I have met since then have been those who have come or gone through here. There have been eight of these and three of their children. There were two other missionaries here also for meetings. More people come through here now than there used to be.

Shucheng, April 14, 1935

Going to conference has taken up some time since my last letter. This was held at Wuhu, about two hundred miles away. The trip took two days going and twenty eight hours returning. There were better connections coming home, but we couldn't do it in two days just a few years ago. There were thirty five missionaries at the conference. Of that number ten were graduates of Biola. Of course, we had a good time at the conference. I was assigned to room with two of the oldest missionaries in the province. Each had been in China more than thirty years. It was good to meet and confer with them. The messages of the main speaker were deep and good. These conferences are held only once in three years, so the four days were far too short. There should have been more time to get acquainted and more time for prayer.

Unfortunately, my fellow worker, Ruth Elliott, has had to go see a doctor. She may have gone as far as Shanghai because it is almost certain she will have to have an operation. She was particularly worried about this because she has a bad health record. At any rate, she is more fit than she was a year ago.

Since Ruth is gone, I will, no doubt, have to play the organ and arrange the program for Easter. We won't have many flowers at that time except tulips.

The colporteur has just been in to discuss his next trip. He is trying to find someone who will take a couple of goats to the Crossetts, a hundred miles from here.

Shucheng, May 8, 1935

Mr. and Mrs. Whipple with their two children came Saturday bringing Miss Kiang, a Chinese lady who will lead some meetings here and at the out-station. Mr. Whipple played the organ at services Sunday and Monday which made the singing go very well, but on Tuesday the Whipples left because there was an opportunity to get to their station by bus. Their seven month old baby girl smiles all the time, and their four year old boy is fine also.

The Christians at the out-station are having a small pulpit made. They intend to have it painted blue. Last year they decorated the chapel with paper flags, chains, flowers, and lanterns. This year they are getting the pulpit. Next year I hope they can buy property for their own chapel.

Shucheng, May 14,1935

Today Ruth has come back with the new worker, Pearl Galloway. Ruth got over the operation she had in Shanghai very well, or she could not have come so soon. I am sure I will enjoy working with Pearl.

Shucheng, May 27, 1935

When we go to the out-station now a number of women come in during the day for us to help them to learn to read. One woman who had been demon possessed stayed with us the last two nights. She declares she is trusting the Lord but she is afraid to pray. We think it is because the demons still have not completely lost their hold on her. She lives in the country so she has very little fellowship with other Christians. This time we made arrangements with them about the keeping of their accounts. One is to do the writing, another is to supervise the accounts, and a third has the money in hand. We have to be very careful about this, for it is so great a temptation for these people to use any money that comes into their hands regardless of whether it belongs to them or not.

We have a hundred and three church members in this county of four hundred thousand people. And yet the three nearest mission stations say "You are so fortunate because you have so many workers." We do share with them some of ours, but cannot hire people to preach as one can a hired man or woman. We have to wait until they catch the vision themselves.

We are about to make a chart of one of the leading families in the church. Half of the church belong to one family. Everyone who comes here says there are so many of them they get mixed up.[10]

Shucheng, June 14, 1935

At the out-station we are teaching a number of women to read. First we teach them to read simple gospel truths. We aim to have all church members able to read their own Bibles. A number like to learn to read the hymns. Among these "Jesus Loves Me" and "There is a Gate that Stands Ajar" are the favorites at first. "What a Friend We Have in Jesus," "In the Cross," and "Follow, Follow" come later. With mature Christians "Take My Life and Let it Be" expresses the desire of their hearts just as it does with us. I hope some day they will learn to appreciate "When I Survey the Wondrous Cross."

We are becoming better acquainted with Pearl Galloway, our new worker. She is more like me than is Ruth Elliott. Ruth and Pearl are the same age, but Ruth is ever so much more capable. Ruth being China born and a college graduate will not always win out though. One thing Pearl complains about is fleas. Perhaps the rest of us get used to them. There are so many annoying things we come to accept as a part of the day's work, the work we love just the same.

Kuling, July 5, 1935

Things were a little unsettled last week, the kind of scare we have met with dozens of times before. Pearl had never met anything like it before so was terribly frightened. Ruth was not much better. The deacons did not want to take responsibility for the two of them since I was going away. We sent our heavier things away the day after the deacons warned us. I talked over plans for the summer with the deacons and the student evangelist home from Changsha. I handed over the supply of Bibles, hymn books, tracts, and posters to him. We turned over the supply of medicines to a church member who has had more then a year of training to be a nurse.

Ruth has gone to stay with her sister, Margaret, for the summer. Pearl and I took rickshas to Tungcheng where we got a bus the next day for Anking. Pearl will stay there for the summer. Eva Knight and Doris Hinckley will be there too.

From Anking I took the boat to Kiukiang. I missed the bus there, so had to take a ricksha across the plain. The distance up the hill is six miles with a four thousand feet climb. This took me ten minutes less than three hours to walk. Some can do it more quickly, but most women and many men can not climb it.

There is not much to write about from here in Kuling. We go out shopping, go to English church services, and altogether live more like anyone at home. The other night I had a great treat. I was given a real orange.

Kuling, July 24, 1935

Being away from the responsibilities and problems of the station for a while is good. Yet no one could be happy without responsibility. Women need some way of expressing themselves. In the past having large families was enough, and that must have been a great satisfaction to many. But I can not see that a small family is enough. Something more is needed.

It is good to be here where it is cool and where I can study with no fear of interruption. It is well that I enjoy studying because there is no end to what could be done. This morning I have read over thirty of the Psalms. There were two or three characters in the Mandarin I was none too sure of. Unless one keeps up the study, much is lost.

About fifteen of us missionaries eat together. Most of them are my age or older. None of them seem to care to walk. Why is it so many folks have so little energy? Many are too fat to get out of their own way, and some are too skinny. I have no excess fat but can step out at a fairly good rate.

Ruth Elliott had a more difficult time getting away from Shucheng. The student evangelist accompanied her. There were no buses out, so they had to walk to the next mission station. They finally arrived two days later than they were expected.

Kuling, August 7, 1935

If the communists confined their propaganda and activities to the realm of economics, which is not my sphere, I might not mention them. Having lost my worldly goods twice at their hands there is a personal score against them. One of the finest Chinese Christian workers with whom it has been my privilege to work, who has walked many a mile with me preaching the gospel and shepherding the flock, lost his life when taken by communists. Because of them it was necessary for me to give up working in Hunan where I knew the dialect and was used to the work. In the last four years three of the C.I.M. missionaries in Anhwei province have lost their lives at the hands of the Reds. Just today I heard someone speak of twenty thousand having been killed by communists in one county. There are probably a score or more counties that could report something as bad or worse. At the present communism is one of the greatest forces the enemy is using against the preaching of the gospel in China. Since I came to China for nothing else, my prayers for those who hold to communistic teachings are for "those who despitefully use us." The best thing I can wish for them is that they get soundly converted.[11]

A letter has come from our station in Shucheng. The Chinese have had some difficulty persuading soldiers not to occupy the station premises. The Christians are busy keeping everything going. This included church services, prayer meetings, Sunday School, Christian Endeavor, besides services at the out-station. Five of the young people helped during the ten days of the Daily Vacation Bible School. This was held in the morning from six to nine o'clock because it was so hot. In the afternoon a Bible class for the young people was taught alternately by the two young men who are studying for the ministry. This had an average attendance of about thirty.

Kuling, August 18, 1935

If it were not raining, I might be at another meeting. There have been so many meetings this summer. I attended only a small part of the Moslem Conference. There are Moslems in our district, probably thousands of them, and so far as I know not one has ever been converted. I should take more time to study means of approach to them. They are not very strict Moslems, even using some lard on the sly when they think no one notices it. So they might not be very hard to reach, but that kind of Christian is very lax if converted.

Shucheng, September 2, 1935

I have been back here almost two weeks and have spent three of those days at the out-station. Those of us who went got up early and had walked the eight miles to get there before nine o'clock in the morning. Things there seem to be going very well. The two seminary students have taken turns preaching this summer. Both of them have fine gifts. They will be returning to their studies in a few days.

There are a number of fine young people in our church. Several of the girls have inquired about going to Bible school. One of these was a girl from the country who was married before she learned to read. Because her husband was ashamed of her, she studied very hard to learn to read. He took another wife anyway. She is really divorced now, but her husband's people have allotted her enough money to keep her.

Pearl Galloway came back yesterday, but Ruth has not returned yet.

Shucheng, October 14,1935

Thank you very much for the money. Since the range of things we can buy out here has increased, money is probably better than parcels because there is no duty to pay. Very likely part of the money will be used for a lamp. Then Ruth and Pearl can use the lamp while I use their books. Ruth has a good many fine Bible study books. These were the part of her father's library which her mother portioned out to her after his death last year. They are very expensive, so I feel fortunate to have them accessible when I prepare messages.

Ruth and Pearl saw to it that I had a lovely birthday. This birthday marks my fifteenth year as a missionary.

One of the Chinese girls has just been in to have prayer with us before leaving for Bible school. She is one who has stood a great deal of persecution at home because she is a Christian. She does beautiful needlework and is earning part of her expenses for school that way. Our seminary student who studies in Changsha graduates in June and has been invited to come back here as an evangelist. He is now a widower, and I have reason to know he is interested particularly in this girl who is leaving for Bible school.

Shucheng, December 18, 1935

The Christians at the out-station want me to come back on Christmas day and stay over Sunday. Even though one nearly freezes when staying there, I plan to go. This will be the first time Christmas has been celebrated there. They have already begun decorating for the occasion. Last year seven of the young men came down here and stayed a few days Christmas time. Before that they were not interested very much.

We have some women in this place who have very little to do. A couple of the statements of the younger women who went to the out-station last time have set me thinking. Such as "When I used to gamble two days and nights in succession, I did not stop to ask anything about what was going on at home, so why should I now?" There are two or three women with very little to do at home, so they can help out more about the church where there is plenty for them to do.

Shucheng, December 23, 1935

This year more than ever we plan to give up our Christmas to the Chinese. In the forenoon will be the Christmas program for the Chinese when we expect about three hundred people. My job will be to look after the ushering, and it makes a hard forenoon's work. After the program is over, one of the women Christians has invited us to her home to talk with some people who have had little contact with the gospel. After that I plan to walk about nine miles to the out-station. We should have a hundred or more people there in the evening. I would enjoy it all more if I did not get so tired. The strength of my youth seems to be a thing of the past.

Shucheng, January 14, 1936

Christmas day went much as we planned. The one exception was that I decided I was too tired to walk to the out-station. When the person went to hire rickshas for us, he found a bus standing waiting. By going by bus we got there at three o'clock in the afternoon.

Ruth, Pearl, and I had our Christmas dinner and opened our presents on Christmas eve. We had numbers of gifts and stacks of cards. Many of the Chinese brought cards.

The Christmas decorations at the out-station were very pretty. They had Christmas greetings written with paper flowers inside and outside the place, also festoons of the flowers and paper chains. This is the first time that town ever celebrated Christmas. The place was packed that evening. The ushering was a bigger job for me in the evening than in the bigger service in the morning in Shucheng. In the morning most everyone came to listen. In the evening it seemed as though most of the children came to make a noise.

I stayed over Sunday at the out-station. If I had not taken plenty of clothing, I would have frozen because the building isn't heated. As it was, I caught a cold that hung on nearly two weeks.

Shucheng, February 12, 1936

Ruth has just received word that she is to move to a station nearer her sister. Except for being nearer Margaret, she is not the least bit happy about going. Most people hate to leave Shucheng.

The last time we were at the out-station, soldiers wanted to stay in our building over night. The two Chinese women with me had never had any experience talking to soldiers. I did not find it especially fun to talk to a group of men each with a gun in his hands. But on the other hand, those who are soldiers are under authority of some sort.

Shucheng, February 24, 1936

Today it is snowing. The house woman is helping Pearl and me fix cushions for the living room chairs. We use bamboo shavings stuffed into cheap unbleached muslin covers. These will then be covered with cretonne.

Last week Tuesday we were seeing Ruth off, and there were people in all day. There was so much more than we could do before Ruth left, and now we are more than ever short-handed. There will be more meetings for me to take, but the Chinese women will have to do more. Pearl has not had as much practice walking as the other girls had, so I will be going off by myself more.

When we leave those who profess to be Christians without enough teaching, they not only do not grow, but they can become a hindrance to others. The best plan I can find is to take as many as possible with me to work at the out-station or other places. Then I can teach them as we go. The last time we were at the out-station we had crowds every evening. The last evening one would have almost needed a shoe horn to have packed in another person. The Chinese women with me preached each night, but the evening prayers and the Sunday morning service I took myself.

Shucheng, March 18, 1936

The changes that are being made now just do throw more of the work on me. The latest change is that the doctor ordered Pearl to leave because he thinks being here she might be put to too great a nervous strain, and so she is to be sent to some other place. In my own experience there are places that are a great deal worse than this has ever been. But so many who come out are not fit to meet any kind of hardship. Of course if anything should happen, having anyone like Pearl here would make it harder rather than easier for me. If worse comes to worse I can travel well over twenty miles in a day on "Old Shank's Mare," but she complains about being all tired out when she only walks three or four. Pearl is sorry to be leaving though, and is taking her time about it. For more than a week now she has been packed up, but some days there were no buses and other days there were other hindrances. I do not know whether she will leave this week or not.

We expect Eva Knight who has been here before most any day, but she will have to try to keep the work going in the next station even after she comes here So she will be away a great part of the time.

Shucheng, March 21, 1936

So far this spring I have only spent six days at the out-station where work is beginning to get established. When I was there the military wanted to occupy the chapel. There are laws against their doing this and I reminded them of it. They stayed out while I was there but another group tried to get in after we left. There are only four male church members in the place. One is middle-aged but was away, and the other three are in their early twenties. They approached one of them and asked him for the key to get in. The door does have two keys. One key we always bring back here and the other we leave in the hands of the Christians. In fact the first young man they spoke to did have a key, but he told the soldiers I had brought it back with us. He left town that day so they hunted up another young male church member. He also told them that I brought the key away and that the place was to worship God in, not to live in. Not satisfied, they broke a fastener and got in. When they saw the benches all arranged and that it was a chapel, the soldiers left. When the soldiers were out of sight, the third young church member appeared who was a blacksmith, and he repaired the door fastener. Two or three years ago the soldiers and the neighbors might have carried off what was in the place and no one would have minded in the least.

Shucheng, April 4, 1936

Yesterday, Sunday, was as full as ever. Before I came down stairs in the morning I was called to attend a funeral which was over two miles out in the country. This was for a young woman in her twenties. When I went to see her Saturday, she did not know me, and her grave clothes were ready waiting on the bed beside her. Funerals are nearly always held within twenty four hours of death. This is partly because they do not embalm and because the women of the house wail as long as the body remains in the house. This woman was young and left three children, so this time most of the grief was real. This woman was a Christian who died of tuberculosis. She had asked me to pray that she be taken home soon.

After I returned from the funeral, I had a group of callers before Sunday School. One of the women I had not seen for nearly two years when I treated a large ulcer on her leg. She brought me two nice chickens and twenty eggs. Then there was Sunday School followed by prayer meeting, church, and communion service. For all of these I was the one to play the organ. After church I took about fifteen minutes off for lunch before making a call with some of the women. We called on a woman who is very ill. She had attended church a few times, but members of her family and others have preached to her until I think she understands. When I came back from that call, there were things to talk over with the Christian Endeavor group. They meet right after church. Then they eat lunch before going out to do evangelistic work in the country. They like to have one of us missionaries go with them to help draw a crowd and help hold up their courage, but this time I couldn't go. I had another group of callers and a number of things to see about before supper. After that there was the usual Sunday evening song service.

Eva was with me a few days before she had to leave again. Last week Monday, three of our Christians went with me to the out-station. About a hundred people came out each evening for the services we held. We did not go out so much, but stayed in the chapel to talk to anyone who might come in. In the afternoon some women came in to study the New Testament. One old woman, who had taken a vegeterian vow, came in carrying a bundle containing her bedding and perhaps all her other possessions tied on her back. She also carried a device that looked something like a spade turned upside down. This had two dangles hung from each side of the iron part. Such things do make a weird sound. One sees them often enough, and they always make me feel as though some of the powers of darkness are not far away. One of the Christian women with me told the old woman that the devil had certainly given her a heavy burden without giving her much compensation.

Shucheng, April 22, 1936

This letter really is being written at Chang-mu-ch'iao, a place over fifteen miles from Shucheng where we are hoping to get some work started. In the other direction it is over thirty miles to the next mission station where there are only about twenty church members. There are still so very many gaps that should be filled in. There is one church member here who lives nearly three miles out, and there are some people interested. That is all the nucleus there is for a church. A woman who used to live out here is giving us the use of a building to start work. Two women are with me. Each of them has a four year old girl along. One is a grandmother and the other has her own child. The younger woman is a very good speaker and does most of the preaching.

Eva did not return to Shucheng until the evening before Easter. Even though she was here to play the organ, she insisted that I accompany the children singing "Allelujah." The piece has some runs that almost anyone would need to practice. The children like to sing something difficult like that.

The day after Easter was Eva's birthday, but we scarcely had time to celebrate it. I even let the cook make the birthday cake.

Evenings there is an evangelistic meeting when about fifty come, and some people come in during the day. Nearly ninety percent of the people have never heard the gospel before. But the Enemy has so blinded the eyes of their understanding that the truths of the gospel make very little impression on them the first time they hear. I remember one day one of the Christians preached to a group of outside women for about an hour, and before they got out of the building one said to the other, "I wonder if it is true". By the time they had probably forgotten all about it. We cannot blame them though, because most people have very little idea of what the preacher has spoken about, and so very few really understand the way of salvation.

Shucheng, April 27, 1936

I returned to Shucheng on Saturday. The road was very muddy, and it is over fifteen miles from Chang-mu-ch'iao. It took well over five hours for me to make it. It was my night to take prayers and there was a Bible class to prepare for yesterday.

Today I have mixed up four different kinds of ointments, had six callers, have written some letters, and have talked over some plans with Eva. After she left for the out-station this afternoon, a telegram came about her going to Shanghai. About that time rain began to pour down, and it has been raining ever since. Sending a messenger after her in this rain would be difficult, and it would be still harder for her to return now. The rain will be an excuse for her to see the changes at the out-station she has not visited for two years. If I had been here when the letter came about Eva going to Shanghai, I would have written a letter of protest. As it is I suppose they think it does not matter. There is more work to do here now than there was four years ago when there were four of us here.

Shucheng, May 15, 1936

Since Eva has gone to Shanghai, and I am the only missionary here, we have been trying to get a women's committee to take over some of the responsibilities for the work. Today three women are out calling. I might have gone with them, but they came earlier than I expected, and my hair was not dry after washing it. Perhaps it was just as well to have them learn to go alone.

I spent eight days at the out-station recently. The young Christians there have decided to have two prayer meetings each week. They give as their reason that they are so few and so new in the faith that the Enemy may get them unless they join together and pray. At a discussion meeting one of them remarked that in order to keep the work up, every church member who was not out of town or ill, must come every time. Then he turned to one of the others and said, "You are not to forget it is prayer meeting night and go off to bed as we found out you did the other evening." This time at the out-station I spent the evenings teaching the Christians. The church members who went out with me had services for outsiders. Then we would have informal talks together for those who lingered.

Shucheng, June 9, 1936

Yesterday there were two letters telling me about my former fellow worker, Eva Knight. In the years we have been together I must have told her a hundred times that she should take better care of her health. Nine times out of ten, she paid no attention but went on her own way. As a matter of fact, I regret having said so much because if there was any result, it was hurt feelings. She has now come down with pneumonia, and as she is so thoroughly run down, there is not much prospect of her recovery. The one who wrote said it was the Lord's goodness that she was where there were doctors, nurses, and equipment. She is having oxygen given her, something it would be impossible to obtain here. In this place I would have had to take care of her myself, as no one in Shucheng has more sense about what to do in a case of illness than I have.

I do miss the others who have worked with me a great deal. This leaves me the only missionary in the "hsien" [county] of a half million people. If someone must be alone, I am glad it is for me to do rather than someone else. There is now a council of four women who are really willing to work to carry on the women's work in our church.

Shucheng, June 24, 1936

Never since I have been an adult, have I felt the loss of someone as I have felt at the death of Eva Knight. In all my life I have never had a more loyal friend. She was always at home wherever she went. When I was gone in April, she straightened out almost every room in the house. She was always willing to put herself out for others. Going off and leaving me alone was not a thing she was happy about at all. Her last letter to me ended, "Love from your little 'un."

A letter has come asking me to pack Eva's things, make a list of them, and send the list to Shanghai. Eva had been told to bring all her things here from Tungcheng, but she had left a good part of them there because she did not want to give up that work there entirely. Unless I am told to do so, I am not going to Tungcheng to pack her things there. One meets enough trouble going through life without looking for it.

The young man who has been studying at the Bible Institute in Changsha has now graduated and has returned here to be our evangelist. He has the idea of doing some real pastoral work for which I am glad.

After Pearl Galloway broke down and Eva Knight died, I have heard the Chinese say things about my looking after myself. Some have said I should get away for a change, but that can not be arranged now. The house is comfortable, and I can stand the heat. I will admit it is lonesome, but I expect company passing through. It has been two months now since I have seen another American, or foreign, woman. At present there are two children on the compound. There is Hsih-chan or Love-Pearl, the child we picked up at the gate more than four years ago. The little girl of her foster parents will be two years old in September. The two girls play together very nicely. The younger is a big, fat baby and needs the older to encourage her to move about. The young child of our evangelist may be here part of the time in the future.

Shucheng, July 17, 1936

The first of this week I went to Tungcheng by bus to make out a list of Eva's things. I tried to get out of it but to no avail. I had a busy time there as so many of the Christians came in to see me. Some of the children especially miss Eva. There is one orphan girl there about twelve years of age who has known no loving except that given by the missionaries. There was such a hard rain Tuesday that I knew the buses wouldn't run on Wednesday, so I hired a ricksha for the thirty mile trip back.

Shucheng, August 4, 1936

Recently I called on a church member whose child had been ill for a month. He looked as though he were in a serious condition. The mother was not much inclined to believe me when I told her the child had worms and that it would be possible to get the child to take medicine. It seems unbelievable to Chinese that there is a good medicine that is not as bitter as gall. I sent the medicine to her, and she was surprised at how easily she got the child to take it but much more surprised about the results. She did not come to church Sunday because instead of having a child who was quiet and limp, she had a cross little boy.

Playing the organ falls to me now. Formerly the other girls would play and look after it, but now I have to blunder through. I am beginning to understand its anatomy rather well. Yesterday I took the reeds out one by one and cleaned them. Is there anything a missionary does not need to know? Bookkeeping, housekeeping, gardening, nursing are a few of the skills required, in addition to a good thorough knowledge of the Bible and its practical applications.

Our superintendent, Mr. Hanna, insists that I am to take charge of the next station at Tungcheng. I wrote and told him it was the last straw, a big straw too.

Shucheng, September 2, 1936

Ruth Elliott arrived a week ago Saturday. It was so good to have company again, for I have been alone most of the time since March. At one time I worked alone in Hunan for five months, but that was in a city where there were missionaries of other missions. Here in Shucheng, which has a population of around fifteen thousand, there is a Spanish or French Roman Catholic priest. I have seen him but have not met him. Very few foreigners ever come here. Sometimes Russians of a very low type come through here begging. To my mind this is a very poor place for that purpose, as the Chinese have a great abundance of their own people unable or too lazy to work.

Shucheng, September 19, 1936

Last week I was away for a few days when I went to a doctor to have my eyes examined. He did not find anything wrong except I need glasses for reading and other close work.

As for the furlough you asked about, when one fellow worker has died and another has had to give up work because of her health, how is the mission to find someone to take my place on short notice? Enough new workers come out, but they cannot stand up under the strain of this climate and some things that go with it. Soft living is another big factor. A person ought to be able to walk five miles without being tired, and able to stand a little heat and cold. Young folks who from childhood have used up the last bit of strength each day and disobeyed other rules about health, as well as not having had a good start to begin with, are of no use in the mission field.

After being alone a long time I get used to it. When company comes, I enjoy having them, but the house is so empty after they leave. It means eating by myself three times a day, and sometimes for many weeks meeting no one with whom I can speak English. There is no use keeping a pet because it is necessary to be away so much. Besides in a land where many starve for lack of the plainest food, I begrudge the rice to feed even a cat.

Shucheng, September 21, 1936

Our colporteur has been away more than a week at a mountain where there is an idol procession. Many of the pilgrims go with a brass bar thrust through their cheeks. Nearly all kneel every few steps as they ascend the mountain. Even when they get to the top, they are not allowed to worship the idol unless they have sufficient incense and cash.

Shucheng, September 28, 1936

In pioneer days in America the spinning, weaving, grinding of meal, carpentry, butchering, making of soaps and dyes, in fact, nearly everything was done at home. I think that the age of machinery is no great improvement over the days when people did not think of having things so complicated or need to be amused all their hours when they are not working.

This city is known throughout all this section of China for its mats. Some of these mats are woven very fine. The Chinese use them to spread on their beds in the summer time instead of sheets. I have one, and it really is much cooler than a sheet. Also there is less trouble about washing it. Every morning it is washed off with a wet cloth. The finest of these mats are quite expensive. Some of bed size can not be bought for ten dollars. The shavings from the reeds used in the mats are of the right softness to use in seat cushions or mattresses.

Shucheng, October 5, 1936

Yesterday ten more persons were taken into the church. This makes an additon of fifty three to this church within the six years I have been here. Besides a new church is forming at the out-station. There was one member there when we began work five years ago. Now there are eleven. There are many more who are interested.

Just now we are having ten days of special Bible classes. Four women have come from the out-station for this and are staying on the compound. Besides these there have been a widow and her two daughters staying here a few days. The other evening while they were at church, their house and everything in it burned. The Chinese have a superstition that there is danger in receiving those whose houses have burned into their homes before the fire demon has been appeased by special rites. This includes inviting the priest to a big meal. The priest brings an idol and performs a ritual. The meal is supposed to be at the expense of the one who started the fire. One who starts a fire that destroys property does not get much mercy.[12]

This year there has been a very good crop of rice, but it is not cheap to buy. There are rumors that it is being either sold to the Japanese or that the Americans are trying to buy up all the rice. There is probably nothing to either rumor.

Tungcheng, October 20, 1936

For the first ten days of this month I had Mr. and Mrs. Weller with me when we had the Bible classes. Four classes were held each day. Mr. Weller took two of these, our evangelist took another, and Mrs. Weller and I did the other. There were some housekeeping problems for me to work out; for instance, my house woman had never ironed a shirt before. The deacons arranged to have a feast in honor of our visitors, but I do not know whether it was by accident or on purpose that this was held on my birthday. Anyway that had been such a busy day that I did not have time in the afternoon to change my dress for the occasion.

Saturday I came down here with two girls who are members of the Shucheng church. When we arrived, we spent some time cleaning the house which has been unoccupied. Sunday we helped with the services and entertained callers. We made a trip seven miles out in the country on Monday. The twelve year old orphan who misses Eva so, is now living with a family in the country. They have taken her in as their future daughter-in-law. From the Chinese point of view this is a very good arrangement. This is a true Christian family where she has gone. Even the dog and the cat are not like those of their heathen neighbors.

Hazel Todd in Chinese dress, 1936.

As to the condition of the church here in Tungcheng, I can not tell what is wrong. The longer I live the more firmly I believe that the Bible is the only attraction the church needs. Other things added to the teaching of the gospel only cheapen and spoil things. "He is altogether lovely".

Clothes are of minor importance to me at this time. Ordinarily I wear Chinese garments made by a tailor who is very reasonable. When I go home on furlough, I will need some new things, but when that will be is hard to say.

Shucheng, October 30, 1936

Miss Reid, a veteran China missionary, came today. She is past seventy years of age. The journey tired her out, so she has gone to bed early.

The colporteur returned from another trip today. He had been in districts where he had to watch his step very carefully because of communists. A young evangelist about two hundred miles from here was taken from his pulpit and dragged outside the city where he was stoned to death. The colporteur knows about this and realizes he must be cautious. In spite of all, he sold nearly a thousand gospels on this trip.

Last evening I was busy making out a four page order for tracts. I ordered more than ten thousand. Some of the Christians help in giving them out. I also keep a fair supply of books and posters on hand. In the office I keep all of one good sized cupboard full of books to sell including Bibles, hymn books, and other Christian literature. My stock in trade also includes a large cupboard of medicines.

Shucheng, November 16, 1936

There are about a dozen things needing to be done today—among other things, I ought to repair the bellows on an old organ so the evangelistic band who go out next week can have it to use. There is a call that should be made today on one of the "wandering sheep" among the flock. Miss Reid who is with me tries to help. She came over two weeks ago and expects to spend a month. The way I rush about almost bewilders her, but there is a variety of things that must be done every day. It is necessary for me to keep in touch with an evangelist and colporteur as well as a fair number of volunteer workers. In the Lord's goodness this is a larger work than that in which she was engaged. More people have been baptized here in the six years since my coming than in thirty or forty years where she worked. It was a difference in the hardness of the place, for I believe that on the whole she is the better worker of the two of us.

Shucheng, November 23, 1936

Miss Reid insisted that I go with her to Liuan, the next station where Mr. and Mrs. Costerus work. One of the Christians could have gone with her, but I think she wanted me to have a change. I had not been there for nearly three years. There always seems to be more than enough for me to do without any extra visiting. Miss Reid was saying the other day that the Lord makes no mistake when He sends so many of us single women to the foreign field. If there were more time, it would have been a good idea for me to have stayed and helped a few days with the work among the women. Many of the women in China are so responsive to anyone who really tries to understand them. Mr. and Mrs. Costerus gave me an urgent invitation to return, but it is good to be back in my own small corner.[13]

Shucheng, December 10, 1936

Day before yesterday I came back from spending a week at the new out-station. I walked the fifteen or more miles out there and back besides doing some more walking out there. There is a small band out there working with our evangelist as the leader. Besides each of the closest mission stations has sent one man to help. The owner of the building being used and my house woman went with me. I slept warm out there because I have a new camel fleece filled comforter. It is light in weight which is a consideration when I need to hire a man to carry my things. The weather was very cold, and there was even snow while we were out. The only way to keep warm besides putting on more clothes was to carry a small earthenware pot with a handle. In this is put a bit of burning charcoal bedded in ashes.

When I began to be a missionary, I usually stayed in and studied when it was cold. In those days there was authority over me. Now those under my authority also stay in when it is cold. In the last few years I have tried to have the out-station trip that would be the last one taken before the worst heat and the first one after, also the last one before the worst cold and the first one after.

Our house woman who came in just two years ago as a raw heathen, has recently become a Christian and a church member. She has learned to read since coming here and can read her New Testament. She takes her Bible with her when she goes to her home twenty miles away where almost no one has the least idea of what the gospel is or that there is a Savior. One time when she was there, she quoted that saying that when an idol falls into the water, it can not protect its own body. Most of the idols are made of mud stuffed with manure so they won't crack. One of the women who heard this saying about idols, went home and put her idol to soak. She came back and reported that it had dissolved.

Shucheng, December 30, 1936

Christmas morning before the program I had packed my suitcase and gathered my bedding together ready to go to the out-station. The Christmas service was a program of carols and scripture. Hsih-chen, the child we picked up at the gate four years ago in the spring, sang two choruses all by herself. She was terribly frightened as there was a crowd of about three hundred people. I played the organ and helped keep order. While I ate lunch, the leaders of the Sunday School gave each of the children a treat. My contribution to this was enough cookies for each child to be given two. These cookies with a bit of red and green Chinese concoction on top were made by the cook under my supervision.

Five of us went to the out-station by bus and two more walked. When we arrived, the Christians were just finishing their program. They had made rather elaborate decorations. In the evening the Christians with me held another meeting with an attendance of perhaps a hundred and fifty. There again as in the morning an address was made explaining the meaning of Christmas.

We stayed at the out-station over Sunday holding a number of meetings. The young people with me organized a society for young people.

A week ago Saturday evening one of our oldest women Christians died. When her youngest son heard of her death, he bought a coffin and brought it home for her. Her sons by a previous marriage had already bought a coffin and put her in it. The sons together decided that the extra coffin be kept for the father. The father died within a week and is ready to be buried in the second coffin. That old man was the first Chinese Christian in this "Hsien" of a half million people. That was over thirty five years ago and was the start of the Shucheng church. Now there are fifty seven male members and same number of women.

In the goodness of the Lord there are many of the native Christians who realize that "the harvest is plenteous and the laborers are few". After all, what are just over a hundred Christians in a district of a half million? The other day the colporteur preached to a man until he exclaimed, "Why did you not tell us before that the gospel is as good as all that?" He replied, "We have been trying to tell you and you merely taunted us for believing in a foreign religion." The colporteur has just been out on a trip for seven or eight weeks when he sold over four thousand gospel portions. It is astonishing how many people he meets who have never heard the gospel before.

Doris Hinckley recently wrote that she expects to be back here with one or two new workers sometime in the spring. If that works out, plans can be made for my furlough. Doris might have had a better furlough, but her mother died after she started home. Then she had word of Eva's death two months after reaching home.

Shucheng, January 11, 1937

There is much about the work here for which I can praise the Lord. It is good for me to know that all three of the places where I have worked in China would like me to continue working there. As far as the Chinese are concerned, I have not altogether been a misfit.

Last week the colporteur started out on Monday with two other Christians to make a trip of over thirty miles, and they expected to be gone a week. They took with them five hundred gospels, which is not as many as I wanted them to take. They came back on Friday because they ran out of gospels. The people where they went have suffered so heavily from communism, and seem to have a longing for something more solid. So many had never heard the gospel preached before. They seem keen to go back again and they want me to go along. I have been wanting to go but it was not safe.

Ch'en Ch'i-kwei, who worked here for six or seven years and is now one of the best known native Christian leaders, will be here soon to hold meetings for a week. This is his first visit back after leaving about fifteen years ago. He will have his meals with me.

Shucheng, January 26, 1937

Thank you very much for the gift of money. This I intend to invest in Bible Institute or Bible Society bonds. Then the interest can be used to help some young person through Bible school.

A Chinese pastor who is known throughout China left here a week ago today. It took him two days to reach the nearest railway station. He came here on a visit, as he had been working here seven years and had not seen the people here for sixteen years. He had a very busy time, as he held two meetings a day besides making calls. On the whole he seemed satisfied with the progress this church has made. A young man who studies in Bible school had business to attend to at the railroad, and met him there when he came. This pastor teaches in the school where the young man studies, and took a real liking for him. He thinks the young man may become a leader in the church of this land, and plans to take some responsibility for his training.

The young man who graduated from Bible school last June seems to be getting along well. He has already made plans to be away more than two months this half year. Now that we do have a good evangelist, the other stations around here (three at least) believe we should share him with them. Those other churches are smaller and are the only ones in bigger counties. This church now has preaching places in two other towns, and hope to start work in another very soon.

Shucheng, February 12, 1937

Since yesterday was Chinese New Year's day, I had prepared for guests expecting fifty or sixty. Only twenty or so came due to the weather. Snow is still falling with five or six inches of it on the ground.

Last week I did have company. The week before that Mr. Rutledge, from a nearby station, sent me word by telephone that he was coming. Then there was rain and snow, and he wanted to send me word that he was not coming. When he went to the office where he could phone, he found the line out of repair. After a while the line was repaired, and I was called to the telephone which is a half mile from here in the post office. Mr. Rutledge was not called to the phone for nearly two hours. So there I was waiting in a cold office without a fire. Mr. Rutledge apologized about it when he and his father arrived unexpectedly a few days later. After all the telephoning they got potluck. Since I have good help here, I really don't need to know ahead when one or two are coming.

Shucheng, March 7, 1937

Thank you for the money order. It has been ample to pay for the next Sunday School supplies for our two churches. Just after the letter with the money order came, I went with five of the Christians to a town over fifteen miles from here and spent a week. We preached to hundreds of people, sold six hundred gospels, and gave away at least two thousand tracts. This was a pretty place, having beautiful rounded hills and a river with water clear as glass. If you ever saw the brown waters of the Yangtze-kiang, you would appreciate this the more. In most places in China, no matter how beautiful the place may be, those who live there do not seem to realize it. What impressed me more than the beauty of the place was the friendliness of the children and how keen they were to show off the sights around the town. Some of them paid very good attention to the preaching and really learned to sing some of the choruses. This is the more remarkable because scarcely any of them had seen a missionary before or ever heard the name of our Lord Jesus.

I had spent hours trying to find two women, to go with me. At last I decided that the house woman and another woman would go. Then one of the other women said, "Do not take your servant with you, or people will think all of us are servants", and she started out to find someone else to go. The first woman she went to said, "Yes, I can go. I have my washing and everything done. I knew I was to go somewhere but didn't know where". I had not had nerve enough to ask her to go because she has children just old enough to go to school who must be left with a fifteen year old servant girl. Three men went too, one being the colporteur. All six of us worked hard, but we enjoyed it.

Shucheng, May 2, 1937

Three experienced workers and a new worker are being sent to take my place where I have been trying to carry on alone the past year. One has been in China longer than I have been as a missionary. Another was born in China as a child of missionaries. Her father has been in the mission for forty years and has written some of the most useful helps for Bible study available in the Mandarin language. She has served long enough to have had a furlough. Doris Hinckley, who has worked with me, has just returned from furlough. The new worker is from Toronto.

To each of the new workers I have written a letter of welcome. Also I have written several letters about finding a school for a very bright blind girl still in her teens. Our young woman in Bible school is doing very well. She writes that she may stay there this summer and work to save traveling expenses to come home to Shucheng. The young man in seminary may have to change schools. The seminary he attends is in northern China where the diet is completely different. Instead of rice they eat noodles and bread. This change of diet has not agreed with him.

I spent a week recently at the out-station at Taochen. I hope to get back there and make some other trips before leaving.

Shanghai, June 11, 1937

There was a great deal of work to pack up and hand over the work to others even when they are as capable as those who follow me. Even yet nearly two weeks after leaving there are yet letters to be written.

According to the present plans, I am to sail from Kobe on the twenty sixth on the Hieyang Maru which will reach Vancouver the tenth of July. Either on that boat or another I expect to go on to Seattle. Do not go to any bother to prepare for my coming home. Probably within two weeks of your receiving this, I will be home, and we can talk things over.

[Hazel's second furlough was spent at home in Strathmore, California, and at the mission home in Los Angeles. She had another trip to visit relatives in Minnesota.]

CHAPTER THREE

On the Front Lines in Anhui: The Final Years, 1938-1941

M/S Tai Yang, November 4, 1938

We were instructed to be on the ship by four o'clock on the afternoon of October seventeen. My brother, Charlie, had brought all my things to the boat. My cabin mate was not so lucky because the transfer company she paid to deliver her things had missed one of her trunks. A hasty trip back into Los Angeles was necessary to get it. In the end we did not sail from San Pedro until eight o'clock.

Shanghai, November 21, 1938

We were delayed another twenty-four hours between Hong Kong and here because of rough weather, so we arrived in Shanghai a whole week late. Mr. Hayman, a provincial superintendent of the mission, came to meet us. I had met Mr. Hayman before and the younger girls seemed thrilled to meet him. He knows the ropes, and while I had to open three of my things and almost needed a shoehorn to put everything back in again, there was no duty to pay.

Shanghai, November 23, 1938

It is almost like being at home again. As yet there has not been time to see the CIM Director Mr. George W. Gibb, so I have no idea about where I will be going.

We had a good time in Hong Kong. We were taken for a drive all around there, so I could see that the bay is just as beautiful as I had been told it was. As the ship had to go into dry dock, we spent two days there, and we found out what it looked like under the ship. The reason they go into dry dock in Hong Kong is that labor is cheaper and is just as good as elsewhere. So on my fifth ocean voyage I saw the propellers for the first time.

Much of the way from Manila to Hongkong and from Hongkong to Shanghai the weather was not good. One night on the way to Hongkong my steamer trunk and suit case slid out from under my bunk, and I had to brace myself in bed. When sitting up on deck, our chairs would start to slide. When it is that rough, I do not even eat or knit, to say nothing of writing letters.

Two of us have been out doing a little more shopping. We go together as we do not want to go around the back streets where things are cheaper alone. I bought a pressure one burner stove, a small German lantern, heavy woolen underwear, a new Chinese-English dictionary and mosquito netting. So far I only bought essentials except for some hand-painted Christmas cards. We are more or less taking this week off to see to our own affairs. Next week we may start going to refugee camps.

Shanghai, November 24, 1938

There will be a wedding here Friday afternoon. The bridegroom had been working up in Sinkiang. As they had to come out by way of India, he and another young man have taken almost five months to get here. He and the bride to be, Katherine Dodd, had not seen each other for six years. I suppose a furlough will be their honeymoon. Katherine was a good friend of the Mrs. Stam who was killed in Anhwei.

Shanghai, December 9, 1938

Although I have been here nearly three weeks, there is not much prospect of going inland. There are parts of Anhwei which may be safe, but anyone who might have gone with me has either been sent elsewhere or has been given something else to do. Now is the time we should be on our way, and the weather has been good so far since we came. As it is, we may have to travel in the coldest part of the winter. For that reason I have ordered a lining made of wild cat fur for my coat.[1]

The last two Sundays I have been out in a refugee camp to teach a Sunday School class if you can call it that.. There were thirty to forty children of widely assorted ages. Because they have been well disciplined, there was little trouble along that line. It is a little hard though to get much of a message across to them because of language. Last week I also had a meeting there with over thirty old women.

There are a number of things that concern us. One is the Costerus family. The last they were heard from, they could not get permission to come here. That was several months ago. It is now nearly two years since they have seen their children who are in school; in fact, there is no opportunity for them to correspond with the children. At another station that I have passed through a number of times was an old Chinese pastor who has worked with the mission for many years. This pastor came to Shucheng to conduct a baptismal service the last year I was there. I had talked with him many other times. When the

Japanese entered the city where he lives, they were almost pumping the well dry. He asked them to use a little less. After that he and another Christian were taken away and have not been heard from since.

Much of what is going on very likely is suppressed. One business man told of how in the defence of Shanghai the Chinese would fight until their ammunition was finished, then throw up their hands. The Japanese would then shoot them all down. The other day we saw a set of dishes, ninety-two pieces in all, for less than five dollars. The reason was that they were marked "Made in Japan". We hear that most of the Japanese shops in the settlement here—and there are not many—are subsidized by the government. The business man who on the ship more or less looked after us has the agency for half a dozen automobile and truck companies for China, and he would not ship any of his stock on Japanese ships. As he told us, he is not the only business man who so discriminates.

This letter will be carried to Canada by a missionary couple and mailed from there. Otherwise I might not have said so much.

Shanghai, December 28, 1938

As yet I have not been able to leave Shanghai because there is no one going in my direction. Before furlough I could have started off on my own. Now it seems essential that a male missionary be along. Formerly I preferred having a Chinese along. Now I am told a Chinese could be a hindrance.

While here I have been out a few times to two different hospitals. At one of them I gave out decorated cards to each patient young and old. The hospital was such a bare place that anything bright was appreciated. This formed part of their Christmas treat. Besides this each patient was given a loose skinned orange and three small caramels. The food in the hospitals is much better than that in the refugee camps. In one refugee camp where there are two hundred and seventy men the mission used nearly four dollars for the Christmas treat. This was a raw turnip and a small piece of bean curd. Many of the men were so keen about the turnips they started eating them without washing or peeling them. Enough money was collected from the CIM group here to give hundreds of others a treat at Christmas, but most of the money was used to buy bed covering for families who have little or none. I am still teaching the Sunday School class every Sunday and am helping with the women's group.

A missionary who worked eighty miles from Shucheng has reported that the church was still standing on our compound. He did not succeed in saving any of our things there.

Shanghai, January 21, 1939

At last they seem to have decided where I am to go for a time. I am going with a young married couple, Mr. and Mrs. George M. Steed. The idea seems to be that I am to return to Shucheng when the way opens. At present Shucheng is in the hands of the Chinese. When I first went to Shucheng, there was an elderly man who had been evangelist in our mission and then for a time in another. He preached once a month but toward the last he often came to preach in the evening. He was so sure the Lord would answer his prayers and that Shucheng would not be taken. When the Japanese did come in, he remonstrated with them about something they did on the compound. Because of this, he was beaten so badly that he became frantic and jumped to his death down the well. It is not possible to get much news of Shucheng, but the church building is still standing and some others as well, but not the house in which we lived.[2]

We were sorry to hear the other day that one of the church leaders in Liuan, the place where Mr. and Mrs. Costerus work, was recently shot. There was some complication over some riff-raff who came onto the compound as refugees when the Japanese took the city. Later when communists retook it, this man, who was leader in more than just the church, was blamed. He had almost full medical training. He is the man who watched the whole night with Mr. and Mrs. Costerus the night their little Elsie died. Then for the coffin he made a wreath of flowers that looked much like Easter lilies.

The plans are for us to go by Japanese steamer to Tsingtao. From there we go to Hwaiyuan in Anhwei, which is a Presbyterian mission station. When we reach there, we will have to inquire about the road before proceeding further.

A call has come for volunteers to teach English to Jewish refugees from Germany. In order to make a living here in Shanghai it is really necessary for anyone other than Chinese to be able to speak a little English. In fact, most Chinese, even ricksha coolies, know at least a few phrases. Were I going to stay much longer, I might have responded to this.

The new Mrs. Schoener, who was Katherine Dodd, has promised to carry this letter out of China.

Fowyang, February 11, 1939

On the twenty fifth of January at least thirty missionaries came down to bid us good-bye before we left the mission compound just after seven in the morning. We were accompanied to the boat by Mr. Hayman. We went to the boat sitting on our baggage in the luggage van. We reached Tsingtao the afternoon of the next day. We went to the house owned by Mr. Scott of the Presbyterian mission where our language training is now given. The two girls who came on the same boat last fall seemed thrilled to see me again. They took me on a walk to a lovely spot yet that afternoon. We were fortunate to spend two nights at that lovely home. We left the house just after six in the morning, but all the girls were gathered on the steps to sing "All the Way My Savior Leads Me" as we left.

We bought train tickets, third class, to Hsuchow. The trains didn't travel at night. The first night in Tsinan we stayed at the YMCA because the mission station was too far away. The second night we arrived in Hsuchow where we were invited to take supper with Bishop P.L. Tsen of the Episcopalian church of Honan. We seldom meet so well educated and fine a Christian. He had been on the train with us on his way back from the missionary conference in India.

We spent an extra night in Hsuchow for our baggage to catch up with us. The next morning we had to look after the baggage by the light of Firefly, the name of my new little lantern which gives a very bright light. On the train that day our luggage was piled on the shelves above us and out into the aisle because nothing could be checked. About fifty rods before the usual place to stop at Pengpu we felt as though we were going over a rock pile. Someone waved frantically for the train to stop. More destruction. Before we got our baggage to the Presbyterian compound, we had hired two sets of coolies. They will not carry beyond certain limits. The compound there was badly damaged in the recent occupation, and there is no missionary there except one woman whose main purpose is to help those passing through. A Chinese man from Fowyang had arrived there a few hours before we got there with the aim of meeting us. From there on the traveling arrangements were in his hands. The next day we did not reach the boat three miles out until late in the afternoon with all our baggage to manage. Then we got to Hwaiyuan station compound when it was almost dark. We were entertained very nicely there, but we could see they were having difficulty just carrying on. The next morning we were shown around the hospital there.

We started from Hwaiyuan on Thursday morning, and it took us until Monday afternoon to go the next seventy miles. We passed two out-stations but met only one Christian. At Mengchen where we got off the boat there is a Presbyterian compound where there is no foreign missionary. There is a Chinese pastor and a gateman. The house built for missionaries was occupied by refugees, so we were given rooms built for Chinese guests. These rooms were much nicer than those we were in the next two nights.

I met several of the women Christians, and it was like being home. Apparently there is anti-foreign feeling there because almost a mob had gathered at the boat and followed us up to the chapel, so it was especially good to see the Chinese Christians.

From Mengcheng we came overland the last sixty miles. There were five carts which were just a platform mounted on ricksha wheels. Four carts were for baggage and one for Mr. and Mrs. Steed. There was a ricksha for me. The tires for the carts were almost worn out, so often all of the carts would be held up while one man would pump up his tires. Other times it would take all six men to bring the carts one by one over the ridge. In all I walked over twenty of the sixty miles in the three days, and Mr. and Mrs. Steed walked as much. The road was just too rough to ride much of the way. The weather had been fairly clear much of the way, but when we got twelve miles from our destination, rain and snow began to fall part of the time. We arrived just as the roads were beginning to get slippery and our things just damp on the outside.

Mr. J.H. Kane, whose wife and child have been in Shanghai, and Mr. Gordon Dunn, a single man, are here. They had been expecting us for some time and had a room ready for me and one for the Steeds. Our rooms both open off a sitting room where a coal fire is kept burning. Due to wind and sunshine both Mrs. Steed and I had burned our faces so badly they are peeling. Otherwise, except for cold sores, the trip seems to have done me no harm. Some of our things were broken on the way including my mirror and fever thermometer. Considering everything it is remarkable that anything was left.

One of the ricksha pullers had come from Shucheng several months ago. He said that one town I had visited and thought so pretty was still intact. A letter has told me that the building where the gatekeeper lived and the church are still standing on our compound.

Fowyang is a large place. Attendance of three hundred at church is considered small.

Hwokiu, March 10, 1939

In Fowyang I stayed nearly three weeks, and the Christians were most friendly. When most of the city was burned, and the people had to flee, the pastor prayed that the church might be spared. The church building which holds nearly a thousand is still there. It is one of the few in China which has a gallery. For months they had no Bibles to sell as the book room burned. The Bibles and the hymn books belonging to most of the Christians were also burned. Because kerosene was so very expensive, they held evening meetings in the dark except for the leader having a small light. They sang hymns and choruses by memory, and the leader would read a sentence of Scripture, and then the congregation would repeat it. This church has its own Chinese pastor and two women workers. When I was there, the rain kept me from getting out to visit. Many of the people didn't have much of a place to stay since the city was burned several months ago. One would have thought though by the send-off they gave me and the way they urged me to stay that I had been with them many years instead of a short time.[3]

We thought we could get here in two days from Fowyang. We started out on a Wednesday and got almost thirty miles, about half way here, the first day. We had a ricksha which I rode at least twenty of those miles. We reached an out-station where there is a very good, self-supporting native worker in charge. About forty people gathered for a meeting the night we arrived. The next day it started raining and continued raining the rest of that week and Sunday. During my stay there I took three meetings and spent hours teaching the women, so my time was not wasted. The church leader told us that there were twenty seven families of the Christians there who do not have sufficient food. Although Sunday was a rainy day, there were at least a hundred at church. When they have a period of prayer there, all pray together, each praying his own prayer out loud.

On Monday we left that out-station by sedan chair. That day I walked about seven miles and rode about the same distance. The chair bearers refused to come farther. Tuesday we came about five miles by native boat, and I walked the remaining eleven miles.

Our efforts to get word through that we were coming had been unsuccessful, so our arrival was a complete surprise to those in Hwokiu, that is Vincent and Margaret (Elliott) Crossett and Ruth Elliott. They are now packing to go home on furlough. Margaret and Vincent now have a cute little girl who was a year old in November. They started the work here so are happy to have someone to carry on. Margaret, Ruth, and I have worked together enough so that we are quite at home together.

Transportation and traveling being so difficult is one reason for things being so very expensive. Some wages have not been raised since I left, but most prices are much higher. Water routes that might be comparatively easy to pass over are brigand infested, so everything has to go the hardest way around. We were talking one day about the roads, and one of the missionaries said that in this section they have gone backward twenty-five years. It did not take me long to prove we have gone back only ten years or less. Most of the automobile roads in this section had been built within the last five years. Now the roads have been torn up, and the buses have gone west. Bus service had never been very well established or organized anyhow. Only in the larger towns can we buy kerosene. Soap is hard to find. I'm glad I brought some prunes and raisins with me because fruit can not be bought now.

Margaret will be taking this letter part of its way to save time and censorship. Thus I can mention that coming from Tsingtao to Pengpu we saw many wrecked bridges and trains and a number of deserted villages. Hwokiu is still in the hands of the Chinese, but there are rumors that it will change soon.

Hwokiu, March 21, 1939

I arrived here on a Tuesday afternoon. Mr. and Mrs. Crossett and Ruth Elliott left on the next morning. I have been in this house by myself for over a week. This is just a shack of a house, and the compound is very tiny. A fellow worker is expected to be here soon. In the meantime I am feeding a black cat, a dog, and a canary. Perhaps my fellow worker will like the canary. Perhaps the cat would appreciate it more.

Although I would like to start going to other places around here before hot weather begins, it is not wise to do so now. For one thing there is some famine relief money in the house. I have not taken any responsibility for distributing it, but it was committed to my care until the right person does take over.

The servant knows nothing about our way of cooking. She can fix rice, meat, and vegetables very well. There is plenty of goat's milk, and eggs are reasonable in price. My largest necessary expense now is feed for the goats. That may be cheaper when there is grass. I can buy kerosene here, but it is very expensive. I have a good supply of wood to burn and some coal.

Shucheng is not much more than a hundred miles from here. I hope to visit there this fall. I have heard that half of the church members were forced to leave there.

Hwokiu, April 7, 1939

Here we are stuck on a boat. Here in Anhwei they do not seem to know how to work a boat. If the wind is the least bit against them, they just tie up and wait for the wind to change. A day or two extra makes no difference to them. Perhaps we may go twenty miles in two days. I might have walked in one day but the woman with me could not do it, and I need to take my bed and bedding. The boatman is rather amused. I woke him up when I moved about to get this paper out of my suitcase to write this letter. At the same time I was doing some rather urgent talking about starting off. The captain aroused, and as the wind was down, he pulled up anchor and started off. A very few minutes after leaving the shore, but too late to call us back, a number of the military came to commandeer boats. A number of boats are following frantically after us. I am surely not very much blamed for waking up the boatman. Anyway we are on our way.

There are eight of us on this small boat. Chengyangkwan, the place to which we are going first, had been open as a mission station perhaps before I was born. I was asked to go there and take charge ten years ago but refused to do it then. Mr. and Mrs. Henry S. Ferguson had worked there so many years that it did not seem right to push them out. She died two years later, and a year after that he was taken by the communists. We suppose he was killed by them because he would not tell where famine relief funds were. That place suffered very heavily through the war last year but the mission compound is still intact. The furniture is gone from the house and the glass from the windows. Many of the Christians were killed or fled. I do not know whether missionaries will ever live there again. The other place to which we hope to go was opened more recently. In other words, these two places are ones in which missionaries have been working but are now vacant because of a lack of workers.

Hwokiu, May 1, 1939

My first two letters have come direct from Shucheng. Some of the Christians there are holding meetings on Sundays in the country. All the furniture that was in the church including pulpit and pews are gone. One can be thankful that the church building is there. An offer has come from Mr. Costerus to supervise putting up some sort of house. At least we have space, bricks, and this offer of help. Timber and lime are very reasonable in price. Nails and glass will be the big expense.

During my time I have attended a number of Bible Conferences, but this last trip of mine was the first time I was the speaker. At Cheng-yangkwan I gave fifteen messages in nine days, and there was an average attendance of well over forty. I had prepared work on the first chapter of First Peter. While there I studied out work on the second chapter. Had I known what was coming, I would have studied more before the journey. At the other mission I visited, Yingshan, I did not hold as many meetings. About as many people came, but on the whole the interest was not as keen.

My next fellow worker is to be Marguerite Goodner. Her home for a number of years was in Hollywood.

Hwokiu, May 18, 1939

My new fellow worker came more than two weeks ago, and we have been together ten days because I left to come to Chengyangkwan. A few days after I return to Hwokiu, she intends to go on a trip. She seems like a very fine person, but we will probably work together only a few weeks. She has always worked in the northern part of the province and I in the south, and north and south in China can meet about like east and west. In the north unless they have noodles as their daily food, they think they have not eaten, and in the south they must have rice. The people in the south think those in the north are dirty and untidy, and those in the north think those in the south are too particular. Those in the north are more awkward as a rule and more straightforward. Those in the south have a bad reputation for their temper and trickiness, and outwardly they are more polite. One usually must use altogether different methods with the two groups. Probably I could learn to work in the north, for they have a proverb that no one blames you for being too polite, but there is such a great shortage of workers further south.[4]

We keep hearing more of Shucheng. There were eight deacons when I went there. One had left the church and another died a few months before I went home. Four other have died since, and only one of them was killed by violence. The body of the man who tried to save our house is buried on the compound. I hear that the evangelist expects to return soon. As a matter of fact, there are three deacons left at Shucheng, as two younger men were elected while I was there. One of the missionaries has gone there. Most of the kitchen is still standing with my stove still in it. The doors of the oven and the lids are gone, but perhaps they can be replaced. The strawberry bed on the compound is still there and is being looked after.

I'd like to ask for a snapshot of Charlie and the truck. Some of my fellow missionaries at least pretend not to believe that a truck can carry fifteen tons.

Hwokiu, May 30, 1939

Last week I did very little else but to prepare and take meetings. There were only fourteen to take. Many of the meetings have really been Bible classes. Marguerite and I between us had these every evening for more than two weeks. The church asked us to do this.

A man from the Swastika Society came to call on me Sunday evening. I should have known better than to touch anything concerning them with a ten foot pole. It seems they have a Red Swastika Society too, which gladly distributes—with some reservation—any funds the Red Cross may turn over to them. They have a report that there was a battle about forty miles from here and that many homes were burned. Now if there is any time in the year when famine relief funds are not needed it is just after the wheat harvest begins, and this time of year people can live in almost any kind of shelter. But the Red Cross would not turn over funds to them without the endorsement of both the missionary in charge of this station (that is myself right now) and the Roman Catholic priest. I promised to write and ask one of our male missionaries about it. Then out of curiousity I asked what the priest was doing about it, and the man told me that he was writing for information also. None of the Chinese had warned me, and none broke in on the man's interview. But two men came in afterwards, one of them almost the leading man in the church, and told me the whole thing is a farce.[5]

Among other things left for me was a black cat. She has had five kittens. Three have been given away, and one more promised to someone. The last may be a drug on the market. The dog is, at least, a good watch dog.

The other day an elderly woman from a place at least fifteen miles away came past our place. The front is just a common sort of shop building, four walls with a roof over it. She only saw posters on the wall and no business carried on. She asked the gate-keeper what the place was used for. He told the woman we used the place to preach to people about the remission of sins. She said at once that she was a sinner, and she wanted to know how to be saved. He brought her in after talking to her for a time We taught her a simple prayer which she readily learned. Often the first time we meet such a woman they are too stupid to learn the first time. The prayer goes, "We beseech Jesus, pity me, remit my sin, wash my heart, and save me". She said over and over again, "I never heard such things before". She left rejoicing after about an hour.

Marguerite is away for a week, and I miss her very much. She is a fine fellow worker. She graduated from U.C.L.A. in 1930.

Hwokiu, June 12, 1939

Marguerite is taking most of the meetings as she is leaving soon. She was just saying her parting gifts to me would be a bottle of vanilla and a bottle of vinegar. Gifts of lemons, bananas, or prunes, not to mention vinegar, are not despised out on the mission field.

My desk is rather fragrant. Gardenias are in bloom, and someone gives us some nearly every day. A couple of fans on my desk are also gifts. These were made from a sort of woven straw. They give us of the best they have of eggs, vegetable, towels, or anything they think we will like. And we can do so little for them in return in some ways.

Another letter has come with word of Shucheng. Services are again being held in the church. Two trees that were too near the wall were cut down and used for new church benches. Before I went on furlough, I refused to have those trees cut down. The lumber was not needed then, but it is now.

Last week I had a carpenter come in to fix our screen doors and the leg on a bench. He wove a wire arrangement on the bottom of the door that will stay put. At the end of the day he inquired about the price of Bibles. The cheapest edition we have has a plain blue cloth cover and no maps and is sold for the same amount of money that is paid for a day's work. He went home with his new Bible instead of wages. His old one had been destroyed by relatives who opposed him for being a Christian. Yesterday we had a woman come in to do our washing. She wanted a hymn book. She was greatly pleased that I did not ask her to pay any money in addition to doing our washing. That was only a paper covered hymn book. Well within three months we have sold thirty-nine hymn books here, over a dozen Bibles, and about as many New Testaments. Many go into the hands of those who never owned a book before.

Sunday the head county official sent word he would like to have us come and show him how to use an adding machine. Not knowing anything about it, of course we both had to decline. There is nothing much a missionary is not supposed to know.

Now we are greatly in need of rain in order to put in crops for the fall. Wheat that was put in early has yielded a good crop, but much had to be put in late because of floods. The floods were caused by the Yellow River having had its course changed last year. These people seem to take it for granted that the river will be turned back to its original course, but one wonders if it can be done even if those in authority want to do it.[6]

In my last letter I mentioned my hesitancy over endorsing an appeal from the Swastika Society to the Red Cross for funds. It was a good thing to hold them in suspense a while until we had returned some bags we borrowed from them. By stalling them off a while, we came to a reasonable agreement about the bags.

Hwokiu, June 27, 1939

Last week I went with Marguerite to Chengyangkwan. There she met another missionary and together they have gone away for the summer. It was necessary for me to go in order to have another American witness for my application for passport renewal. Chengyangkwan is twenty miles from Hwokiu by boat. One can walk the fifteen miles quicker than getting there by water, but in hot weather that was not our choice. In Chengyangkwan I led three meetings over the weekend. If I had been in Hwokiu, I would have had more.

Last week I had another letter from Paul Hsu, the young man who was in seminary before I left Shucheng. At present he is working to support his foster mother and his brother. He wrote in English, "I have asked the Lord to guide me to leave the present circumstances and to take service for Him."

My Chinese newspaper has begun to come. It is five or six days late but is cheaper and quicker than anything I can get in English. This place has no means of communication with the outside world except by post.

A mother has been bringing a small boy to me for treatment for his eyes. When I first saw him, his eyes had been swollen shut about a week. The first couple of days he screamed when I tried to do anything with him. After that he seemed to have changed his mind about me. His mother half apologized for bringing him one morning saying he wanted to come as soon as he woke up. His eyes seem all right now. I used drops of argyrol then bound on pads of boric acid. I have a good supply of argyrol which I buy solid. I weigh it with grain scales mixing a small quantity at a time.

Hwokiu, July 17, 1939

The last two weeks I have been having Bible readings every evening Brevity was not what was desired, and many having reached the place where they like to look up a dozen or more references, it is just as well to give them what they want. Having plenty of books to refer to here, I spent a good deal of time in preparation. We had an average attendance of at least thirty. As for Bible teaching, the Chinese church seems to be demanding more of it than ever before. One may well put up with some inconvenience in order to give it.

We were having some trouble with soldiers coming to borrow our benches and doors two weeks ago. They usually did return benches within a couple of days after they said they would. It came to a climax a week ago Sunday morning. A group of soldiers came in to occupy the room facing the street which is used for evangelistic services. Seeing me appear, they were very nice about it and declared they had only come in to rest a while. As a matter of fact, they did leave just before the church service began. Church service was scarcely dismissed when another group of soldiers were here to borrow our doors and benches. In desperation I went up to the one who seemed to be the leader with my card. I asked him to kindly take it to his superior officer and tell him I was putting in a request that no more benches and doors be borrowed without their bringing a card or some written order guaranteeing that said articles be returned. I might have noticed that the Christians were making themselves scarce as I talked. The soldier said something about how other doors had already been taken, and thinking he was only mentioning a precedent, I said my permission had not been given. When I went back to where the other Christians were, they were grinning. They then informed me that I had been talking to the superior officer. Within a short time all the doors and benches were back on the compound, and no soldier has been here to borrow anything since. None of the Christians seem to ever mention this affair without a smile.

I have met some of the young girl soldiers recently. One only eighteen years of age had escaped from Nanking. A soldier's uniform could not hide her attractiveness. In times of peace she would be in a sheltered home, the only suitable place for such a girl. One's heart rebels against the fiendishness of the system that makes that impossible. She was a professing Christian.

Mr. Kane and Mr. Dunn at Fowyang have been having trouble about cashing checks. Mr. Dunn came the sixty miles here by bicycle over bad roads two months ago. He has been having malaria, so this time sent a Chinese Christian after money.

Last week I received some Bibles I ordered more than three months ago. It gives you some idea of how difficult such supplies are to obtain. It is easy enough to say "do without." We can do that about food and clothing, using what the people use. But medicines and literature are what make the real problem. One has to be very hard boiled about only selling medicines to Christians. One must overlook the slight fact that lives may be lost because of this, but it is impossible for us to try to keep on hand anything like an adequate supply of quinine, for instance.

Hwokiu, August 14, 1939

Two weeks ago the refugee baby that the missionaries before me rescued died. She had been exposed too long and she always did have a cough. The Chinese who took care of her didn't know how to feed and care for her very well. I felt very sorry about the way she was buried. Not having seen a child's funeral here, I wanted this to be an example. (I have never forgotten the results of my first storm about this in Hunan. Not so long afterward a child apparently died during the night, but the father said he must wait until morning to have some sort of service because the new missionary was most unusually particular about such matters. In the morning the parents discovered that the child had not died.) In this case the foster mother had gone out on an errand after the baby's death. While she was gone the foster father came in unexpectedly, grabbed the child with only her underwear on, and took her out and buried her. Even the neighbors were displeased with him. The foster mother had even laid out some of the clothes which Margaret and Ruth had furnished, for the burial. The deacons declared it looked too much as though he did it to get the clothes for his own children and asked him to bring them back to the church. The foster mother told me her husband had so disposed of five of their own children. I was telling her something of our customs along this line, and she answered that she thought it wouldn't hurt so much to have it done that way. It seems as though at every turn heathenism makes all the harder experiences in life so much the worse.

There is a vegetarian woman who has come in to see us twice. She likes to hear us tell about the Lord. But she seems to put it from her when it comes right to the issue, saying she cannot break her vegetarian vow. Those with spiritual understanding out here know that mixing faith in vegetarian vows and trusting in the blood of Christ is impossible.

Hwokiu, September 4, 1939

Yesterday Mr. and Mrs. Steed arrived, so I will be able to leave within a week. The people had wanted to have a feast of welcome today for the Steeds and as a farewell to me. In the first place, they need the money to buy new property. Secondly, this is not a time for feasting in this time of floods and war. Third, I do not care so much for these things. Instead a tea will be given tomorrow on the compound.

Last week we heard that the city where there is one of our nearest mission stations had been wrecked by bombs. As I hope to go there soon and as there is no one else of our mission within a hundred and thirty miles, I sent a messenger to find out about them. They had heard that we were in a similar plight and were glad to get our messenger's report. There was something to the report we heard, as about sixty people were either killed or wounded there in a city of about forty thousand people. As for us there was nothing to report. From the military point of view this place is of no consequence.

Chengyangkwan, September 16, 1939

I stayed in Hwokiu more than a week after Mr. and Mrs. Steed arrived. The people of Hwokiu wanted to give me something, but I insisted that they use their money for the church. Several did give me gifts of some sort. The shoemaker whose small son I treated for sore eyes would not take any money for putting half soles on a pair of my shoes. He used material now very difficult to obtain.

My woman servant from Hwokiu has come with me. We may be here two weeks or more because again I must wait for someone to accompany me. While I am here, I have been asked to take some Bible classes. I hope to take up the eleventh chapter of Hebrews and perhaps draw a few lessons from the book of Proverbs.

I received a letter in English from the girl in whom Paul Hsu is interested, She graduated as a nurse in the spring and is a capable Christian girl.

Chengyangkwan, September 29, 1939

Mr. and Mrs. Costerus, who will be my traveling companions and with whom I will work for a time, have been held back from coming, so I am still stuck here. In the meantime I have been working. I have had the tiles on the roof relaid. The masons found a piece of shrapnel on the roof while working. This could be from a year ago, for this place has changed hands twice.

Last week I had meetings twice a day taking some lessons from the book of Proverbs. Verse one of chapter twenty eight will be remembered because many of the outsiders got excited and prepared to leave last weekend. Apparently there was little foundation for the rumors.

For the present the mission has cancelled all furloughs. Just what other measures they may need to take one does not know. I will try to continue to write home twice a week to someone. Many of the people here love beauty as much as we do. The other day I saw a straw thatched roof covered with coreopsis of different colors blooming. The Chinese often do so much with a tiny piece of ground. Many people are too tired or discouraged to carry on, but you would be agreeably surprised to see how quickly they are trying to cover the scars.

One woman I have spent considerable time with over the past two weeks is about thirty-five. She was the only and petted daughter of a wealthy family and did go to school a few years. After she had only been married a few years, her husband died. He also had been very fond of her. As a matter of fact her husband was slain by communists. Her children both died and her mother-in-law's people cheated her out of her beautiful things. They often made her do the work of a servant and did not give her enough to eat. They sometimes have beaten her severely. Do you wonder why she went crazy? For some strange reason she takes a special liking to me, and does talk rationally to me. She is very thin and her color not at all good. Her husband's people only hope she will die so they can be free of feeding her. While they are not altogether rigid about a widow here in China not marrying again, it is rather frowned upon except by the very poor. But the lot of a widow without children is apt to be hard. Having sons greatly improves matters for her.

Chengyangkwan, October 16, 1939

This morning I managed to buy some white enamel to paint the old rusty galvanized tub I found here. Galvanized iron is most difficult to buy, so some in any condition is not to be despised.

From my window I can see a man spinning cotton. He works all day by himself with simple equipment and is out in the air while doing it. Most of the trades are carried on with one side of the house open even when there is snow.

Famine conditions prevail here. It is said the average home has one meal a day, and those who have two meals a day are considered well off. Prices for rice and wheat or for vegetables of a sort are not excessive. But so many just do not have money to pay for things. Living conditions must be a real problem. So the woman servant being allowed to eat with me during my brief stay here considers herself as having a very special privilege. Even at that, I do not share with her the fruit, tomatoes or small amount of powdered milk I use. On the other hand she eats a good deal more rice and vegetables. She says she praises the Lord even when she wakes up for having three meals a day.

Liuan, October 30, 1939

In all I spent five weeks in Chengyangkwan before Mr. and Mrs. Costerus arrived. They came as the men were finishing the whitewashing and an hour after I put the last coat of paint on the bathtub. Another thing I did was to apply kerosene to the bed to make sure no bedbugs were lurking in it. Then I scalded and rescalded it. We were delayed in starting off because we had to get passes.

The next morning after their arrival we, Mr. and Mrs. Costerus, the house woman, and I, were on the boat ready to start. The river was anything but straight, and part of the way there was a strong current against us. Fortunately, part of the time there was a favorable wind. We started on a Thursday and arrived here Tuesday noon. Sunday the rain kept us from traveling, and the boat was tied up on the bank well before dark each evening.

Within twenty four hours of arriving in Liuan there were two air raid alarms. Those who are used to them wait until they hear the planes before taking shelter. The two men missionaries here while Mr. and Mrs. Costerus were gone had a dugout prepared.

Now I am preparing to go to Shucheng to stay over Christmas. I can take little more than what a man can carry over forty miles. I must take bed and bedding, some things to eat, and a quart of kerosene. Today a letter came from a woman at the out-station. She said they are beginning to have Sunday services again and they want me to come to give them more Bible teaching. To do this I would willingly go without a number of things. It was so good to get that message the day before starting in that direction.

Shucheng, November 13, 1939

It took us the best part of two days to come over forty miles here. I had a sedan chair but walked about a third of the way. A bicycle would have been of no use for most of the way. The path had never been good because of the heavily ladened narrow tired wheel barrows incessantly run down the center. Now much has been done to make it worse. I saw six crews of men working at not road building but tearing it up some more. Often times they had dug pits lengthwise of the path plenty deep enough to bury horses. Getting here was a tremendous job. We are forty miles from "no man's land" in one direction and eighty miles in another direction.

This paper would catch fire and burn very quickly if an attempt was made to explain or give my opinion of the situation here. Most of the church is scattered; many of them hundreds of miles away. The missionaries who followed me were advised to leave, so a great opportunity for witnessing as to the keeping power of our Lord was lost. Perhaps that is the greatest loss of all. The house might cost a thousand dollars to rebuild plus months of work. Most of the Chinese quarters are gone. It would take hundreds of dollars more to replace the other goods. We have ten benches left out of forty with backs. Most of those missing were borrowed by the military. Since I came back, after going to their headquarters three times to see them about this, they have returned two more.

I am staying in a room about ten by ten feet which is a part of the lean-to built on the back of the church. It is the only room left on the compound with a board floor. My woman servant has a room like mine without the flooring. The first few nights neither room had a door. Then I had a carpenter fix things; however, there was only one door left on the compound. That one had had four panes of glass in it. Not being flat, this door would have been of no use for a bed so was not taken. For the first ten days here the furnishings of my room consisted of my camp bed and a pile of bricks on which to set things.

Everyone seems glad to see me, the outsiders too. But what an impression for us missionaries to have given to make the people think we only work in peaceful times or places! My furlough coming when it did has required altogether too much explaining.

Since coming here I have spent two days at the out-station at Taochen. I met four of the church members. There is no rented place for meetings now, and no good place for me to stay there.

Shucheng, November 25, 1939

This morning I have been out calling to try to stir up some more people to come to church. Some of them declared they had nothing good enough to wear. In this case, there is truth in the excuse, and one's heart aches to see the rude shelters where some must spend the cold winter. This district is better off than some with enough food of a sort, but they can not all afford salt or oil to go with their vegetables.

Coming back to this once beautiful compound to see the house and so much more gone has been very difficult. So much more sad is that about two thirds of the Christians have either died or moved away. I have been trying to visit every Christian within a dozen miles. There are still about eight within that distance I have not seen since coming back.

Yuin San-chie, or Mrs. Fang, my servant from Hwokiu, trails along with me wherever I want to go and acts as a general servant. She is not quick or showy about anything she does, but she is faithful. I do not know what I would do without her. She has no strings to keep her from working for me. Her father was killed at the hands of the enemy last year, and her worthless husband died years ago. It was easy for her to find someone else to work her small fields. Her younger sister who is a trained nurse had taken on the responsibility for her only child.

This is something against the rules of the mission, but do you suppose you could find ten dollars somewhere for an organ? I do need one badly. My voice is not strong enough or true enough to lead singing. The church will have to buy new benches and repair the building, and I am having so many extra expenses now. One of my tiny bits of charity this week was to give money to buy material for warm shoes for the three orphan children of a former teacher. [7]

Shucheng, December 9, 1939

This week I went to a place nearly twenty miles from here. The road there is a fairly good path, so the servant and I walked. The place is very crowded as so many people have fled there. Because of that the inns are not very accommodating. The first afternoon I took care to be there by four o'clock. Even then we asked at every place in town without finding a place to take us in. Then one inn-keeper said, "I believe your doctrine and will think out a plan." When we were shown to a room he proposed for us, we found it already had two occupants. One came forward to meet us at once and gave us a great welcome. She was the young woman who had done the embroidery on the banner and on the pillow slips I brought home. This was the first time I had seen her since furlough, and she now lives about twenty miles in the opposite direction from which I came. We both arrived at that inn on the same day. I was glad to tell her how much everyone admired the work she had done on those things. She is now working in a government position. The room we shared was not much, but we managed for one night and found better quarters next day.

We had intended to stay a week to work there but came home earlier because the situation was so difficult. Due to problems from planes we could not walk the streets or gather crowds, and the inn keeper did not want us to have many visitors. A few Christians welcomed us in their homes where we could teach. The place has changed hands four times, yet it seems quite prosperous.

Our church register seems to be lost. I wish now I had kept a personal copy, but it never occurred to me that with two registers, one in Chinese and one in English, that everyone would run off and leave them. My ideas of what things are important and what should be done seem peculiar to others, I'm afraid. Perhaps I can duplicate a good share of the register from memory.

For more than a year there was no communion service here. Cups, tray, plates, table, and all were gone. At last I bought a table that could be lent for this purpose, and I found some wine cups for a reasonable price on the street. A tray and plates were borrowed. To cover the elements I used some material bought for curtains. This did have a narrow blue stripe, but no piece of white material large enough was available. The church members were most appreciative of the communion service.

Within the past two days I have received three Chinese letters. One was from the colporteur. He had both of his daughters and the little girl, Pearl, the child we picked up at the gate, placed in an orphanage. He longs to return, but since he is so nervous, that might not do. We have had at least three air raid alarms today, and once we heard planes when there was no alarm. There is plenty of work to do if he were to return, but one wonders about him when he didn't stay near his job. None of the other church members gave away their children! One of the other letters was from Hunan where some are still determined to return.

Liuan, December 28, 1939

The three deacons who are left here came in Christmas afternoon to discuss plans for repairing and rebuilding. I let them do much of the buying and consulting workmen.

While in Shucheng I had a two room shed recovered. I bought almost two tons of a certain kind of yellow grass to use on the top of the mud part of the compound wall and to thatch the house. This is the best time of the year to buy the material, but not the best time to do the work. According to Chinese this is the time to build. As this is a heathen belief, we do not wish to follow it. They themselves do not like it that weddings and building should come when it is freezing cold. There are unlucky days to be born and to die, and their dead are often placed in substantial coffins to wait months for a luckier time to be buried. The Lord knows how difficult it is for many to break through all of this.

Before Christmas I stayed two nights at the Taochen out-station. While there I had to depend on the hospitality of the Christians. They gave me of their best, and had me take four meetings while I was there. They told me what they did with their well-stocked tract cupboard when they had to flee. They took the tracts with them to the mountains and distributed them to others there. Because the hills are hide-outs for brigands, we missionaries seldom if ever have an opportunity to go there. The one who told me about this said the tracts were not sufficient, so she wrote out about a hundred copies of a chorus to give out. When people asked her and the others if they were refugees, they answered that they were Christians. Many listened to their testimony gladly.

My woman servant has gone with me everywhere I went. It is good to find a woman able and willing to walk with me. When I left Shucheng, she planned to go to visit her young son. She had let him go before I hired her, so that is not on my conscience.

While in Shucheng I lost another five pounds. We do without butter now and are trying more than ever to live only on Chinese products.

Liuan, January 13,1940

Sunday I had my first experience in seeing bombs dropped. There was quite a loss of life and property although only one of the planes that flew over dropped bombs here, and one bomb dropped in the river bed where it did the least possible damage. This house is well built, but it shook like in an earthquake. The two Alsatian shepherd dogs were certainly frightened. As the planes came nearer, we went to the cellar. Much of our routine has been disturbed since then.

Mrs. Costerus spends most of her morning in the dispensary. Sometimes I help her. Most of her time is spent treating ulcers. Many are three inches across. Mrs. Costerus likes this kind of work better than I do. I would rather not be tied down but prefer to be free to do preaching and Bible teaching. While here I have been asked to take two meetings a week, and I expect to do some calling.

Margaret Elliott Crossett had a baby daughter born in September. She now has two girls. The family is now in the States on furlough. The news was three months reaching me.

Liuan, January 15, 1940

Supplies are going to be harder to get. We may have to learn to do without many things, but tooth brushes, baking powder, and sugar still seem essential to us. We are now using milk made from soy beans. It may be almost as good as rnilk, but does not taste as good without some salt. Some sweetening might help too.

Liuan, January 31, 1940

We have been having a great deal of snow, and it is cold. Many who are living in mat sheds are suffering. I hope the weather does not prevent me from going back to Shucheng soon. The heavy shoes which were bought for me when I was home have really helped me. The chillblains on my feet do not amount to much. One sore on my hands though has broken open. It is the first time I have had anything like it.

This week we were pleasantly surprised to have a valuable supply of quinine come through. This was a donation from the American Relief Committee and should be the means of saving many lives. This means a great deal to us because it is not pleasant to turn away those who desperately need it as we had to do a number of times in the past months. The nearest missionary doctor managed to obtain a special pass to have the medicine carried through both lines.

There have been many coming to the dispensary with eczema, impetigo, and scabies. A soldier came in the dispensary one day while I was there, with scabies on his hands. Mrs. Costerus sold him some sulphur ointment for it, but he was disappointed that she did not use a needle on him. Two, who came in after the air raid, we had to send to the Presbyterian hospital in Showchow. One had broken bones, and one needed a piece of shrapnel removed from her hip.

Cloth is rather expensive now, so one sees patch upon patch on the garments of the Chinese. I am trying to use only a moderate number of Chinese garments. One can wear things now more shabby because nearly all do. A person who wears a garment that has never been patched is considered very well off.

Liuan, February 17, 1940

Yesterday we were invited to a feast. It was not as elaborate as it might have been a few years ago. The family where we went have had ten children. Four died and three were taken away as refugees, so they only have the three little ones at home with them. The husband of one of the guests was shot as a traitor by some worthless officials who have since been disciplined. The fact that he was a Christian and an earnest one at that had much to do with the false charges brought against him.

One hopes it will be possible for me to return to Shucheng next week. I need to get the well repaired. Also we want to mortgage or rent something at Taochen, the out-station. What we need is about two or three rooms for another woman and myself to stay when we go there. There are Christians who are prepared to open their homes for meetings but are not prepared to entertain us. I have spent two days and they seemed to be glad to welcome us for that much time in two homes. But one could so easily wear our welcome out.

Shucheng, March 2, 1940

I have been back here just a week. We were delayed because there was rain on Monday, the roads were muddy Tuesday, then the men wouldn't start until after the Thursday holiday. The trip took two days, and the men were afraid they couldn't get food on a holiday. Anyway I was back for church Sunday.

Shucheng, March 17, 1940

One of our young girl church members has been away as a soldier. Her first question after church was, "Where are all our church members?" I was interested in the pronoun she used and in her desire to enter into things again. The poor giri is scarcely twenty, and she, no doubt, has been through a great deal. I gave her a New Testament when she told that her Bible and hymn book had been burned. At one time she was a hundred and forty miles from here, and she walked home in five days.

Shucheng, March 18, 1940

One of the deacons came in two miles from his home and spent the night on the compound last night. At least four persons have been taken for ransom from the area near his home within the past week.

On my last trip to the Taochen out-station two rooms were rented. Unfortunately the young man who should be in charge there, was called as a soldier. One of the women is in charge now. We used borrowed benches and held some meetings in the rooms we rented.

About seventy or eighty were here at church Sunday. It was a beautiful day, and two different men walked eight or more miles to come to service. One came from the east of the city and one from the south.

This is the second time this morning that I have heard the distant rumble of a bird of passage.

Shucheng, April 6, 1940

Since the first of March I have received five Christmas cards from America. When my Christmas presents from home came at the end of January, my fellow missionaries remarked that they must have been sent early. No one that I have heard of has received any mail from America that has been mailed since Christmas. The Costerus girl who is studying in the States has always written regularly. Any telegraph or telephone connections to this place are in the hands of the military.

Shucheng, April 15, 1940

Between eighty and ninety people were here yesterday, about forty of them being women. Usually the proportion of men is greater. Perhaps this is because more men have returned to this border city. Certainly the fact that men can come in from a greater distance has something to do with it. Very rarely does one ever see more women than men in the Sunday congregation in Shucheng. Even in China it is mostly the women who attend church, and usually it is the women who worship idols. Many a man who would scorn to worship an idol himself will gladly furnish the women in the household the wherewithal to worship them. Also it is the women who are the most loath to give up heathen practices as a rule. Often these practices are delegated to the most menial servant in the home. There are times when they have begun to profess to be Christians that they think for one person to attend church is quite enough. We are still trying to get some building done. The carpenters at least should finish their part of the work this week. The men who do the thatching should begin their work either tomorrow or the next day. Having no floor and very little finishing work to do makes the work much more simple. The carpenters have already done most of the work of making the windows and doors. We have to buy the logs, have them sawed and then have all doors and windows made. Those who thatch the roof have already sorted the straw into bundles of equal length. Over the rough, heavy beams a rough network of bamboo is made, leaving spaces between the bamboo about six inches one way and a foot the other. Next, if it can be afforded, are spread rush mats with the smooth side down. As they do the pleating of the bamboo work firmly, the result is not a bad-looking ceiling. They fasten and pleat the grass down using a bit of clay to help make things firm. This kind of thatching is usually guaranteed for five years or more. If it leaks during the first two or three years or more, one calls the man who did the work to come back and do it over again. It is done by farmers a good deal, who only spend a few months each year at it. What we are having built now is three rooms and a kitchen. Glass for the windows will be the largest single item of expense. We do not know when work can begin on our dwelling house. It might be wise to wait until peace is declared.

Shucheng, April 27, 1940

The ten dollars for the new organ was here when I came back from Taochen yesterday. This is enough for a good organ made in Shanghai. All Chinese materials are used for these organs except for the reeds. I'll be thankful to have it for my own and church use.

The rooms at the out-station are not too satisfactory, but they will serve as a base until we can find better. We did get aquainted with more women and girls. Many are really trying to learn to read and to find out more about the gospel. My servant, of course, goes with me. She shares meetings with me, and the Chinese women like to have her talk things over with them.

The church at the out-station has just three benches which look like sawhorses. These benches are their own precious possessions because the people contributed the money and bought them themselves. Their very rough table does not look so bad to them for the same reason. They plan to do some whitewashing before they put up the posters the superintendent left for them.

Our strawberries have begun to set on the plants, and that is one reason I am not thrilled about going away to conference. The fact that I am now senior missionary in this province gives me a place of honor at the conference, at least, among the Chinese. Mrs. Costerus is somewhat older, but they count years in China more than age.

A number of things have gone wrong with the building today. The mats we sent a man thirty miles to purchase are not sufficient. The bamboo was not strong enough, and some propping had to be done. The carpenters put the hinges on wrong. But the thing that made me the most cross was the fact that the men thatching the roof used our new wooden well bucket to carry mud.

Shucheng, May 11, 1940

The people here love all kinds of noise. It seems the more the better if it is a funeral or a wedding. They use fire-crackers and very noisy musical instruments with either. There is a two stringed fiddle played by blind fortune tellers. There are gongs used by priests as a signal to open the way for departed spirits. There are bamboo flutes and drums. The drums are mostly used to escort idols when they are taken to homes of the sick. Cymbals are used in the same way. Flutes are more generally used for weddings and funerals. Nearly everything played is in a minor key. The Chinese usually pick up a tune quickly except they change it some way to make it sound strange. If they start a tune in the wrong key, in spite of everything, they go through it to the bitter end. I have heard that the cymbals and drums are used at their noisiest when new Buddhist priests are initiated and have their heads branded. Some of the sounds people delight in the most are used in the service of the devil, and there will always be sounds to make sin seem a pleasure.

A college graduate was in yesterday to borrow a Bible. He said he had read the New Testament but not the old. I lent him a Bible with large print.

The Chinese sometimes must lie awake nights thinking up ways to wangle money out of us missionaries, as we have the reputation of being fabulously rich. A favorite way, although it does little to loosen my purse strings, is to claim their father or mother who was a Christian has died, and money is needed for the coffin. They can weep and wail and put on quite a show for my benefit as well as kowtow. Usually there is no invitation to attend the service. Anyway I usually pay them a bit for the show, not enough to buy a meal.

If there is a way to hang a door or window wrong, the carpenters working on the building have found it. While I was at the out-station, the windows were all hung so the glass would have been put on the inside. Then the workmen tried to make me think that was the Chinese way to do it.

Shucheng, May 27, 1940

Shucheng is the county seat, and before the war had a population bigger than Visalia, but my last letter was sent late because the city had run out of stamps of a large enough denomination to mail a letter to a foreign country. The city has been reduced in population now, of course. Much of the big street is being rebuilt, although much that is being put up is just shacks. On the side streets there are ruins as far as one can see. Business has increased since I returned, but has in no way reached what it was when I left for my furlough. I found some window glass last week, but the shopkeeper would not cut it. I bought three panes for places where we can adjust the frames.

Last week we moved into the new rooms. They are indeed a great improvement over where I have been even though there are no floors and not enough window panes. This simple building will later be used as women's guest rooms. The masons are plastering the last room today.

One of the out-station Christians wrote me last week. She has a new baby about five weeks old, a boy named Dawning Grace. Her six year old boy's name is Bestowed Grace and the three year old girl is Chosen Grace. The woman has learned to read enough to read her Bible within the last five years. She is the one who told me, "Of course, I must keep my house clean, cook, and keep the children clean, but it is not necessary to do the embroidery work on my children's clothes. I can use that time to learn to read." She now lives more than twenty miles away and is probably the only church member in a good sized town. Other Christians meet with her for worship, and for these she has asked for tracts and booklets to help her in teaching them.

Shucheng, May 29, 1940

Yesterday there was a funeral. The woman who is our out-station leader told me it was the second Christian funeral she had attended. Afterwards at the Bible class I explained some of our Christian customs about these things. "That ye sorrow not as those who have no hope" I have emphasized. With the Chinese, even the Christians, there is likely to be so much of that loud, bitter wailing, much of it being for the neighbors lest they be criticized for being unfilial. Still we must not do things in such a simple way that the heathen criticize us for not caring for the dead and tempt some weak Christian into trying some heathen practices. Our service can be an opportunity of testimony before the heathen relatives, friends, and neighbors we might no other way reach.[8]

Shucheng, June 6, 1940

After making a trip to the out-station I hope to call in masons to repair the old kitchen. It must have been very damp not to have burned with the rest of the house. Where the idea came from that kitchens must be built as an well so they will not catch the rest of the house on fire, I do not know. In this case it saved the kitchen. It was built of bricks laid on the ground, so one nearly freezes his feet in the winter, and a low tile roof that keeps it very hot in the summer.

Some of the out-station girls have been earning money for hymn books by shelling peanuts. The peanuts are smaller than those at home, and they must shell about seventy pounds to earn enough for a hymnbook. They have been so proud to do this because in most cases this is their first book. Then comes the task of learning to read.

One of our Christian girls in the country is blind. A missionary taught her to read Braille just after I went home on furlough and gave her copies of Matthew, Mark, and Genesis in Braille which she has almost memorized. She also wants a hymnbook. I tried to arrange for her to go to a school for the blind, but she was already too old for entrance age. The family, although more intelligent than the average, had not heard of a school for the blind.

Shucheng, June 7, 1940

Sunday one woman walked in ten miles from the out-station to be baptized and join the church. Mr. Costerus came to conduct the service. Besides he brought the news of a telegram that informed us that Ruth Elliott is in Shanghai and expects to leave there the seventeenth of this month on her way toward this station. She likes this compound as I do, and she likes to do some of the things I don't care to do like working with the young people and children. Also she plays the organ and takes care of the music. She will have a great welcome.

Shucheng, June 21, 1940

While I was at the out-station recently there was a special effort beseeching the idols to send rain. No pigs were to be killed for three days. They set the idols out in the fields, so they could see how hot and dry things were. It did rain on the evening of the third day. Otherwise the idols would have been beheaded. Since it did rain, there were to be three days of theatricals. The Christians, of course, were busy learning to read and studying the Bible as they progressed. Being able to read may not be a requirement for becoming a Christian, but scarcely ever can one stand as a Christian among heathen surroundings unless he can get Bible teaching.

Today I have been trying to impress on the compound people the difference between the well bucket and the mop bucket. Of course, we boil all water before drinking any of it, but I would still prefer that these buckets aren't changed about.

Shucheng, July 8, 1940

We have one woman church member, a widow who has seen better days. She was baptized the fall before I went home on furlough. Just before that her house and all its contents were burned. For ordinary occasions the women go about in trousers with a blouse, but for special occasions, or all the time if one bears the name of teacher, there should be a skirt worn. She felt that for such a special occasion as seeing me off when I left to go home she should have a skirt. She bought cloth which she could scarcely afford and had a skirt made. The next year when she met brigands, they stole the bundle of clothes she had in her hand but left her with her skirt hanging over her arm. This year she met brigands again. They stole the money she had on her person but failed to see the bundle she had in the back of the sedan chair as it was hidden by her skirt. The bundle contained enough money to last her several months, most of her clothes, her Bible, and hymnbook. She is very sure now that the Lord guided her about obtaining that skirt. She could sell it now for more than she paid for it as cloth is now much more expensive, but she is not thinking of doing that.

Liuan, July 12, 1940

The trip from Shucheng was not easy. It was necessary to spend a night in an inn on the way. Between the room being hot with little air and the bedbugs, that was not a comfortable night. There were still nine of their representatives left in my mosquito net when I arrived here, and that in spite of the fact that I had used insect powder.

The weather had become too hot for Ruth Elliott to come across to Shucheng, and the mission does object to my being alone during the heat. The mission has given me a great deal of rope since I returned from furlough, but there is no advantage in hanging myself with it. They have granted money now to build the house in Shucheng and are giving me Ruth as a fellow-worker.[9]

It is good to be here with Mr. and Mrs. Costerus. Mr. Costerus has been asked to supervise the building of the new house for me. He is Dutch and, before coming to China, was a carpenter by trade. The house will probably be as big on the ground floor, but the upstairs will be made smaller than the one that burned. There are a good many bricks which can be used, and the building will be made on the old foundation. Our first difficulty will be obtaining the timber.

Liuan, July 27, 1940

Ruth Elliott arrived last week bringing the organ I ordered with her. It seems like a very good one. The one Mrs. Costerus has is of the same kind, but hers does not have as much volume. The Shucheng Christians will be thrilled when they hear it. They were so disappointed that the old one was lost in the fire.

Ruth brought some more of my things from Shanghai. We must order glass, nails, locks, and window catches from Shanghai, and perhaps the rest of my things will come through with that order.

Here in Liuan there are church services of some sort every evening and three times on Sunday, but the attendance is never very large. The chapel could not hold more than two hundred. The city is three times as large as Shucheng, and when I went home on furlough the church membership was half as large as the Shucheng church. It may be some time before we get back to that proportion again. The work Mr. and Mrs. Costerus do in the dispensary is a great part of the effort here.

We are hoping the trip back to Shucheng will be as easy in some respects as coming over. I was stoppped only three times on the way for questioning. All three times I showed my card and it was handed back. The last time the soldiers on duty apologized for troubling me. When out of earshot my chair bearers began discussing about how much more they would have troubled their own people and without apologizing either.

Liuan, August 10, 1940

The most exciting thing we have seen this week was the lightning striking the tower over a gate about a block from here. The tower was higher than anything else in this neighborhood, and it had some military telephones in it. More than once we have watched the enemy planes, and this tower seemed to be their target. The lightning struck truer; however, it can still be repaired. That night after the lightning struck, a special idol was put up there, and people burned incense before it until midnight when the military made them quit.

Yesterday we received word that soldiers were occupying our chapel and at least one of the rooms I had so recently had rebuilt. We have appealed to the military authorities here to send word to them about getting out. We expect to return there next week.

While I have been here this summer I have had a women's meeting once a week, so it has been like a vacation for me. I have used cutouts on a flannel board some. With my easy program I have gained back some of the weight I lost.

Shucheng, August 28,1940

We arrived back here on the twenty first after a hot trip and one bad night spent on the way. There are rolling hills all the way, and the birds and the wild flowers were interesting. The prettiest thing was the crape myrtle in bloom.[10]

Perhaps I mentioned in my last letter that we were to come back early because soldiers came in and occupied our premises. You see they would pay no attention to those left to look after our place, but they told the soldiers when we were expected back. They moved out of the rooms in which we lived the day before, and the next day after we came they all moved off the compound. They had been on the compound sixteen days although I was only away six weeks to a day. They were not as much to blame as the city authorities who were responsible for finding them a place to stay. They all know they should keep off our mission compound. We think they did enough damage in sixteen days even though it was mostly nail holes in new plaster. We recognized a bench which once had a back as having been ours. They borrowed it from some other place, but needless to say they did not get a chance to take it away.

Shucheng, September 2, 1940

One of our deacons is on the compound for a few days. He has been very ill. I am glad his sister who is a trained nurse has come to take care of him. She is the one I helped prepare for the mathematics part of her entrance examination to enter the hospital. She passed as well as other girls who had been in school much longer.

We have not had the opportunity to go out much recently. These last few days it has rained. Some of the rice here that nearly died has sprouted again. Cotton and beans too were needing the rain. Our roof leaks rather badly and that is a trial. It was supposed to have been guaranteed for years but the man who did it did not know his job. I am very much disgusted with some of this building work.

Shucheng, September 27, 1940

We are not progressing very well with plans for our new house. Everything is going up in price. It has been decided that I am the one to "bell the cat", in other words go to the nearest towns across the lines after the necessary hardware for the house. To tell you the honest truth, I would almost prefer to go without the house than to go. Yet we often have some ticklish thing to do. This morning I shut the door in the faces of about a score of soldiers who very much desired to occupy our chapel. They had their guns with them. I often have had arguments with those fellows about borrowing of doors, benches or use of our premises. There is no use giving in to them even an inch, for we would soon see them in control of the place, and their telling me where to get off if I showed any sign of fear. What probably happened this morning was that the petty officers went to talk with their superior officers, who knew our mission stations are not public or even private property they can lay their hands on at will. Had I opened the door to those soldiers this morning, they would have despised me for being weak.

My bargaining for materials for the house has not been very successful. The custom here is to argue over prices of everything we buy. I get tired holding out over long arguments. Ruth, having been born in China, is much better at this game.

Ruth is starting a choir. She leads the altos, but does not find it easy to teach the sopranos. She has tried to teach our woman servant to sing although without much success.

Ruth minds this camping out kind of living. We still do not have floors, window panes, or screens. Ruth was upset the other night because she found a centipede in her bed. Such things worry her a good deal. Still, after being told by the Chinese for the 'steenth time that she is not as brave as I, she is learning to take things more calmly.

Food becomes rapidly more expensive. Many will have to boil turnips with their rice this winter to eke it out. Still this is a great improvement over having to eat tree roots and bark. There is genuine famine in many parts of China, but I have yet to see a real famine here. Every year they seem to raise plenty for the people living here. There would be plenty this year if so much had not been shipped out. I have bought nearly half a ton of rice to sell out at cost to the servants when it becomes more expensive so as not to have to increase their wages. We are now keeping three. This includes a man to look after goats and the garden as well as to run errands. He may have to go over twenty miles after kerosene and carry it back next week. Your last letter had been opened by censors.

Shucheng, October 7, 1940

I am surprised the mission is sending out a fair number of young men this year, more of them from England than the U.S.A. It seems to have been like that during the last war, and all the time the mission gets a high grade of men and women. The trouble is that Christians in America know nothing about our mission and do not care to know about it, even though no other so-called "Faith Mission" would compare with it and only one denominational mission surpasses it when all their fields are combined. In China very much of all but the most accessible places has been allotted to our mission to evangelize. To urge people to support only denominational missions is to support only those missionaries who work in large enough places to have hospitals and schools, and to leave most of the hard places to reach untouched. As a rule they work among up and outs and we among the down and outs. We also can generally get closer to the people just because we do live in closer touch with them.[11]

I may get started for Hofei later this week. We have ordered a hundred and fifty panes of glass when a hundred and twenty would be ample. When one considers the sort of punishment it will get on the way, breakage is expected.

More wild animals are around now. Until the corn was husked, night after night we heard the weird shrieks of those who were frightening away jackals. We hear much more now about wolves and their taking away children. Some Christians who used to be in the habit of sleeping outside are now afraid to do so.

Last night our servant told me that twice during the day she saw a baby girl left with only her napkin under her but no garments on her. Of course now that times are hard there is no orphanage to which to take her. The servant said she thought the child was blind. Very likely when night came, dogs would dispose of the child. We must be careful about collecting such babies or we would encourage those who can care for their children to abandon them.

Shucheng, October 23, 1940

The Chinese love to rush the season and considered it quite the thing to count my last birthday the fiftieth. (Actually forty seventh). They would have liked much better to have had some more publicity too, but being one of the first days I was around after being ill, too much of a disturbance would have hardly been the right thing. As it was, it was a little too much. The three deacons had my presents carried through the streets. They had things arranged on a special tray so everyone could see what they brought. There was a length of red cloth to use later as decorations for Christmas and weddings. It was not silk but more expensive than silk would have been a few years ago. There was a pair of scrolls with characters lauding me to the skies, about thirty eggs, several pounds of good spaghetti, four packages of their candy, and two plates especially arranged. The spaghetti is supposed to go with birthdays and had a red paper lace drapery over it. The plates had three cornered buns on them and a garnish of heavenly bamboo and various figures done in paste. One had dragons and various fruits and vegetables on it; the other had flags. You see, my birthday comes on their national holiday, about equivalent to Fourth of July.

Since my birthday I have gone to Hofei after the hardware. I have been through "No Man's Land" and back. I took seven men with me and had to hire two more. A damper was put on things from the start because the men took a wrong road, so bandits relieved them of most of their money when we had gone only eight miles. They might have met with rougher treatment still had I not been with them. I did not have much money with me, but the bandits did not find any of it. We had met the bandits just before we got to our out-station. When we passed through there, I met two of our enquirers. The men with me were wanting to turn back. The enquirers assured us that they would be praying for us, and we would be all right.[12]

As we were crossing lines, I brought foreign things to wear. Of course, I could not talk to the Japanese at the gates they control, but some polite phrases to use with their Chinese interpreters helped.

It was good to get back into civilization in Hofei for a few days. I had not seen a car actually going since a year ago in January. The missionaries in Hofei have radios with wind chargers, pianos, and a few other things that go with modern life. The men talk about coming back into the hinterland if worse comes to worse. To the women though it was a mystery how a woman could travel around here as I do. Being acquainted with the people and having the language make a good deal of difference. These missionaries gave me some seeds and plants, and I bought a few groceries and some medicines from them.

We were delayed in Hofei an extra day to get permits to carry two tins of kerosene and the glass out of the city. The man who finally gave me the permits objected to the number of men I had with me, but it takes four men to carry the hardware.

It was not particularly to my liking to sleep on tables at the inn on our return. The pigs were brought in for the night, and there were other conditions that were not pleasant. Many places had been burned, and people were more or less camping out.

Recently I have not been good for much work. There is nothing much wrong except anemia. Getting good food is difficult. Even when I can get good food, it is an effort to eat it.

Shucheng, November 4, 1940

So far we have found only one of the hundred fifty panes of glass brought from Hofei broken. I think there is just about enough hardware unless it be bolts for the windows. We can get those made to order, both brass and iron being available. We have heard that after much urging from Mr. Costerus, what was stolen from us on the way is to be returned. I am afraid the chair-bearers will be punished. They are suspected of being in league with the bandits. First, because they insisted on starting a day late, and on the morning they left they delayed starting as long as possible. Second, they insisted on travelling on a road they were told not to go on because we always had heard it was not safe. They had made a remark at the time of the robbery too that helped cast suspicion on them. I was told that a Chinese would have had them arrested at the first town we passed through after it happened.

Hofei is thirty miles from Shucheng, and I walked much more than half of the way. All the way whenever we met soldiers of either side, it was necessary for me to walk ahead to face the music while the seven or more husky men with me walked a safe distance behind.

Since my return, progress on the house seems to be better. The brick walls are nearly finished, and upstairs partitions are being put in. Men are starting tomorrow to go after reed mats for lining under the tile roof. The contracts have been made for the rest of the boards for flooring and for making the doors and windows.

Shucheng, November 18, 1940

We had intended to use mats under the tiles for insulation, but the men who went after them met bandits, and the money was stolen. We had a bamboo net made instead. All the way through it had been much like building or making bricks without straw. Labor and local products are becoming more expensive. It costs less for a day's work than for a half pound of nails. Do you wonder that the nails are kept locked up and are counted out when they are used?

Shucheng, November 21, 1940

Last Sunday three men who desire to be baptized were here. They came over twenty miles carrying all the food they would need while away from home. They each bought a Bible and two hymnbooks. One of the deacons wants to visit them in their homes before their baptism. They expect to be back for that at Christmas. One of them looked at my poster of the prodigal son. He read the Scripture portion printed underneath in Chinese until he came to the place where it says he woke up or came to himself. He commented, "I just woke up myself. Before I did not understand."

Shucheng, December 8, 1940

Some letters are coming through from home in one month, and some are taking as much as three months. I feel all the mail is not going through. Perhaps I should have used even more discretion about what has been written. Having been accustomed to nothing but our American liberty, we do not always realize what it is worth. Anyway there may be times when we must keep even the most important items of news to ourselves.

Last week I made over a gallon of green tomato pickles, over two quarts of orange marmalade, and some chili sauce. We cut up some ginger to dry. We hired a woman to scrape the root, but, believe it or not, she was slower at it than I was. I did a good part of it myself. The knives the Chinese use are more like cleavers. They do not know how to use a paring knife, and when they try, they cut away from themselves. When chopping up anything, they do it quicker and better than we do. Just watch a Chinese in an eating house cut up an onion some time. But when we get a new cook, we have to teach him how to peel a potato. A good many things we would pare they leave the peeling on. This includes carrots, turnips, cucumbers, and most squash.

Shucheng, December 27, 1940

The Sunday School had been disbanded for two years. Ruth started it again in September. Since then the children have done very well with their memory work. For the Christmas program the children repeated Luke:1-20, Matthew 2, some verses from the first chapter of John, and some from the ninth chapter of Isaiah. They sang one song and some choruses. After the program each child who took part in the program was given a card, some cookies, and some peanuts. Those who did not take part were given peanuts. Ruth and I gave the cookies and the cards. Years ago we gave parcels of Chinese candy. Then we found that the children preferred the homemade cookies. The cookies are no more bother, and they cost us less.

We will soon be moving into our bedrooms in the house. The office was done in time to use last Sunday.

Shucheng, December 28, 1940

The carpenters and workmen could not come today because no one was allowed on the streets this morning. An inspection is being made of who is home and what the business of each one is, and more. In order to go ten miles now, we must have passes. We can make out our own though. With our seal they are as good as those from the officials.

Lately we have had trouble with petty thieves. I have lost a few things of moderate value, a sheet, my old wool sweater, and three garments of lesser value.

Shucheng, January 6, 1941

Usually quarterly accounts are less than a third as much work as they have been this time. The masons had put in over three hundred days of work, the carpenters well over a hundred days, and other workmen three hundred and fifty-one days. Besides we bought logs, different kinds of tiles, lime, glass, nails and other hardware, paper, straw, sand, dirt, bamboo, hemp, boards, different kinds of bricks, and other things in building. I am glad that part of the accounts is done.

We are using part of the house, but much remains to be done. We plan to have as much as possible built in, so it can not be easily stolen. One big disappointment about the house is that the roof leaks, and that is blamed on the fact that Mr. Costerus did not see that the structure was strong enough. Although much about the house is cheap, we do have solid brass door knobs. They are as cheap here as anything we could get.

Today the carpenters killed a wildcat in our kitchen. It had crawled under the stove. Ruth and I had seen it before. The wild animals we have seen on the compound this year include plenty of rats, a weasel, a badger family, and now this wildcat.

An evangelist came and spent the weekend here a week ago Sunday. The church hopes to have him come and spend a year in the district. We certainly need some help. It has not been possible to visit two groups of believers more than twenty miles away. The leading deacon has too many other things he must see about. Out here they have a system of having a man in charge of each ten families and another man over each group having a hundred families. Our deacon is sort of a deputy officer over the hundred families, and they are having meetings continually, sometimes even on Sunday. He almost always gets out of the Sunday meetings as he has Sunday service most of the time.[13]

Banditry in the country falls off sometimes for a few days, but every few nights we hear shots. It makes Ruth rather nervous at times. We old hands are not expected to be affected by such little things. On most clear days we hear planes. There is a commercial flight that is routed almost directly overhead, passing Shucheng on its way from Nanking to Hankow.

Shucheng, January 20, 1941

Several days ago I received the liver extract you sent, and I began to take some at once. Ruth and I both seem to need tonics at times. For the past few months we have lived almost entirely on Chinese food. We are not used to living almost on rice like they are. Thank you for sending the medicine.

We have moved into the house although every room lacks some carpenter work. The sitting room needs the window seat and book shelves finished. The office will have a book cupboard. All three bedrooms lack closet doors, and two of them lack flooring under the dormer windows. The stair railing and the veranda floor are not done. To fix the roof so it won't leak some special tiles that must be made to order are needed. Six men are working today. Four are carpenters, and two are sawing timber to make door frames and panels. We have found some carpenters who take pride in doing finer work. Since there are heavy rains here, we are considering having eaves troughs made to save the soft water. Our well water is hard, and the soft water would make a saving in use of soap.

Since my last letter, two of the men from the place more than twenty miles away have been here to church. We do wish someone had the time to go there for a few days to work. I am afraid I have not the strength to walk that far. Besides the "powers that be" have ordered me not to go so far from the home base. There should be someone to go to Taochen to rent premises there, but there are several reasons for not going now. My last trip was a little too much for me. After renting premises to me, the landlord rented the place to someone else. The deacons here think I should give in about it. After making about six trips in all there, most for the purpose of renting premises, someone else can try their hand at it. It is very difficult to find what we need, and the place we used to rent is too big for us now.

There are a few surgical instruments here on this compound from the nearest denominational hospital on the other side of the lines. Not even the Chinese Christians know about this. The nearest foreign surgeon does not propose to be entirely without tools should he have to journey in this direction. It is partly because of such possibilities that we want to get this house built and the compound into better condition.

Shucheng, February 3, 1941

These last few days our weekly newspaper has not come nor have we had mail from home. We have heard shots recently. Soldiers were fighting bandits. For a few weeks our Taochen Christians could not come here and we could not go there. But last week three of them came in and reported that the coast is clear. They also asked for tracts and gospels as well as posters as they hope to make a trip out preaching. One place they hope to go is where there has been very little witnessing done before.

Yesterday we must have had at least a hundred and fifty people here at church. Such a crowd would have been about normal before my furlough. But everyone says that there have not been more in attendance since the Japanese came. We do not have benches enough to seat so many people now. The church has enough money in the treasury to buy timber for new benches, but the wood will need to be seasoned before it is used. There are new doors on the church. While I was away, the old ones all vanished. One of the church members who is away serving as a trained nurse, heard that there were new doors, so she sent home money to have them painted. When they had the boards behind the pulpit painted, they had the text for John 3:16 painted there with a floral border. My opinion was not asked about doing this, but I had reason for telling them since that it is beautiful. Chinese characters lend themselves to anything like that, making much more beautiful shop signs or mottoes. They are very ornamental as written even with nothing for a border.

Last Monday was Chinese New Years day. A good many people came in the first day of the new year, and most of the church members come to see us these first few days. After that Ruth and I started paying calls. During the first week possibly I called on a third of the homes nearest at hand. We spent two full half days out calling. All the carpenters and other workmen are laid off from work for a few days, so that frees us for a while.

One of the women who came to church yesterday walked about eight or nine miles to get here on Saturday. Her husband, who comes almost every Sunday, walked in with her, but needed to go right back. She returned home today. Her small feet are a hindrance and also the fact that in a few weeks their family may have an addition. But she had not had an opportunity to partake of communion since she was baptized last June, so she wanted to come. There has been no other Christian woman who lived within five miles of them. One of our other Christians plans to move within a half mile of them soon. When there are two Christian families, they can have their own services. Then others would probably join them.

Shucheng, February 16, 1941

We still do not have many letters, and we think some go astray. It has now been more than three weeks that our weekly newspaper has gone astray. That is too long in these days to go without news. I suppose our newspaper fell into the hands of censors. They were not protected as Ruth's special stamps were. She collects stamps, so her brother uses some of the rarer ones on his letters to her. Often these were missing when the letters arrived. She wrote back to him about her letters arriving without stamps. The next time he wrote beneath the stamps, "These stamps were stolen by a lousy thief". That time the stamps came through.

We had less than thirty people at church today, although the last two Sundays we had a hundred and fifty. So many come in from the country. Most women who live in town came this time, but none from the country.

Some have come in this afternoon to perhaps stay a few days. There are five girls on the compound who have been frightened by soldiers, and well they might flee. Apparently the soldiers are some that revolted, and we only hope they continue to stay away from this place. Soldiers that submit to authority leave us alone. One is not sure about what those who are free lancers may do. These ex-soldiers are helping themselves to anything they see that they want, including bedding, clothing and chickens as well as other food. Bedding and clothing have become so very expensive that none but the well-to-do can replace any stolen from them. Last year there was not a good crop of cotton, and so much more is used locally now.[14]

We have started at least with our New Year calls. Nearly every family that can afford it invites us to a meal once a year. Ruth has been to three places, and I to two places. Most families can not afford to invite us. Some of these give us a few eggs or some very finely ground rice flour. Sometimes they have given us sesame seeds, beans or some special sort of foods seasoned just right.

Shucheng, February 17, 1941

We have just heard that the relative of three of the girls who brought them in has been pressed into service to carry things about thirty miles. One can not wonder at their being disturbed because of it. He had promised to bring them food. At least he left some money with them to use. He had some money which came from his son two or three years ago. I know about this because he came in to get our mission stamp on the money order so he could get his money.

Shucheng, March 5, 1941

So many of our things had disappeared that we were forced to fire all of our servants. Whoever took the things paid attention to not taking all or any one thing except one kind of medicine for which we might some time have desperate need. Ruth and I each lost one sheet and a new piece of cotton material. Right now we can not replace these things. Some help has been given by church members. One of the deacons sent in his hired man the very same day. He guards the gate, carries water, looks after the goats, and does a little work in the garden. A church woman came in to help two days. She does not let her relatives and friends know that her needs are well supplied. If they knew she had money they would want to borrow it. A church member and his son came in today to dig a drain.

We have sent for the dog that was offered by Mr. and Mrs. Costerus. The servants we dismissed left threatening us with thieves. We need a dog in these times on a big compound like ours.

Our out-station at Taochen needs attention. I must go there when I can get away from here.

Only four men came to our early morning prayer meeting. They came before we had breakfast. We have it in the morning because they can not come in from the country in the evening.

Shucheng, March 10, 1941

Your Christmas card and gift came Saturday. This parcel bore official marks of having been censored in Hongkong. Parcels may very soon be prevented from reaching Shanghai. Once reaching there though we could probably find a way of obtaining them. Some of the things I brought back from furlough are still in Shanghai. These I consider my reserve supply, for while on furlough I bought for eight years to come. When one considers that the shops at home look like fairy land to us being away so long, one can understand that we enjoy this shopping while on furlough. Again, thank you for the remembrance.

The streets of Shucheng look a little better than they did when I returned over a year ago, but there is plenty of room for improvement. People we meet are shabbily dressed. Clothing is for the most part made of hand woven material, though now it would be difficult to tell the original color of the goods. Almost every garment we see worn, even to church, is patched.

We are training new servants. We have hired a young woman for general servant and a young man for gardener, but today this man is mopping floors. Ruth and I could manage nicely without this help were it not for our missionary duties, and of course, that is what we are here for. Our temporary gatekeeper left today, so we are still short handed.

Shucheng, March 24, 1941

A week ago Saturday I went to Taochen where I stayed until Tuesday. One of the church members went with me, and she cooked for me while I was there. A church member there had enough rooms in her house to let me have a room by myself. While I was there, I had four meetings and made a number of calls. We made final arrangements to rent a few rooms for the work.

We have begun to take a daily paper. They usually come three or four at a time. We received an order of a thousand gospel portions and a few Bibles last week, but the reference Bibles have not come yet. As much as possible I want the Christians who take meetings to use reference Bibles.

The Chinese Christians expect me to locate any passage of Scripture they mention instantly, and they expect me to tell them what the Bible teaches on an obscure point almost as fast. One of my fellow workers asked me once how one knows such things. Far be it from me to claim having attained unto this.

In one way I am glad my furlough came when it did. Those who go now face the possibility of not being able to come back. Many of our missionaries are now stranded in Europe and can not come back until the war is over. As for safety, one wonders what place is more safe than another.

Shucheng, April 10, 1941

The recent thefts here in this house can not be passed over too lightly lest there be a repetition of them. The deacons came in yesterday, and we got no satisfaction out of hours of questioning. I think one trouble is that they would all so much rather tell a lie than than to lose some face. Even when all evidence is against them, they say with a straight face that they know nothing about it. As a public example all three servants have been disciplined, with the promise that, when the thief is found, Ruth and I will make a public apology before the church for their being unjustly branded as thieves. Had they not been church members, they would have been turned over to the police. That would have been so much disgrace to the church that we would have suffered as much as they would.

Shucheng, April 12, 1941

Today I bought a hundred and forty pounds of lime for finishing the house. It was four times as expensive as what I bought a year ago. Last fall I bought rice for ourselves and the servants for the year. It is now about four times as expensive as when I bought it then. It makes a great savings on the servants' wages now for we pay them partly in rice.

Sometimes it is so hard to think of what it is you may want to know, and there may come times when we either can not tell you what you may want to know or may have our lines of communication cut. It is come to this—if we go to Shanghai, it is difficult to get a pass back if one can get it at all, and if one goes home, they may be kept from coming back. Those who have children in Chefoo feel this keenly. Mr. and Mrs. Costerus have not seen their children now for nearly two years, yet they have no prospects of seeing them for another year.

Shucheng, April 22, 1941

One thing I have not understood for years has been why our country allowed the selling of scrap iron and such things to another country when this will be used to fight democracy. If our country can not control the affairs of private individuals, how could they plow up fields of cotton and wheat and destroy suckling pigs? Right now I wish that planes had not been invented. They are doing more harm than good in China.[15]

Shucheng, April 28, 1941

Some tiles, bricks, and lumber for built-in furniture are still needed for the house. The screening is paid for, but we must get it from across the lines. I am glad Ruth has begun to talk of going after it.

What sort of registration numbers do my brothers have? One can not imagine their having to go abroad, but in this awful war one can not tell from which direction the enemy will hit next. The thing is more manifestly satanic than many wars in the past.

Shucheng, May 12, 1941

This is a dull day with a heavy rain. Ruth went on a trip almost two weeks ago, and while it keeps on raining like this, there's a question about when she can return. This is about the busiest time of the year for many people. Many of the women are feeding silk worms. A few of them may be starting to spin the cocoons. The farmers have just cut their colza or rape seed which is grown for oil. The next big job is planting rice. This rain is good for that, but would bother those who are harvesting.

When I was in Shanghai after my furlough, someone recommended my buying some Prontosil which is a Bayer product used for blood poisoning. Until ten days ago this lay on the shelf. Then the brother of one of our deacons came to ask me if I had anything for blood poisoning. A cousin of theirs had been infected from a rat bite. This medicine, which is very expensive, worked like a charm right from the start; in fact, it was a life saver. Very likely this product is not sold in the states. It is really not a remedy for the laity to handle, but we are not competing with the doctors. There are no doctors within thirty five miles, and scarcely anyone has the courage to journey that far.

One of the men was in from Taochen last week to report that all was going well there. One or two new persons are interested. He had been spending several days at fairs selling gospels and giving out tracts. The fairs are like big open markets where people from far and near bring their surplus especially of things they have made to sell. There are some things sold that one never sees in shops.[16]

Our gardener belongs to a family of generations of Christians. He was quite amused the other evening when he told about two families in town who had had funerals that day. After the funerals the families discovered that the burials had been on a very unlucky day for funerals. For that reason they dared not spend that night in their own homes because the dead would become alive and come home to visit. Such are heathen beliefs. This is the best gardener we have had. He really takes an interest. He dug out all the grubs in the strawberry bed, so we had some berries this year.

Shucheng, May 26, 1941

Perhaps the rains have been the reason that Ruth has not returned, or she may be held up by some red tape. Ruth was willing to bring back supplies, but in weight she is not likely to bring more than I did last fall. Two other mission stations though are expecting her to bring back supplies for them. She is to bring back the screens for the house, kerosene, and sugar. Also she was to have her physical examination. She is needed back here too for a number of reasons. For one thing her silkworms need attention. She expected to ride a new bicycle back. That is harder than one might think because the roads are so bad.

Getting medicine is likely to be a problem. At present I do have a supply of quinine furnished by the American Red Cross for sale. People come for it as far as fifteen miles. Just to have quinine to sell at a nominal sum so we have funds to renew the stock is a great boon. I am selling it for slightly more than one fourth of what they would have to pay for it any place else. Strange to say, people are not begging for me to give them medicine, but they are asking to buy. They say they can not buy it elsewhere or the other places give them imitations of the real thing.

Sunday after church six or seven women came in for more Bible study. One of these women claimed that some years ago I had given her a tract. This she took home and pasted on her wall. She says she has believed the gospel since then. The oldest woman who came was very interested in our flowers. We promised her some seed of coreopsis if she would come back later.

A letter came from Paul Hsu today. He is now going to a university in west China. Formerly he studied at a Presbyterian seminary. Paul wrote that he had heard that the girl to whom he is engaged had married someone else, and he was asking me to investigate. I do not believe the rumors, but I will make inquiries.

Tungcheng, June 13, 1941

Ruth returned from her trip all right. She did not succeed in buying any kerosene and could get only the twenty pounds of sugar that we ordered. Besides the screens she brought back some vegetable seeds and some medicines.

One of our church women came with me to Tungcheng yesterday. We came thirty five miles and were on the way thirteen hours, but the chair bearer thought we made good time. Of course, I walked part of the way. All the way everyone we met knew I was from the mission. About fifteen miles from Shucheng a man asked to buy quinine. I did have a little with me that I could sell. Later a woman asked for help for her baby that had convulsions. The Chinese doctors had told her there was no help for the child. Perhaps the life could have been saved at a first rate hospital, but the only thing I could do was to tell the crowd of women who gathered how to prevent such a thing happening with another child. The woman with me repeated everything I said partly to help them understand and partly to make it more emphatic. When we came within five miles of this place, I met a chair bearer who asked, "What are you doing here, Miss Tao, walking by yourself?" In China instead of hellos there is a question of what are you doing or where are you going. The answer may be given by pointing your chin in the direction headed whether the intention is to go that way ten feet or a hundred miles. As a matter of policy I am usually vague.

Tungcheng is much richer than Shucheng and has suffered, so far, much less from the war. The work here, however, is much poorer. The compound is very small. As there has been no missionary even to visit for three years, the house has been neglected; in fact, it is full of bedbugs. The man who has charge of these buildings and the man who carried my things here are making visits in the country today.

Shucheng, June 25, 1941

Yesterday we returned from Tungcheng. In the week and a half while I was there I led small meetings each night and an extra one on Sunday. We made a few trips to the country where we gave out tracts, held some meetings, and visited people.

For some time we have been anxiously awaiting the return of a young family from Hunan. A servant of their parents had been sent out to meet them to help carry their things and the children, but he missed them. Anyway they, the young couple, their two children under three years of age, and their eight year old nephew, arrived in Tungcheng the last night we were there. They had been on their way for three months and had come through Nanchow and Changteh where I have worked. Another had some money for them, and I could help too. The next day we rented two barrows, one for the family and one for the woman and me. I got off and walked some of the distance. The main reason for this family to return is that the young man has tuberculosis so wants the family home with his parents and hers too.

We stayed over night about eight miles from Shucheng, We walked the rest of the way back. The young man had to walk slowly, and the children were taking extra time, so we were ahead. We met the father of the young man two miles out from his home. He had come to meet me because he thought I might have heard of his son. I told him to keep going another mile to meet the family. I knew there would be joy in seeing his grandchildren for the first time, and he would be happy to help carry them home. There was a little extra walking to tell the others of the family that the reunion was near. I expect to go back to celebrate with them as soon as there is an opportunity.[17]

In all, while on that trip, I walked no less than fifty miles. As I have not been doing that much walking recently, I lost a few pounds. We are seeing numbers of planes. Everyone is saying the invaders will be here soon. Ruth and I have had no leading though that we should prepare to flee.

Shucheng, July 8, 1941

The house is not yet finished. At least we are through with the mason and we have a good roof over our heads for the time being. The carpenter is not yet finished, and we have only begun to talk about paint although we have lived in the house six months.

Since my last letter we have had an abundance of rain, practically assuring this large district of a bumper harvest. How one wishes men might learn to praise the Lord for all His goodness. We are praying that there may be no hindrance to the harvesting.

Something happened these last two weeks that I am very sorry about. My mistake in psychology has cost a life. A mother brought her eighth child for me to examine. All the others had died. It took very little discernment to find out that the child had worms. I suppose what I should have done would have been to feel the pulse of both hands and charge her about ten dollars. Instead I sold her a dose of santonin for thirty cents (my usual price for a child that size). The mother very much disliked my suggestion that her child had worms, or that the santonin must be followed by castor oil. So she took the santonin home but did not give it to the child. Instead she took him to a so-called doctor who probably knows even less than I do about treating children. He gave the child a hypodermic needle of something—probably morphine—and charged ten dollars. Knowing the child's condition was desperate if there was delay in giving him santonin, I returned the thirty cents and got the medicine back. Two days later she called in a doctor from the country. He told her the child had worms and it was too late to give the proper remedy even if he had it, which he did not. The next morning the child died as worms were crawling from his nose. You may say, why not charge more for santonin? It is just that not every child is an only child, and not every parent has money. So many times the Christians will have santonin given to their children long before their condition becomes desperate. One can not help feeling sorry for that mother as she realizes now that she actually had the right remedy for her child in her hand, and did not give it to him because she thought it was too cheap. As a matter of fact, probably no one else within twenty and possibly forty miles has santonin to sell. What an illustration this is of the way so many reject God's way of salvation because it seems too easy.

Ruth celebrated the Fourth of July by not being able to eat anything all day. She must even yet be careful of what she eats.

For a long time those on the compound came in each evening for prayers. Now we usually have more from outside the compound than those here. Among those attending is a young man school teacher and a number of school boys. Ruth and I take turns leading.

Not long ago I heard a missionary say that her idea of something terrible would be to have to go through a summer without soap. We may run out of laundry soap in the fall if we can not buy more. The one who filled our last order ignored the zero when we wanted to buy forty cakes of laundry soap. We have toilet soap though to last us through next year.

Shucheng, July 21, 1941

Today two men are mixing paints, but no carpenters came. We do not let the workmen work on Sunday nor do we pay them for that day. Some go other places to work then and may not return until the middle of the next week. This can be annoying when we want a job done,

Ruth left on Friday to go visit her sister, Margaret, and family. She decided to walk the first forty miles, but changed her mind after going half that far. The last sixty miles she will go by boat. Ruth is paying her own way for this visit with her relatives. The two little nieces both have birthdays in the fall. One will be four and the other two years old.

Today I have such a cold I hardly know what to do with myself. Still I had seven persons come in for medicines of one kind or another, and I started to treat a badly infected hand. I had some calls to make and have prepared for a meeting tonight.

Another church member, Mrs. Wang, returned to Shucheng last week. She has spent days going visiting with me. I am surely glad to have her available to help again. This woman can afford a servant so is free to help.

More than even before now I am a saver of paper and string. Any left over newspaper can be sold. Three pounds of paper would buy a chicken. I save the wrappers that come around the papers to wrap up pills and doses of salts. Good string is just as precious. I use the waxed paper that comes around soap to wrap up ointments.

We still live in uncertainty. While I was at Tungcheng, Shucheng was bombed. Two or three persons were killed. One of our women church members got two bad bruises from falling tiles, and a piece of shrapnel fell within two feet of her. Since then Tungcheng has been bombed. We have church services very early in the morning so people can get out of the city before bombing planes arrive.

Since Ruth is gone, I will have all the evening meetings. The Sunday School on Sunday afternoon which Ruth organized again, is now in my care. There were twenty five here last Sunday, and with all ages from four to twenty, that is enough for one to handle. The leaders we had before my furlough have all gone away.

Shucheng, August 4, 1941

This morning I have turned away two outsiders and have treated three people or sold them medicine. It is not ideal perhaps to only do for the Christians, yet when one's time and strength are limited, it must be "First to the household of faith". And that seems to mean the others get left out. When callers follow callers, we can not do other things, and since looking after the callers is our job, other things must be let go. When we have time to get to the kitchen, we have something better to eat too. One thing I have been treating for several weeks is a sore on the back of a hand. This had begun as a carbuncle, and without proper attention could have easily caused an old woman's death. She and her friends know this too. Now after much attention the sore is down to a comparatively small size.

A number of people near here were bitten by a mad dog within the last two or three days. Fortunately the people here have some prescription in which they use common native herbs that seems effectual in preventing rabies from developing. They also use this for their water buffaloes. What concerned me are the many large bites several received. Diptheria has also broken out near here. The son of one of our church members died of it last week. There was no way to get antitoxin in time to save his life. Eighty two persons came here to the house for injections against typhoid and cholera last week. Many more would have been done if we had not run out of serum. We may see about obtaining more of it.

Shucheng, August 5, 1941

Today three callers came before I was through eating breakfast, all on comparatively important matters. Then three newspapers and some other mail came just after breakfast. The newspapers from Shanghai are never less than a week old. As many as five may come the same day. Just now one of the first questions many ask me is about what our newspapers say about the world situation. Many of the people know a considerable amount about what is going on outside of China as well as the affairs of their own land. None of them seem to misunderstand why Chinese assets in America have been frozen. I suppose within a week after that happened most thinking people in China knew about it too.[18]

There are some things that really amuse the Chinese. Those on the compound nearly split laughing about what happened yesterday morning. A woman came in with a very sore finger. When I started to look at it, she pulled away saying, "Oh, no, miss, I am afraid you will hurt me". Then I drew back and told her I was more than willing to leave her hand alone. The gardener intervened by grasping her hand firmly and did not let her withdraw until I had opened and drained it. She had to admit when I was through, her finger felt much better.

We continue to have plenty to eat at least. Crops are good, but some find it hard to get on. A widow has been sewing for me for a few days. She felt keenly having to pay two days wages not for regular taxes but for a special emergency tax. At the end of last week I gave her more rice and salt than she could earn in a day. To her, salt is a luxury not eaten every day. A day's wages here does not buy a whole pound of salt unless one has some skill as a carpenter or mason. Even then it would be only a pound of coarse salt like ice cream salt.

Ruth seems to be having a good visit with her older sister Margaret a hundred miles from here. She will be back, no doubt, by the end of the month.

Shucheng, August 18, 1941

On Sunday word came that my quarterly accounts were lost in the mail, so they asked me to make new copies. It took almost a half day to do it, not counting the interruptions of which there are plenty. I sell quinine to some who come many miles for it, but I am trying to shut down on selling medicines to all but Christians. Even then it leaves plenty for me to sell to.

There is one well-to-do man well known around here who was cut off from being a church member before I came. At the time of the threatened persecution (about the time of my first furlough), he and his family deliberately went through heathen rites and pasted up posters outside their home denouncing Christianity and declaring they had no part nor lot in the church. One can hardly blame the deacons for taking him at his word. All this happened long ago, and the last two or three years the man has come to church about once a year so he could drive some hard bargains with us. He sold us some bad tiles for this house at higher than market price, and wanted to sell me some special tiles later at twice the usual price. They tell me all his dealings are like that. When his daughter-in-law died Saturday, I was rather puzzled about the invitation to the funeral because of not remembering the woman. One of our deacons concluded that we were invited because our Christian funerals are not nearly as expensive as their heathen rites. He thought that identifying ourselves with such people would spoil our testimony.

Among my many callers this morning was a young man who is a member of the church. We talked shop because he is just setting up a medicine shop. He does have a good deal to learn although there are many things he could teach me. He lost a case of cholera Sunday morning partly because he does not have the proper equipment. What one needs most in that case is apparatus for running a saline solution into the vein. He has unlimited confidence in himself, so would have used the equipment if he could have obtained any. There are some simpler methods I have used, but they are not as effective. We are all going to have to use more of the native drugs to take the place of those things obtained from foreign sources.

Shucheng, August 31, 1941

We have had rain today. People are none too happy about it coming while they are harvesting their rice. They thresh much of it the day it is cut. But they depend on the straw for fuel and to make up beds. When our woman made a trip with me recently, she was surprised at how prosperous the place to which we went was. She based her conclusion upon the fact that the stubble had been left in the fields to rot instead of being gathered for fuel. As a matter of fact, as long as people must be paid to burn all the grass by the roadside, I am not very greatly impressed myself about people being hard up.

Our new chiang is far too salty. When I was told how much salt to use, those who told me had not counted on my being present to see it put in. What we use in meat and vegetables will be all right. We have to fix more beans to stretch out the salt in the rest. If you do not understand the over salting, perhaps the statement of an American business man in China might help. His remark to me was, "I could easily support you on the money you could save me if you were around my house to look after things."

The new freezing order means we get no more remittances for a while. However we have plenty of food in the house, and also money enough available to last us several months. Ruth has written that she hopes to be back this week, but I have no hope of seeing her before next Tuesday.

Shucheng, September 1, 1941

Ruth came back from her visit more than a week ago. It is certainly good to have her here. You might be interested in the way our deacons solved a problem. The problem was a church member who is a hunchback and more warped in mind than in body. We missionaries and others have tried to help him by giving him money, but he soon squanders it. He will not work steadily at the lightest work. What bothers most is his disreputable appearance when he comes to church services. The deacons bought cloth and hired a woman church member who is a widow who needed work to make the hunchback a suit of clothes. One of the deacons takes charge of the clothes and allows him to wear them just to church. Without this precaution he would take the clothes out and pawn them. I had nothing to do with this matter from beginning to end.

Shucheng, September 3, 1941

Many of the Chinese ways of thinking and talking remain strange to us. The other day I heard one servant tell another he should tie a string around his ear to help him remember something. What I still object to is that they want to put clothing on shelves and dishes of things in drawers. I suppose they think their reasons are as good as ours. The painter, if we would let him, would pay all the attention to the doors and do almost nothing to the floors.

Today the gardener could not work outside, so he polished our brass door knobs. He has made them shine like mirrors, and with the new paint they look fine.

Ruth and I talk of inviting some missionaries from near here on a visit. So far there have been no foreign guests in the house. We can not wait until the house is really finished before having people come.

We have recently heard how to make powder from soy beans to use in place of milk powder. When we buy a stone mill to replace the one that was stolen, we hope to make some. Then we can make more peanut butter too. Our chiang is made with a sort of broad bean. The shelled beans are covered with flour, as much as the beans will absorb. Then the beans are spread on trays and covered with a fragrant weed. They are left in a dark room until they are covered with a deep mold. The beans are then put in crocks with plenty of salt and sesame oil, and sunned until black. When ripened this has a nutty flavor. Those who like cheese would appreciate chiang.

Shucheng, September 17, 1941

It is high time a letter was on its way to you even though it is not easy to think of what to write when letters have not come through from home. My letters are written regularly every two weeks. Please do give me some idea as to whether you receive them or not. There is such a temptation to steal the postage stamps and destroy the letters when we put on as postage half of an ordinary man's wages to send a letter.

We have been kept from going out much recently because of heavy rains. Our roof leaked some this time, but it would take a very good roof to protect one in such a storm. The cotton has been damaged and also some of the late rice.

Yesterday a Chinese girl came to help us for the next few weeks. She is a Bible School graduate and is very earnest. Women are expected to come in from places miles away for a few days of Bible study. After that Ruth wants the young woman to go with her to Tungcheng for a while. Our other autumn work will need to be done after her return.

This weekend I hope to go to Taochen for a few days. There are several matters at the out-station that require my attention. For one thing, the Christians there are not happy with the place we are renting. We may need to find another place to rent.

We received a letter this morning from a missionary doctor who, as he puts it, has just been a pawn on an island. He has worked only forty miles from here in Hofei. He has just been allowed to come back to pack up his things, settle his accounts, and make other arrangements before leaving. I suppose he will be in the U.S.A. by the end of next month. He mentioned that we might be having some sort of tea party soon. Since the letter was written eight days ago, Ruth and I do not think there is much to that.

We have heard that Paul Hsu's foster mother, who went to west China, will be back here soon. I am sorry for Paul because the girl to whom he was engaged, without saying anything, married someone else. My last letter from him was written in May.

Most of the Christians who left Shucheng got homesick. Some have returned, and more are on their way home. One family started home more than three months ago and have not arrived yet. There are so many things to delay them. In Hankow they must wait about twenty days for a pass. We hardly know how to count our blessings when we can come and go at will.

These last few days I have been treating the eyes of a girl almost going blind. Even though I have looked after her eyes twice a day, I still have very little hope of being able to save her sight. Such a prospect for a fourteen year old girl, and her sight certainly could have been saved had she come two weeks sooner. I charge so very little that they could have afforded it. If it had been a boy it might have been attended to sooner. There always was plenty of blindness in China, and there is more now than ever.

Shucheng, September 29, 1941

We are having a conference on Bible school these days and have nearly a dozen extra grown people on the compound because of it, not to speak of children. They make for plenty of trouble.

Today another married couple returned from Hunan after being away more than three years. A little girl about four years old died on the way when they were only seven miles from home. They went away over a thousand miles and had been gone more than three years. Both the father and mother are church members. Their children hardly know the the way around home any more. This is because the houses and roads have changed so much.

Shucheng, October 7, 1941

We have come to probably the last contract for painting the interior of the house. The painter is taking plenty of time before he will agree to the price the deacons say is enough for this. Prices for everything used in the house have gone up, many doubled. Much of the material would be difficult or impossible to get now. Ruth and I were saying the other day that no one else will know how to appreciate this house, not knowing what a task it has been to supervise its rebuilding

Three women and a young girl came from Taochen for our ten days of Bible classes, and they stayed on over Sunday. Two stayed because they had not had the opportunity to take communion for a long time, and the other two wanted to see what communion was like. One woman came from a place twenty five miles from here. She stayed a few days, but she understood very little. From this same place another woman wanted to come; however, she felt she couldn't manage with her children. She sent a boy to listen for her. He was the only male in attendance, and he listened very attentively. Some women came from a place some miles east of here. One of these women was keen to pay attention in spite of her baby who was seven months old. Her husband told her before she came that he wanted the baby dedicated. She was troubled because she did not have shoes or stockings for the baby. She brought along money to buy some, but in Shucheng, which before the war had a population of far over ten thousand, none could be bought. Since this was to be a special service, and since the mother was so anxious to have shoes and stockings, we decided to do something about it. Ruth and I donated some cloth, and some Christians worked until almost midnight making the baby a cute pair of shoes.

There were two girls here part of the time whose husbands do not want them. It is not because either is lazy. The older one took a definite stand to become a Christian while here, and there would be plenty of other homes open to her. She has a knack for doing things quickly and well. That trait seems to make a girl desirable anywhere.

The girl who came to help teach our Bible classes made the remark more than once about my being rich. Her idea was that to have plenty of Bibles, New Testaments, hymnbooks, tracts, and other Christian booklets for sale when they are so hard to obtain in the interior constitute possessions more precious than gold.

This fall I have bought more rice than I did last year. Already it could be sold for at least a twenty percent profit. If I sell any of it though, it will be later on to some of the very poorest at cost. This is a form of relief I know would be greatly appreciated, and after all a good many people are glad to do some work or put forth an effort to keep their self-respect. Any who are like that are the ones we most want to help.

Ruth has gone away and may not be back for a month. We have another station to look after and the two of us can hardly do justice to this one.

Shucheng, October 20, 1941

These days I am alone again for a month. It will be two weeks tomorrow since Ruth went to Tungcheng. We have the oversight of that station as well as this, and there would be plenty to do without going there. In these two districts together there must be fully a million people. We are so near the border that we do not like to say too much about wanting help, but we do need it.

Neither of us minds a great deal being alone when things go smoothly, but there are so many queer things that go on. Last evening one of the two girls staying on the compound locked a young man in the room her brother had occupied. He had not yet removed his things from the compound. There was a suspicion that there was an extra man on the compound when we went around inspecting, but the girl refused to let me have the key. We found the man, though, by standing on a bench and looking through the window, and we escorted him off the compound. The affair is more serious than it may sound, for police or soldiers often inspect premises. I as head of this place would be held responsible if we were harboring a thief or other lawbreaker. We found this man too early in the evening for him to have done much mischief. Today I made one of the girls who was responsible leave the compound. I expect to let the parents of the other girl know what happened and let them deal with her, but if she ever does anything like it again she will leave too.

Until today I have been selling considerable quinine. I ran out this morning. There is so much malaria about I hope I can get more quinine, but medicine is becoming increasingly hard to obtain. There is Chinese medicine for many things, but it is more difficult to prepare.

Today it may be settled whether our gardener will be drafted or not. My difficulty is that it is so hard to get good help. We need an able bodied man to do some of the work on the compound. Carrying water and chopping wood are too hard for most of these women. Besides at night we ought to have a man on the compound.

We keep hearing about more of our people starting home from Hunan. Our leading deacon has just sent for his eighteen year old daughter who has been away more than three years. She probably would have been glad to come home sooner if he had been able to send the money sooner.

Our newspaper continues to come eight to ten days late, and never sooner than a week. One would surely like to comment on some things, but one had better not. The letters coming to me are marked "censored" although nothing has ever been blotted out. Anyway news is a big topic of conversation, and the Christians do try to keep informed.

The stores ordered in July have not come yet and will not come this week. A detailed list of things has to be sent in, and ours was sent last week. Passes have to be obtained to bring in medicines and many other things we need.

The blind girl who had learned to read Braille died during the summer. She had so very little help. She had had the opportunity to go to church for only a very few months. She never had anything more to read than four books of the Bible, yet she knew more about prayer than some who attend church all their lives. The woman relative who helped her come in contact with the gospel said because she could not see natural things, heaven always seemed more real to her, and she spent all the more time praying. Her step-mother was very horrid in the way she talked to her, but the blind girl often did not seem to hear. There was much she could not do, but she kept all the rooms dusted and kept track of everything in the house for the family.

Ruth and I had a long talk one day about living in dangerous places. Our conclusion was that we lived in a safer place than most people. You see we are not in danger of being run over by a car when we cross a street. It has been a year since I have seen a car with an engine in it. There are compensations for living in the interior of China.

The painter is still at work in the house and it s not likely that he will be through this month. He takes his time at it even though he works by the job. Today I had a mason here with a boy working mostly on repairs.

They sent us a good remittance again, but we have received word about not ordering more stores from Shanghai. We already use a Chinese vegetable oil lamp for the kitchen, and we may have to begin using one in our other rooms soon. We have not opened our last tin of oil but will soon do so. Ruth is trying to be as economical as possible, for she has nearly run out of money. I do hope I can find someone to take some to her.

Probably Thanksgiving will be over before you get this message, and Christmas soon to come. Perhaps I had better wish you a Merry Christmas in this letter lest I be too late.

Epilogue

Before Hazel's last letter of October 20 had reached her parents in Strathmore, California, they had received an air mail letter telling of her death on the seventeenth of November from typhus fever. Because of disrupted communications in wartorn China, this news was more than a week late in reaching the Shanghai headquarters of the China Inland Mission. The news was then cabled to the center in Philadelphia and relayed back to California reaching the Todd family on November 27, 1941, ten days before Pearl Harbor.

After some delay with hopes of hearing further details from China, a memorial service for Hazel was held at her home church, St. Andrews Presbyterian in Strathmore, California, on December 28, 1941. A month after that the Todd family received letters from her fellow missionaries, Mrs. Costerus and Ruth Elliott, both of whom were with her at her death. They then learned that Hazel had not been a victim of typhus.

Ruth wrote that at first Hazel's illness was thought to be malaria, a peculiar kind. Later it seemed to be typhoid or para-typhoid. As soon as it was discovered that neither atebrin nor sulfapyridine helped, the illness was diagnosed as typhoid and Mrs. Costerus was summoned. Until Mrs. Costerus arrived, the Chinese nurse had done a splendid job. Hazel began to improve as soon as Mrs. Costerus, a good friend and an excellent trained nurse, arrived. By November 15 her temperature was normal and remained so. At her ten o'clock feeding on the morning of November 17 (she was on a two hour schedule of liquid diet from six in the morning until eight in the evening) Hazel seemed bright and cheerful. She talked of what she was going to do as soon as she was able. The first thing she was going to do was to write a letter to her mother. A few minutes later Ruth and Mrs. Costerus were standing at the foot of the stairs when they heard a peculiar noise. They rushed upstairs to find Hazel having a heart attack. Ruth quickly got hot water bottles and boiling water. Mrs. Costerus gave two injections and did everything possible working swiftly, but all was to no avail. In less than ten minutes she was gone.

Five hundred dollars was paid for a fine wood coffin. It was one that old Deacon Teng had purchased for himself a dozen years earlier. Until the time of the funeral, Christians came in one by one and in groups, weeping and mourning. Some of the church young people made some very pretty wreaths of evergreens with paper flowers and chrysanthemums. On Wednesday morning Mr. Costerus arrived, and the funeral was held that afternoon. The deacons had bought white cloth for the Christians to wear at the funeral, long pieces to be worn over the shoulder and tied across the body at the hip. The Chinese custom is to give this material to those who attend funerals, but during those troubled times, it was felt that this would draw enough people to actually cause a riot. The decision was made to have this cloth kept for subsequent funerals thinking Hazel would have approved of this. All the Sunday School children were given pieces of material a foot square to wear on their shoulders. These they were allowed to keep.

Mr. Costerus and a deacon presided at the funeral. Both paid tribute to Hazel's life and her love for the Lord. They told instances of how she did not spare herself, truly giving everything to the Lord's work, not counting her life dear to herself. Hazel was buried on the compound under a spreading tree in the garden she loved.

Ruth and Mrs. Costerus sorted all of Hazel's things. These articles mailed back for her family were completely lost. Ruth and Mrs. Costerus bought some of the household items, and some were packed to share with other missionaries. When Mrs. Costerus returned to Liuan, Ruth went along, arriving there December 2. From there she expected to go on to Chengyangkwan to be with her sister and family for Christmas. Just before they left Shucheng the order of goods had arrived from Shanghai including the ninety pounds of sugar.

In March of 1945 a letter was received by the Todd family from Paul Hsu. He and his wife were then teaching in Tungling Middle School, Tung-ling, Hunan Province. Portions of this letter are quoted:

"It will make you surprising when you receive this letter, so I must introduce myself. I am one of Miss Hazel Todd's best friends. She led me to believe the Lord in the year 1933 when I was a student of a middle school in Shucheng. She also led my mother to be a true Christian.

"Because of the great war we have not seen Miss Todd after her furlough in the year 1937, but I have received her letters during I studied in the National Chungking University. Afterwards I came to Kwangsi and Hunan Provinces in teaching in middle schools. I did not know Miss Todd had gone to the Lord's home until last year. What a sorrow it was!

"My mother returned to Shucheng in September. She likes to visit Miss Todd's tomb in the compound often. Do not be anxious about her tomb as we shall keep it all right. She did a good work for God at Shucheng. We shall remember her forever. We Christians have a great joy, for we will meet again in paradise. May God be with you."

Conclusion

In the less congenial postcolonial world of the twenty-first century, American Protestant missionaries still maintain the evangelical enterprise, much in the spirit of Hazel Todd and her CIM colleagues two generations earlier. A contemporary account of these persistent, if often frustrated, efforts chronicles the life of an American family living in an isolated area of northern Kenya. As itinerant evangelists among the Samburu, one of the most determinedly non-Christian peoples of eastern Africa, Richard and Carrie Maples proclaim a steadfast conviction to do God's work. Thus sustained in the face of continual financial insecurity, considerable personal hardships, and the casual indifference of those whose cultures and time-honored values they seek to transform, these ex-California suburbanites resolutely pursue their "calling." When author Daniel Bergner explained his fascination with the Maples family and contemporary African missions in general, he noted that "one of the things that interests me about missionaries is that they are able to measure success in tiny increments and are able to stay committed for long periods, often for their entire lives."[1]

Measured by her recounted experiences in China, Hazel Todd would assuredly have understood that modest logic of computation and that high level of personal dedication. Her prolonged term of service and commitment to the CIM could indeed be measured in small yet tangible increments. Struggles to master a daunting language and its regional variations, endless days of walking to and from scattered mission outstations selling gospel tracts and preaching, repeated efforts to engage the predicaments of rural women and their families, basic medical care and counseling regularly dispensed to local residents, the unrelenting daily tasks of mission stewardship and providing ordinary household needs, managing imminent threats to mission personnel and property in recurrent times of civil disorder, revolution and war—these were among the common indices of Hazel's two decades of ministry in the hinterlands of Hunan and Anhui.

Hazel Todd sought to transform the religious beliefs of individual men and women in a time of mass revolutionary transformation of Chinese politics and ideology. Twenty years of encountering traditional Chinese belief systems and the increasing militancy of Chinese politics gave Hazel little sympathy for either. The diffuse and pervasive character of indigenous Chinese religion had long presented Christian missionaries with tortuous spiritual and cultural problems of accomodation or rejection. To Hazel that heritage was, simply stated, a formidable obstacle at worst and a minor obstruction at best in getting the Word to China's millions. For her, as for CIM missionaries in general, China in this respect epitomized a protracted battle against an enemy wearing various guises in many separate encounters. Her letters obliquely testify to the continuing vitality, or at least the tenacious endurance of traditional rites and beliefs that even the post-1949 Communist party-state would fail to suppress.

While Hazel could not have known it, her arrival in China in the early 1920s coincided with the rapid recession of a progressive vision of Chinese modernity compatible with Protestant Christianity. In the apt words of Ryan Dunch, "What emerged instead to dominate the history of China in the twentieth century was the militant, mobilizing, censoring party-state that cornered the market on envisioning and creating 'new Chinas.'"[2] While detesting the chaos and brutality of China's seemingly endemic warlordism, Hazel was alienated by the strident nationalism of the Guomindang during the 1920s, which linked the Christian missionary enterprise to imperialism and cultural subversion. By the 1930s she was even more repelled by the irreligion and social revolutionary violence of Chinese communism, which spasmodically targeted both foreign missionaries and Chinese converts. The last three years of Hazel's life and mission work were punctuated by the hardships of China's struggle for national survival against Japan, whose outcome remained darkly undetermined at the time of her sudden passing three weeks before Pearl Harbor.

The recollections of Hazel Todd are a counterpoint to those of others in her generation who maintained a higher profile and greater vocational visibility in the China mission field. Associated with enduring, prestigious institutions such as clinics, hospitals, schools, and colleges in more developed areas of China, American medical missionaries and educators have frequently given voice to their personal and professional experiences through their correspondence and published writings.[3] Far less common are the records of the day-to-day experiences of those evangelical generalists of the CIM and kindred organizations situated in makeshift sites in "hardship posts," the traditional villages and market towns of China's vast, underdeveloped countryside. Respecting this unsubtle division of labor and status within the missionary community, in late 1940 Hazel Todd lamented that "the trouble is that Christians in America know nothing about our mission and do not care to know about it . . . In China very much of all but the most accessible places has been allocated to our mission to evangelize. To urge people to support only denominational missions is to support only those missionaries who work in large enough places to have hospitals and schools, and to leave most of the hard places to reach untouched. As a rule they work among up and outs and we among the down and outs. We also can generally get closer to the people just because we do live in closer touch with them."[4] As her letters testify, indeed she did.

Notes

Introduction: China, the Missionary Project, and the Career of Hazel Todd

1. One of the better introductions to this period remains Jonathan Spence, *The Search for Modern China*, 2nd edition (New York: W.W. Norton and Company, 1991).

2. See Ka-che Yip, *Reconstruction in Nationalist China: The Development of Modern Health Services, 1928-1937* (Ann Arbor: Association for Asian Studies Monograph and Occasional Paper Series, Number 50, 1995), 13.

3. See the extensive discussion of both Roman Catholic and Protestant missions in Kenneth Scott Latourette, *A History of Christian Missions in China*. (London: The Society for Promoting Christian Knowledge, 1929 —reprint, Taipei: Ch'eng-wen Publishing Company, 1970), especially chapters XVIII-XX.

4. A dated but still useful survey of the controversies surrounding missionary activities is Jessie G. Lutz, *Christian Missions in China: Evangelists of What?* (Boston, Mass.: D.C. Heath and Company, 1965).

5. See John K. Fairbank, "Introduction: The Place of Protestant Writings in China's Cultural History," in Susanne Wilson Barnett and John King Fairbank, eds. , *Christianity in China: Early Protestant Missionary Writings* (Cambridge, MA: Council on East Asian Studies, Harvard University Press, 1985), 2.

6. Eva Jane Price, *China Journal 1889-1900: An American Missionary Family during the Boxer Rebellion* (New York: Charles Scribner's Sons, 1989).

7. See Kathleen L. Lodwick, *Educating the Women of Hainan: The Career of Margaret Moninger in China 1915-1942* (Lexington, KY: The University Press of Kentucky, 1995), and Lawrence D. Kessler, *The Jiangyin Mission Station: An American Missionary Community in China, 1895-1951* (Chapel Hill: University of North Carolina Press, 1996).

8. Lodwick, *Educating the Women of Hainan*, 3.

9. Kessler, *The Jiangyin Mission Station,* 158-159.

10. Lodwick, *Educating the Women of Hainan,* 2.

11. *China's Millions* 37.1 (January 1929): 2.

12. See Latourette, *A History of Christian Missions in China,* 382, and also *Christian History* 15:4 (issue 52, 1996), a special issue on "Hudson Taylor and Missions to China." For an excellent comprehensive history of the early years of the CIM, see Alvyn Austin, *China's Millions: The China Insland Mission and Late Qing Society. 1832-1905* (Grand Rapids, MI: William B. Eerdmans, 2007).

13. See the incisive overview provided in Austin, *China's Millions*, 1-30 and 91-92; Latourette, *A History of Christian Missions in China*, 385-386; Valentin H. Rabe, *The Home Base of American China Missions, 1880-1920* (Cambridge, MA: Council on East Asian Studies, Harvard University, 1978), 19, 87 and 148, and the overview provided in Marshall Broomhall, *The Jubilee Story of the China Inland Mission* (Philadelphia: China Inland Mission, 1915).

14. *China's Millions* 37.1 (January 1929): 2; note also Austin, *China's Millions*, 18.

15. M. Searle Bates, "The Theology of American Missionaries in China, 1900-1950," in John K. Fairbank, ed., *The Missionary Enterprise in China and America* (Cambridge, MA: Harvard University Press, 1974), 142-155; see also Austin, *China's Millions*, 446-448, which establishes that this shift toward fundamentalism was deliberately engineered by leaders of the American branch of the CIM in the early twentieth century.

16. *China's Millions* 37.1 (January 1929): 2; see also Austin, *China's Millions*, 313.

17. Stephen Neal, *A History of Christian Missions* (New York: Penguin Books, 1964), 336.

18. Latourette, *A History of Christian Missions in China*, 386, and Bates, "The Theology of American Missionaries in China, 1900-1950": 142-143.

19. *China's Millions* 37.1 (January 1929): 2.

20. See John Hersey, *The Call* (New York: Alfred A. Knopf, 1985).

21. For comparison, see the excellent studies by Jane Hunter, *The Gospel of Gentility: American Women Missionaries in Turn-of-the-Century China* (New Haven: Yale University Press, 1984), and Lodwick, *Educating the Women of Hainan*, 1-5.

22. *Interview* with Winifred Todd, October 6, 2004.

23. *Billy Graham Center Archives*: Collection 215 (6-11): The Records of the Overseas Missionary Fellowship (China Inland Mission), United States Council: Register of Candidate Information, 1898-1934, p. 166.

24. Kathleen Lodwick's analysis of Margaret Moninger's teaching career in Hainan during roughly the same period as Hazel's work in the CIM offers an interesting parallel: "Like those who preceded her to the Hainan mission, Margaret came from an America that did not ask questions about cross-cultural exchanges. Americans were convinced of the superiority of their culture and government and did not question their rights of extraterritoriality in China, gained and kept as they were by the gun. Margaret, like many, if not all, missionaries, came from the segment of American society that centered its life around the church and thought it their Christian duty to pass their religion and their lifestyle on to peoples of less-blessed countries." See Lodwick, *Educating the Women of Hainan*, 6. The quote is from Hazel Todd's letter of August 4, 1936, in Winifred Todd, compiler, *Letters from Hazel* (Fresno, CA: Liberty Printing Company, 1977), 84.

25. Jessie G. Lutz and R. Ray Lutz, "Karl Gutzlaff's Approach to Indigenization: The Chinese Union" in Daniel H. Bays, ed. *Christianity in China: From the Eighteenth Century to the Present.* (Stanford: Stanford University Press, 1996), 288. Note also Hunter,*The Gospel of Gentility*, 3.

From Yangzhou to Hunan: The Early Years, 1920-1930

1. Hazel's brief description of some basic features of Mandarin Chinese is accurate enough; for an excellent general analysis of the language see Jerry Norman, *Chinese* (Cambridge: Cambridge University Press, 1988).

2. Yangchow (Yangzhou) in Jiangsu Province, given its location at the confluence of the Grand Canal and Yangzi River, had been one of the most important urban centers of the Lower Yangzi region since the Tang dynasty.

3. Chinese resistance to "going to law" has often been exaggerated. Recent scholarship supports the notion that civil litigation has been a constant feature of life in China over the past several centuries. See the numerous examples cited in Madeleine Zelin, Jonathan K. Ocko, and Robert Gardella, eds. *Contract and Property in Early Modern China* (Stanford: Stanford University Press, 2004).

4. Yangchow's salt merchants, who had traditionally monopolized the distribution of this essential commodity, were among the city's wealthiest civic elite. On their background, see Ho Ping-ti, "The Salt Merchants of Yang-chou: A Study of Commercial Capitalism in Eighteenth Century China," *Harvard Journal of Asiatic Studies* 17 (1954): 130-168.

5. "Out-stations" were rural branches of the central mission church in an area, usually situated in villages and small market towns. A good overview of this Protestant mission strategy in operation in the Lower Yangzi region is found in Kessler, *The Jiangyin Mission Station,* 20-22.

6. Situated on Lushan Mountain adjacent to Poyang Lake in northern Jiangsi Province, Kuling was one of the select few "hill station" resorts and convalescence centers for foreign expatriates—conventionally missionaries and businessmen—in early twentieth century China. After 1949 the location became much more renowned for periodic Chinese Communist Party plenums. A vivid nostalgic account of Kuling as Hazel would have known it appears in Elsie Hayes Landstrom, *Closing the Circle: An American Family in China* (Fort Bragg, CA: Q.E.D. Press, 1998, 110-118. The development of such colonial places of refuge in the tropics and subtropics is aptly traced in Barbara Crossette, *The Great Hill Stations of Asia* (Boulder, Co: Westview Press, 1998). Crossette excludes "semicolonial" China from her survey, however.

7. Latourette's discussion of the Bible Union is worth repeating here. "So strongly were the more aggressive among the conservatives convinced that 'modernism' threatened the very life of the Church in China that in 1920 they organized under the name of The Bible Union ... [The Union's] convictions were not new, but were substantially the position always taken by the great body of Evangelicals and still held by the majority of missionaries in China."

What was new was that the organization actively lobbied to exclude "modernist" missionary candidates from service and vigorously promoted conservative Bible curricula. By 1923 the Union had enrolled over two thousand members. As Latourette concludes. "The result was discord: Protestants were at odds with each other during the years when they were facing the most difficult situation which had yet confronted them in China." See Latourette, *A History of Christian Missions in China,* 795-796.

8. As assistants to female missionaries, Chinese "Bible women" were social intermediaries, and often essential ones at that, in the task of evangelizing women in rural areas; note here Hunter, *The Gospel of Gentility,* 16-19.

9. In stating "the neighbors are held responsible for what happens," Hazel undoubtedly refers to the *baojia* system, a state-imposed surveillance network of community responsibility for local law and order. Developed in the eighteenth century under the Qing dynasty, it remained in force under Republican authorities; see F.W. Mote, *Imperial China 900-1800* (Cambridge, MA: Harvard University Press, 1999), 918-919.

10. The "richest clan in Nanchowting" refers to an important lineage in that area—lineages being defined as extended kinship groups tracing their origins and descent to common ancestry and usually holding both property and rituals in common. Lineages were central features of Chinese rural society, particularly in central and southern China. The support or opposition of lineage members could significantly help or hinder missionary evangelism; see, for example, Jessie G. Lutz, and Rolland Ray Lutz, *Hakka Chinese Confront Protestant Christianity, 1850-1900: With the Autobiographies of Eight Hakka Christians, and Commentary* (Armonk, NY: M.E. Sharpe, 1998), 204-208.

11. Hazel here appears to describe a botched case of the usage of moxibustion, a traditional Chinese medical technique involving the local applications of heat to the skin. It is frequently but not exclusively associated with acupuncture.

12. Regarding instances of "demon possession," note here Alan Hunter and Kim-Kwong Chan, *Protestantism in Contemporary China* (Cambridge: Cambridge University Press, 1993). As these authors point out (p. 146), "Calling on spiritual beings for healing and exorcism has long been a core feature of Chinese religious life. Its Christian version requires a new orientation of the believer, but is not a radical innovation; on the contrary it maintains the essence of the tradition."

13. The "anti-Christian movement" as formally organized among China's students began in 1922 as an offshoot of the wider iconoclastic leftist intellectual currents of the New Tide or Chinese Renaissance. It denounced Christianity both as an unscientific superstition and as an ally of China's capitalist and imperialist oppressors, and gained momentum as tensions rose between China and the foreign treaty powers in the mid-1920s. See the excellent summary in Latourette, *A History of Christian Missions in China*, 694-699.

14. Situated on the Hupei-Honan (Hubei-Henan) provincial boundary north of Hankow, Kikungshan or Chikungshan (Jigongshan) was another well-frequented hill station for the rest and recreation of missionary expatriots. See Latourette, *A History of Christian Missions in China,* 672.

15. The term "wenli," as Hazel indicates, refers to the literary or classical Chinese written language in which was encoded the bulk of China's vast literary tradition down to the early twentieth century.

Above and apart from fluency in the vernacular (in this case, Mandarin Chinese), protracted and demanding study was necessary to master the classical language's archaic usages and forms; see Jerry Norman, *Chinese,* 83-110.

16. Hazel here begins to experience the persistent problem of warlordism, which plagued and also critically shaped China's politics between the fall of the Qing dynasty in 1911 and the onset of total war with Japan in 1937. Edward A. McCord

sees it as a defining feature of modern China's "crisis of political authority." As he states, "The militarization of politics that drew military commanders into the political arena also empowered them by making the military force they controlled the main determinant of political power." See Edward A. McCord. *The Power of the Gun: The Emergence of Modern Chinese Warlordism* (Berkeley: University of California Press, 1993), 311.

17. Orthodox Confucian moral standards harshly maintained that, regardless of the age at which they were bereaved, widows were forbidden to remarry; the custom was not frequently disregarded among the poor in rural China for pragmatic reasons, however.

18. The colporteur's primary task was to sell translated Bibles and other Christian religious literature in the Chinese countryside; like any salesman, his income depended on periodic assessments of his sales volume.

19. Over several centuries a dense network of periodic markets had developed in China, and itinerating missionaries made good use of them in CIM's evangelical work; see, for example, D.M. Campbell, "Systematic Visits to Seven Markets," *China's Millions*, 49:3 (March, 1941), 37-38. For a superb analysis of the periodic marketing system, see G. William Skinner, "Marketing and Social Structure in Rural China, Part I." *The Journal of Asian Studies* 24: 1 (November 1964): 3-43.

20. Note here Daniel L. Overmyer, *Religions of China: The World as a Living System* (San Francisco, CA: Harper and Row, 1986), 72-73. China's local deities and their worshipers were bound by reciprocity and mutual obligations; if gods failed to live up to their end of the bargain (in this case, bringing rain), they themselves might be rejected. Some telling illustrations are provided in Arthur H. Smith, *Village Life in China* (Boston, MA: Little, Brown and Company, 1970), 125-127.

21. Among other things, "modernists" generally espoused the social gospel of progressive reformist action in the world, scientific textual criticism of the Bible, and acceptance of Darwin's evolutionary theory, while fundamentalists reacted by affirming the priority of evangelism in an increasingly sinful world, Biblical inerrancy, and traditional Christian creationism. A fuller comparison is offered in Martin Marty, "North America" in John McManners, ed., *The Oxford Illustrated History of Christianity* (Oxford: Oxford University Press, 2001), 410-415.

22. Hazel identifies the interchangeabilty of soldiers and bandits, just one element in the endemic problem of banditry in early twentieth-century China. The areas of Hunan and Anhui provinces where she worked were both hotbeds of banditry. See the exhaustive analysis of Phil Billingsley, *Bandits in Republican China* (Stanford, CA: Stanford University Press, 1988), 1-39.

23. General Feng Yu-hsiang (1882-1948), popularly known as "the Christian general," was one of the most important warlords on the national stage at this time. By the mid-1920s his political career subordinated Christian influences to national revolutionary goals, including the alliance with the Soviet Union. See the capsule assessments of Feng in Latourette, *A History of Christian Missions in China*, 777-779, and Edwin Pak-wah Leung, ed. *Historical Dictionary of Revolutionary China, 1839-1976* (New York: Greenwood Press, 1992), 112-114.

24. From 1924, regulations proposed or adopted by various government agencies sought to gain greater control of China's extensive network of Christian educational institutions in the interests of revolutionary nationalism. Foreign and

native Christian educators were deeply divided over these efforts, particularly efforts to curtail or eliminate compulsory religious instruction. Responses over the next several years varied from total compliance to outright rejection of the regulations; see Latourette, *A History of Christian Missions in China*, 814-815.

25. Sun Yat-sen (1866-1925) was of course revered by Chinese across the political spectrum as the founding father of the Chinese Republic, its first president, and a tireless advocate of national unification. Hazel's elation at his death on March 12, 1925, while understandable in the light of increasing threats to the foreign presence in China at the time, was sadly misplaced. Sun's death only widened the serious and growing political and ideological tensions within the nationalist movement. For a biographical sketch of Sun Yat-sen's career, see Leung, ed., *Historical Dictionary of Revolutionary China,* 393-394.

26. As Reinders notes, "The association of Buddhism and a non-meat diet has been so strong that many Christian missionaries have felt the need to attack vegetarianism, not in any abstract or generic form but adapted specifically to counter Buddhist rationalizations." The issue of vegetarianism surfaces several times in Hazel's letters; see Eric Reinders, *Borrowed Gods and Foreign Bodies: Christian Missionaries Imagine Chinese Religion* (Berkeley: University of California Press, 2004), 146 ff.

27. The "true Jesus denomination," while a "false sect" to Hazel, was an indigenous form of Pentecostalism founded in 1917 in northern China. Its followers rejected mainstream churches and missionaries, emphasized charismatic faith healing and speaking in tongues, and avowed a communal living style. By 1949 it claimed about 120,000 adherents in China, and additional believers in Taiwan and Hong Kong. See Hunter and Chan, *Protestantism in Contemporary China,* 120-121.

28. In the Boxer Protocol of 1901, an indemnity of 450 million taels had been exacted from China by eight foreign powers as restitution for the destruction caused by the Boxer Uprising of the preceding year. The sum amounted to almost half the Qing empire's annual budget. The United States used its share to fund a program allowing Chinese students to study in America, hence Hazel's resentment of the ingratitude of China's nationalistic students. See Spence, *The Search for Modern China,* A 48.

29. Calumnies against Christian missionaries for alleged atrocities such as the use of people's vital organs for medicine were common as early as the late eighteen hundreds; they were a significant factor in provoking the well-known Tianjin "massacre" of 1870, in which nineteen foreigners were killed. See Spence, *The Search for Modern China*, 202-204.

30. The custom of using mediators or middlemen was an ingrained feature of many transactions in Chinese society; this is evident in property disputes in the late imperial period, for example. See Ann Osborne, "Property, Taxes, and State Protection of Rights," in Zelin, Ocko, and Gardella, eds., *Contract and Property in Early Modern China*, 145-146.

31. Chang Tso-lin or "The Old Marshall" (1873-1928) was the dominant warlord of northeast China (Manchuria) and a power broker on the national stage until his assassination by Japanese Army agents in 1928. See the numerous references to his career in Edward L. Dreyer, *China at War, 1901-1949* (London: Longman, 1995). T'ang, "the leader in the south of China," was T'ang Sheng-chih (1890-19??), a

Hunanese militarist who played a key role in winning central China for advancing Nationalist armies in 1926-27. See his biography in Howard L. Boorman, and Richard C. Howard, eds., *Biographical Dictionary of Republican China, vol. III: Mao-Wu* (New York: Columbia University Press, 1970), 236-239.

32. Opium frquently presented itself to both Chinese and foreign observers as one of modern China's most enduring problems. For excellent recent analyses of the multidimensional nature of opium production, consumption, and efforts at suppression in late imperial and Republican China, see Timothy Brook and Bob Tadashi Wakabayashi, eds., *Opium Regimes: China, Britain, and Japan, 1839-1952* (Berkeley: University of California Press, 2000).

33. The military episodes in Hubei Province which Hazel discusses were the leading edge of the Northern Expedition of 1926-1928. Until mid-1927 the Nationalist (Guomindang) and Chinese Communist parties temporarily collaborated in military campaigns to defeat warlords, oust foreign imperialism, and unify China. Use of the term "Reds" at the time by anxious foreigners thus indiscriminately referred to both Nationalists and Communists. For an exhaustive account, see Donald A. Jordan. *The Northern Expedition: China's National Revolution of 1926-1928* (Honolulu: University Press of Hawaii, 1976).

34. The CIM established a school at Chefoo (Yantai) in Shandong Province in 1880 for the offspring of missionaries and the business and diplomatic communities in China. With a curriculum patterned on the British system as well as the expected emphasis on religious education, the school survived in various locations until the CIM finally withdrew from the People's Republic in 1951. See the website maintained by the University of London's School of Oriental and African Studies Library on the history of the CIM (www.mundus.ac.uk/cats/4/904.htm).

35. In the summer of 1926, in response to a local warlord commandeering foreign ships for troop transport, two British gunboats bombarded the port city of Wanhsien (Wanxian) on the Yangzi River in eastern Sichuan Province. The attack caused massive fires in the center of the city, and provoked national outrage and a boycott of British vessels over the next several years. See Harold Isaacs, *The Tragedy of the Chinese Revolution*, 2nd revised ed. (New York: Atheneum, 1966), 124-125.

36. Although she understood relatively little about that faith, Hazel's dismissal of Buddhism is hardly surprising. By the time she arrived in China, there was a long-standing tradition among Protestant missionaries of denouncing Buddhist beliefs and practices. See the various examples cited in Reinders, *Borrowed Gods and Foreign Bodies.*

37. For a fuller account of the antimissionary rioting in Nanchow, which details the destruction of church property and the limited threat posed to mission personnel, see G.F.Draffin, "Under the Red Flag," *China's Millions* 35:2 (February 1927): 25-26.

38. The policies of encouraging labor militancy and discouraging Christian schools that Hazel refers to appear to signal the onset of the Wuhan Regime, the leftist wing of the forces of the Northern Expedition. By mid-1927 the Wuhan Regime had disintegrated in favor of Chiang Kai-shek's conservative and anti-Communist National Government. See Leung, ed., *Historical Dictionary of Revolutionary China,* 468-470.

39. The concept of using posters in evangelical campaigns may owe something

to the increasing presence of commercial advertisements for products such as cigarettes and patent medicines in the Chinese countryside. See Charles Best and S.J. Garland. *"Advertising the Gospel," China's Millions* 31:1 (January 1923): 10-11. For excellent examples of the type of posters used in village evangelism, which also employed indigenized imagery, see *Billy Graham Center Archives*: The Archives Bulletin Board, October, 2000, "Chinese Village Evangelism Posters," www.wheaton.edu/bgc/archives/docs/chinaposters01.htm

40. The festival of the fifth day of the fifth lunar month (*duan wu*) is better known as the Dragon Boat Festival. Together with the New Year and Mid-Autumn Festivals, it is one of China's three great traditional holidays celebrated throughout the country. See the detailed account in H.Y. Lowe, *The Adventures of Wu: The Life Cycle of a Peking Man*, part 1 (Princeton, N.J.: Princeton University Press, 1983), 141-148.

41. In considering Hazel's reaction to the temples of Lushan, Reinders' discussion is appropriate: "Most Protestant categorizations of the religions of the world were ultimately quite simple: there was the true religion, and then there was idolatry. The term *idolatry* could be applied to any and all non-Protestants, including Chinese Buddhists, Catholics, and the prophets of Baal.

Theologically, idolatry was the worship of anything other than the true God, and the term could be used in relatively abstract ways but most often had a very tangible, visible reference: people bowing to an object." See Reinders, *Borrowed Gods and Foreign Bodies*, 8-9.

42. As Hazel reports, Communist forces led by Peng Dehuai seized and held Changsha, the capital of Hunan Province, for three days in July 1930 before being driven out. The attack represented the so-called Li Lisan line of seizing major cities instead of the subsequent Communist strategy of consolidating control in several rural base areas. See Dreyer, *China at War*, 158.

43. The "three practically new workers" who were to accompany Hazel to Anhui were among the two hundred recruited by CIM between 1929 and 1931 to replace people who had retired from service during the 1927 evacuation, as well as to extend the mission's efforts into hitherto unreached areas of China. Alvyn J. Austin notes that "The coming of 'the Two Hundred' meant a proportional increase of the CIM from 14 per cent of the total missionary population in 1922 (960 out of 6,636), to almost one-quarter in 1935 (1,359 out of 5,816) . . . Their arrival also shifted the balance within the mission, making it more American in personnel and outlook." See Alvyn J. Austin, *Saving China: Canadian Missionaries in the Middle Kingdom 1888-1959* (Toronto: University of Toronto Press, 1986), 233-234, and also *Billy Graham Center Archives*: The Archives Bulletin Board, March, 2003, "China Inland Mission's Call for Two Hundred Workers," www.wheaton.edu/bgc/archives/bulletin/bu0303.htm

Reassignment to Anhui: The Middle Years, 1930-1937

1. Known as *tongyangxi*, the custom of having future mother-in-laws bring up adopted daughters as future daughter-in-laws was widespread in China, especially in the central and southern regions of the country. It obviated paying a high bride price later for a mature young woman, and placed unfortunate young girls firmly

under older women's domination. See Lowe, *The Adventures of Wu*, part. 2, 191.

2. Student desire "to fight the Japanese" in late 1931 was a patriotic reaction to the Kwantung Army's conquest of Manchuria (soon to become the Japanese puppet state of "Manchukuo") in September of that year, and the temporizing response of Chiang Kai-shek's Nationalist government. See Dreyer, *China at War*, 170-172.

3. Hazel was quite accurate about the uncomfortably close location of "a hotbed of communists and bandits." Otto Braun, who was the Comintern's chief liaison with the CCP during these years, offers the following information on the Oyuwan Soviet: "The second-largest soviet area, with a territory of over 40,000 square km and a population of 3 million, lay in the Honan-Hupeh-Anhuei border triangle north of the Yangtze River and east of the Peking-Wuhan Railway. The 4th Corps . . . with 12,000 to 15,000 men and about 10,000 rifles, provided its regular armed forces." The largest soviet area was of course the Central Soviet Area in neighboring Jiangxi Province. See Otto Braun, *A Comintern Agent in China 1932-1939*, translated from the German by Jeanne Moore (Stanford: Stanford University Press, 1982), 15.

4. Female literacy rates in rural areas, indeed throughout China, were even by this time (the 1930s) abysmally below those of men. To cite a relevant contemporary example, in his 1930 investigation of Xunwu County in southeastern Jiangxi, none other than Mao Zedong noted the following: "We can say that essentially no women can read, for no more than 300 women in the whole county are literate." Mao estimated that forty percent of Xunwu's entire male population (the county's population totals are unspecified) had at least rudimentary literacy. See Mao Zedong, *Report from Xunwu*, translated with an introduction and notes by Roger R. Thompson (Stanford, CA.: Stanford University Press, 1990), 190-191.

5. Another perspective upon Hazel's relatively few disputes with her missionary subordinates Margaret and Ruth Elliott is reflected in archived transcripts of their own historical experiences in the field. While Margaret openly criticized Hazel's management style and handling of day-to-day problems, Ruth expressed little apparent dissatisfaction on either account. See *Billy Graham Center Archives*: Collection 287-Margaret Rice Elliott Crossett, T4 Transcript, T5 Transcript. www.wheaton.edu/bgc/archives/trans/287t04.htm and *Billy Graham Center Archives*: Collection 187-Eleanor Ruth Elliott, T4 Transcript. www.wheaton.edu/bgc/archives/trans/187t04.htm

6. The missionaries' dampened holiday spirits apparently arose from an extremely belated report of the 1932 U.S. presidential election results, a resounding victory for Democrat Franklin D. Roosevelt over the incumbent Republican president Herbert C. Hoover. One is still left to wonder why the news of this major political event took over a year to reach them in Shucheng.

7. With or without the devotional excesses illustrated here, well-organized pilgrimages to sacred sites in the quest to acquire spiritual merits have long been a conspicuous feature of China's popular religious traditions. See, for example, Lowe, *The Adventures of Wu*, 1, 79-95 and also Susan Naquin and Chün-fang Yü, eds., *Pilgrims and Sacred Sites in China* (Berkeley: University of California Press, 1992.

8. The brutal executions of John and Betty Stam in December 1934 in southern Anhui by Chinese Communist guerrillas made them undoubtedly the most

publicized Christian martyrs of the time. For one recent hagiographical account (out of many) of their careers as itinerating CIM evangelists, see Vance Christie. *John and Betty Stam: Missionary Martyrs* (Uhrichsville, OH: Barbour Publishing, 2000). Further details about the episode were recorded by Elsie H. Landstrom, whom the Stams had befriended as a child. They were abducted from their CIM station at the town of Tsingteh and soon thereafter beheaded in the village of Miaosheo. The couple "were in the path of a Communist army of 6000 . . . Later identified as the Red-Northern-Campaign Anti-Japanese Army, which had been driven from its headquarters in Kiangsi by Chiang [Kai-shek], their commander called the villagers together to witness the punishment of foreigners who represented a government that was helping Chiang to destroy them." The miraculous survival of the Stam's infant daughter Helen Priscilla thanks to the efforts of local villagers did much to enhance the legend. See Elsie Hays Landstrom, *Closing the Circle: An American Family in China* (Fort Bragg, CA: QED Press, 1998), 138-139.

9. By "playing with fire," Hazel apparently refers to the perceived improvement in U.S. relations with the Soviet Union in the years immediately following diplomatic recognition of the USSR by the Roosevelt administration in 1933.

10. This is yet another instance (see note 10 above) where "lineage" should properly be substituted for the term "family," given the large numbers of local church members who were sharing a common surname.

11. Conversion to Christianity was not the Nationalist government's preferred mode of dealing with actual or presumed communists. In her own letter dated a month later than Hazel's, Ruth Elliott had the following comments about the "Reds" in Shucheng: "During the summer here the soldiers rounded up a lot of people who had signed up with the Reds and executed them. Altogether more than 200 were killed. An average of 16 a day taken out and shot. That seems to have discouraged Reds around here. The Red suspects taken from across the street . . . got off by paying a lot to the officials and buying some guns for the soldiers. Money talks." See *Billy Graham Center Archives: Collection 187(1-7, September 10, 1935)*: Eleanor Ruth Elliot, Papers 1910-1981, n.d.

12. Chu Jung, the God of Fire, seems to have had benign origins, but "popular tradition has gradually led the people to believe that this is the god charged with meting out punishment by setting people's houses on fire. Worshiping the God of Fire is therefore a precautionary measure to prevent the divinity from visiting the worshippers' establishments in the wake of which there is often a fire accident." See Lowe, *The Adventures of Wu*, 1.210.

13. Hunter remarks that "by 1919 the American missionary force in China consisted of nearly equal numbers of single women, married women, and married men . . . Not only were single women represented in the mission community well beyond their numerical proportion in the United States, but their work appeared to be central to a mission organization in need of new strategies and additional personnel . . . In 1919, 13 percent of all missionary centers in China were entirely staffed by single women." See the full discussion in Hunter, *The Gospel of Gentility*, 52 ff.

On the Front Lines in Anhui: The Final Years, 1938-1941

1. The chaotic conditions prevalent in the interior are well described by Ruth Elliott in a letter to her family from Hwangchuan, Honan (Henan) in December, 1936: "We were bombed for 10 days, gassed, shelled, and had fighting all around our compound, were under Japanese rule for 2 months and couldn't leave the premises without a permit good only for one day. Then when the Japanese withdrew, guerrillas came in shooting into the air and hunting for spies. They rioted the Catholics, driving them out of town, looting their premises . . . the officials sent a guard to escort them back. And that's where we are now. The 200 refugees have returned to their homes, praising God for the way He cared for them and supplied every need." See *Billy Graham Center Archives: Collection 187(1-10, December 6, 1938)*: Eleanor Ruth Elliot, Papers 1910-1981, n.d., and note the description of the same incident in Timothy Brook, "Toward Independence: Christianity in China Under the Japanese Occupation, 1937-1945" in Bays, ed., *Christianity in China*, 324-325.

2. Japanese atrocities in occupied China are most notoriously symbolized by their gruesome massacres in the Nationalist capital of Nanking (Nanjing) in late 1937 to early 1938. See here the controversial but influential work of Iris Chang, *The Rape of Nanking: The Forgotten Holocaust of World War II* (New York: Basic Books, 1997). A more complex picture of accommodation as well as brutal oppression is depicted in Brook, "Toward Independence" in Bays, ed. *Christianity in China*, 317-337.

3. Hazel's upbeat picture of Fowyang's Christian community is echoed a year later by a published report; see J.H. Kane, "A Thriving Church," *China's Millions* 48:7 (July 1940): 101-103.

4. The traditional cultural stereotypes of North versus South China have endured down to the present, with provinces such as Anhui, Jiangsu, Henan, and Shaanxi bisected by such distinctions; see, for example, a concise discussion of "North China and South China" in http://encycl.opentopia.com/term/North_China_and_South_China .

5. The Swastika Society, more properly known as the Red Swastika Society (hongwanzihui), was a voluntary Chinese "redemptive" organization which had sponsored a wide variety of educational and charitable activities since its foundation in the early Republican era, and managed to flourish even under the Japanese occupation. See Prasenjit Duara, *Sovereignty and Authenticity: Manchukuo and the East Asian Modern* (Lanham Md.: Rowman & Littlefield, 2004), 89-90 and 103-110.

6. In early June 1937, Chiang Kai-shek ordered the Yellow River dikes blown open to halt the Japanese advance into Central China. The southeastern shift of the river's course flooded much of Henan, Anhui and Jiangsu provinces, resulting in the drowning or death by famine of several million local inhabitants. This desperate "total war" measure cost the Nationalists heavily in political capital both during and after the Sino-Japanese War. See Dreyer, *China at War*, 228-229.

7. By requesting dollars for the purchase of the organ "against rules of the mission," Hazel refers to strict CIM regulations banning the collection or the personal solicitation of money by its missionaries. These rules, as well as fundamental

CIM theological precepts, were constantly reiterated on the masthead of the organization's monthly journal *China's Millions*.

8. Reinders' remarks on Protestant missionary views of Chinese rituals such as the funerals Hazel refers to are significant: "Ritual was consistently described as useless, degraded, empty, and ridiculous. It had no power to effect salvation. China was perceived as uniquely engulfed in ritual ... Chinese ritual was presented as a kind of absurd theater, in which 'a nation of actors' engaged in stylized fictions full of sound and fury but signifying nothing." See Reinders, *Borrowed Gods and Foreign Bodies*, 96 ff.

9. The grim wartime conditions Ruth Elliott faced in normally impoverished northern Anhui en route to Shucheng that summer are vividly described in letters to her family: "The inns where we stayed enroute defy description. They are the poorest I've ever seen. In most of the rooms where we stopped there was no furniture we could use—no table, no chair and even no bench ... The food in this district is the world's worst. In one place all we could get was dough strings made of course wheat full of grit ... [and] they were far from cooked through ... The tea for which we paid one cent a bowl was frankly made of mulberry leaves ... and had about half a teaspoon of solid mud in the bottom." See *Billy Graham Center Archives: Collection 187(1-13,June 30, 1940)*: Eleanor Ruth Elliot, Papers 1910-1981, n.d.

10. Ruth Elliott also described her late August trip with Hazel from Liuan back to Shucheng, and what she found upon their arrival: "Everywhere the city is in ruins. It is estimated that 9/10ths of the city was burned as a result of incendiary bombs. I believe it, too, because I've seen very few houses indeed that are intact. But it's encouraging to see how people are rebuilding ... money is scarce and prices are high. However, living expenses are just about half—at least a third less—than they are in Liuan ... But travelling is terrifically expensive ... Our heavy things, which came up by barrow, cost over $60.00. They charge much more than they used to because the road is dreadful. The Chinese have cut it up so the Japanese can't use it, but it harms themselves more than the Japs. The road is nothing but gullies and mounds ... It was nice to get here to the compound again ... The ruins of the house are rather desolate to see, but we have the prospect of seeing the house rebuilt within a few months." See *Billy Graham Center Archives: Collection 187(1-13, August 29, 1940)*: Eleanor Ruth Elliot, Papers 1910-1981, n.d.

11. Hazel characteristically doesn't report it, but at the time this letter was written she was recovering from a serious bout of illness, as reported by Ruth Elliott on October 7: "Hazel has been sick with dysentery. She is lying on my chaise longue at present, having been in bed for five days and ailing for six or seven. I'm glad she's feeling so much better ... We hope Hazel will be well enough to celebrate her birthday on Thursday." See *Billy Graham Center Archives: Collection 187(1-13, October 7, 1940)*: Eleanor Ruth Elliot, Papers 1910-1981, n.d.

12. Hazel's personal encounter with bandits on the road to Hofei is recounted more fully by Ruth Elliott in her correspondence: "The report we heard that Hazel and the party were robbed on the way to Hofei was true. Two men held up the party with seven husky men in it. But we have reason to believe that at least one of the chairbearers was in on it, so if the coolies had tried any rough stuff on the bandits, the bearers would have helped the bandits. They actually got away with only what the coolies were carrying in money. From all of them together they actually got

about $70. The bandits got Hazel's suitcase out and started hunting for her money. She had it in the side pocket, an arrangement they don't have out here in suitcases, so though his hand was right near the money he didn't find it. After a minute Hazel got rather mad and slammed the suitcase down on the man's hand and told him to leave her things alone. The bandit started to hit her but our servant, Yang, caught his arm and told him he'd better think twice before he hit a foreigner. That sort of scared them so they left. As they left they said, 'Don't forget, we didn't take anything of yours.' But Hazel answered, 'But you opened my suitcase and hunted.' After Hazel got back and told us about it, Mr. Costerus went to the official here and reported the matter. He was disgusted to find a mere boy there who was indifferent to the matter. So Mr. Costerus told exactly what was what. He told him that he was responsible for what happened in his district... Since that visit we have found out more about this official. The Chungking government issued an order that beginning on Jan. 1, 1940, the position of 'Ch'ü' official, which is just under the county official, would be abolished and all who were in such positions would have to make arrangements for other work. The Ch'ü official here thought this a cushy job and didn't want to hunt another, so he just decided to stay. He commandeers taxes and puts on an extra one now and then so he can have plenty of cash at his disposal. He has been living this way all year and no one dares to report him. So now when Mr. Costerus innocently said he would report to the American embassy if nothing was done, that man is in the soup unless he forks out that $70." See *Billy Graham Center Archives: Collection 187(1-13, October 29,1940)*: Eleanor Ruth Elliot, Papers 1910-1981, n.d.

13. This traditional community security apparatus, called the *baojia* system, has already been described (see "The Early Years," note 9 above).

14. As noted by Ruth Elliott, the rapacity and unruliness of the soldiers or ex-soldiers Hazel describes was also attributed to a new (and evidently poorly provisioned) division of Chinese troops sent in to garrison the Shucheng area. See *Billy Graham Center Archives: Collection 187(1-14, February 16, 1941)*: Eleanor Ruth Elliot, Papers 1910-1981, n.d.

15. The obvious reference made here, amid Hazel's criticism of New Deal economic policies at home, is to the continued U.S. exports of strategic raw materials to a thoroughly militarized Japan, even as diplomatic relations between the two countries were progressively deteriorating.

16. The reference to "fairs" is further confirmation of the logical evangelical strategy of utilizing the periodic marketing system in the Chinese countryside (see "The Early Years," note 19 above).

17. In Hazel's temporary absence, Ruth Elliott reported continued sporadic Japanese bombing raids on Shucheng at this time that stimulated considerable local panic; see *Billy Graham Center Archives: Collection 187(1-14, June 20, 1941)*: Eleanor Ruth Elliot, Papers 1910-1981, n.d.

18. On July 25, 1941, President Franklin D. Roosevelt issued an executive order freezing *both* Japanese and Chinese assets in the United States. While the national security imperatives for the action taken against Japan are well-known, in China's case it occurred at the behest of the Nationalist authorities themselves. As an official communique reads, "At the specific request of Generalissimo Chiang Kai-shek, and for the purpose of helping the Chinese Government, the President has, at the same time, extended the freezing control to Chinese assets in the United States.

The administration of the licensing system with respect to Chinese assets will be conducted with a view to strengthening the foreign trade and exchange position of the Chinese Government. The inclusion of China in the Executive Order, in accordance with the wishes of the Chinese Government, is a continuation of this government's policy of assisting China." See *The New York Times*, July 26, 1941, as excerpted in www.jewishvirtuallibrary.org/jsource/ww2/usjapanchina.html.

Conclusion

1. See Daniel Bergner, "The Call," *The New York Times Magazine* (January 29, 2006): 40-47 and 72-75 (the author's comment is on p. 6).

2. Ryan Dunch, *Fuzhou Protestants and the Making of a Modern China 1857-1937* (New Haven and London: Yale University Press, 2001), 201.

3. See the works by Kessler, Landstrom, and Lodwick previously cited, and also M. Christina Zaccarini. *The Sino-American Friendship as Tradition and Challenge: Dr. Ailie Gale in China, 1908-1950* (Bethlehem: Lehigh University Press, 2001).

4. See Hazel's letter of October 7, 1940, from Shucheng, Anhui on p. 188 above.

Sources Consulted

Manuscripts and Other Primary Sources

Billy Graham Center Archives: Collection 187(1-4, 1-7, 1-10, 1-13, 1-14): Eleanor Ruth Elliot, Papers 1910-1981, n.d.

Billy Graham Center Archives: Collection 215 (6-11): The Records of the Overseas Missionary Fellowship (China Inland Mission), United States Council: Register of Candidate Information, 1898-1934.

Interview: interview with Winifred Todd on October 6, 2004.

Whitworth University Archives: China Inland Mission, Letters from Hazel Todd, Folios 1-48.

Books and Articles

Austin, Alvyn. *China's Millions: The China Inland Mission and Late Qing Society, 1832-1905*. Grand Rapids, MI: William B. Eerdmans Publishing Company, 2007.

Austin, Alvyn J. *Saving China: Canadian Missionaries in the Middle Kingdom 1888-1959*. Toronto: University of Toronto Press, 1986.

Barnett, Susanne Wilson, and John King Fairbank, eds. *Christianity in China: Early Protestant Missionary Writings*. Cambridge, MA: Council on East Asian Studies, Harvard University Press, 1985.

Bates, M. Searle, "The Theology of American Missionaries in China, 1900-1950," in John K. Fairbank, ed. *The Missionary Enterprise in China and America*. Cambridge, MA: Harvard University Press, 1974, 135-158.

Bays, Daniel H., ed. *Christianity in China: From the Eighteenth Century to the Present*. Stanford: Stanford University Press, 1996.

Bergner, Daniel. "The Call," *The New York Times Magazine* (January 29, 2006): 40-47 and 72-75.

Best, Charles, and S.J. Garland. "Advertising the Gospel," *China's Millions* 31:1 (January 1923): 10-11.

Billingsley, Phil. *Bandits in Republican China*. Stanford: Stanford University Press, 1988.

Boorman, Howard L., and Richard C. Howard, eds. *Biographical Dictionary of Republican China*, vol. III: Mao-Wu. New York: Columbia University Press, 1970.

Braun, Otto. *A Comintern Agent in China 1932-1939*, translated from the German by Jeanne Moore. Stanford: Stanford University Press, 1982.

Brook, Timothy, and Bob Tadashi Wakabayashi, eds. *Opium Regimes: China, Britain, and Japan, 1839-1952*. Berkeley, CA: University of California Press, 2000.

Broomhall, Marshall. *The Jubilee Story of the China Inland Mission*. Philadelphia: China Inland Mission, 1915.

Campbell, D.M. "Systematic Visits to Seven Markets," *China's Millions* 49:3 (March 1941): 37-38.

Chang, Iris. *The Rape of Nanking: The Forgotten Holocaust of World War II*. New York: Basic Books, 1997.

Christian History 15:4 (issue 52, 1996), special issue on "Hudson Taylor and Missions to China."

Christie, Vance. *John and Betty Stam: Missionary Martyrs*. Uhrichsville, OH: Barbour Publishing, 2000.

Cochran, Sherman, Andrew C.K. Hsieh, and Janis Cochran, trans. and eds. *One Day in China: May 21, 1936*. New Haven: Yale University Press, 1983.

Crook, John. "In the Midst of a Bombing Raid," *China's Millions* 46:3 (March 1938): 40-41.

Crossette, Barbara. *The Great Hill Stations of Asia*. Boulder, CO.: Westview Press, 1998.

Draffin, G.F. "The Loss of All Things," *China's Millions* 39:3 (March 1931): 41-42.

Draffin, G.F. "Under the Red Flag," *China's Millions* 35:2 (February 1927): 25-26.

Dreyer, Edward L. *China at War, 1901-1949*. London: Longman, 1995.

Duara, Prasenjit. *Sovereignty and Authenticity: Manchukuo and the East Asian Modern*. Lanham, Md.: Rowman and Littlefield, 2004.

Dunch, Ryan. *Fuzhou Protestants and the Making of a Modern China 1857-1937*. New Haven and London: Yale University Press, 2001.

Dunn, G.T. "A Bicycle Trip Through Central Anhwei," *China's Millions* 46:6 (June 1938): 86-87.

Fairbank, John K., ed. *The Missionary Enterprise in China and America*. Cambridge, MA: Harvard University Press, 1974.

Hersey, John. *The Call*. New York: Alfred A. Knopf, 1985.

Ho Ping-te. "The Salt Merchants of Yang-chou: A Study of Commercial Capitalism in Eighteenth Century China," *Harvard Journal of Asiatic Studies* 17 (1954): 130-168.

Hoste, D.E. "A Re-Statement of Policy," *China's Millions* 37: 1 (January 1929): 3-4.

Hsiung, James C., and Steven I. Levine, eds. *China's Bitter Victory: The War with Japan 1937-1945*. Armonk, NY: M.E. Sharpe, 1992.

Hunter, Alan, and Kim-Kwong Chan. *Protestantism in Contemporary China*. Cambridge; Cambridge University Press, 1993.

Hunter, Jane. *The Gospel of Gentility: American Women Missionaries in Turn-of-the-Century China*. New Haven, CT: Yale University Press, 1984.

Isaacs, Harold. *The Tragedy of the Chinese Revolution*. 2nd rev. ed. New York: Atheneum, 1966.

Jordan, Donald A. *The Northern Expedition: China's National Revolution of 1926-1928*. Honolulu: University Press of Hawaii, 1976.

Kane, J.H. "A Thriving Church," *China's Millions* 48:7 (July 1940): 101-103.

Kessler, Lawrence D. *The Jiangyin Mission Station: An American Missionary Community in China, 1895-1951*. Chapel Hill: University of North Carolina Press, 1996.

Landstrom, Elsie Hayes. *Closing the Circle: An American Family in China*. Fort Bragg, CA.: Q.E.D Press, 1998.

Landstrom, Elsie H., ed. *Doc: Surgeon in China Through War and Revolution 1924-1949*. Fort Bragg, CA: Q.E.D. Press, 1991.

Lary, Diana. *Warlord Soldiers: Chinese Common Soldiers, 1911-1937*. Cambridge: Cambridge University press, 1985.

Latourette, Kenneth Scott. *A History of Christian Missions in China*. London: The Society for Promoting Christian Knowledge, 1929 (reprint, Taipei: Ch'eng-wen Publishing Company, 1970).

Lee, Joseph Tse-Hei. *The Bible and the Gun: Christianity in South China, 1860-1900*. New York: Routledge, 2003.

Leung, Edwin Pak-wah, ed. *Historical Dictionary of Revolutionary China, 1839-1976*. New York: Greenwood Press, 1992.

Lodwick, Kathleen L. *Educating the Women of Hainan: The Career of Margaret Moninger in China 1915-1942*. Lexington, KY: The University Press of Kentucky, 1995.

Lodwick, Kathleen L. *The Chinese Recorder Index: A Guide to Christian Missions in Asia, 1867-1941*. 2 vols. Wilmington, Delaware: Scholarly Resources Inc., 1986.

Lowe, H.Y. *The Adventures of Wu: The Life Cycle of a Peking Man*. Princeton, NJ: Princeton University Press, 1983.

Lutz, Jessie G. *Christian Missions in China: Evangelists of What?* Boston: D.C. Heath and Company, 1965.

Lutz, Jessie G., and Rolland Ray Lutz. *Hakka Chinese Confront Protestant Christianity, 1850-1900: With the Autobiographies of Eight Hakka Christians, and Commentary*. Armonk, NY: M.E. Sharpe, 1998.

Lutz, Jessie G., and R. Ray Lutz, "Karl Gutzlaff's Approach to Indigenization: The Chinese Union." In Daniel H. Bays, ed. *Christianity in China: From the Eighteenth Century to the Present*. Stanford: Stanford University Press, 1996, 269-291.

Mao Zedong, *Report from Xunwu*. Translated with an Introduction and Notes by Roger R. Thompson. Stanford: Stanford University Press, 1990.

McCord, Edward A. *The Power of the Gun: The Emergence of Modern Chinese Warlordism*. Berkeley: University of California Press, 1993.

McLean, Cynthia, ed. *Gleanings from the Manuscripts of M. Searle Bates: The Protestant Endeavor in Chinese Society, 1890-1950*. New York: The China Program, National Council of Churches of Christ in the U.S.A., 1984.

McManners, John, ed. *The Oxford Illustrated History of Christianity.* Oxford: Oxford University Press, 2001.

Mote, F.W. *Imperial China 900-1800.* Cambridge, MA: Harvard University Press, 1999.

Naquin, Susan, and Chün-fang Yü, eds. *Pilgrims and Sacred Sites in China.* Berkeley: University of California Press, 1992.

Neal, Stephan. *A History of Christian Missions.* New York: Penguin Books, 1964.

Norman, Jerry. *Chinese.* Cambridge: Cambridge University Press, 1988.

Osborne, Ann. "Property, Taxes, and State Protection of Rights." In Madeleine Zelin, Jonathan K. Ocko, and Robert Gardella, eds. *Contract and Property in Early Modern China.* Stanford: Stanford University Press, 2004, 120-158.

Overmyer, Daniel L. *Religions of China: The World as a Living System.* San Francisco: Harper and Row, 1986.

Price, Eva Jane. *China Journal 1889-1900: An American Missionary Family during the Boxer Rebellion.* New York: Charles Scribner's Sons, 1989.

Rabe, Valentin H. *The Home Base of American China Missions, 1880-1920.* Cambridge, MA: Council on East Asian Studies, Harvard University, 1978.

Reinders, Eric. *Borrowed Gods and Foreign Bodies: Christian Missionaries Imagine Chinese Religion.* Berkeley, CA: University of California Press, 2004.

Skinner, G. William. "Marketing and Social Structure in Rural China, Part I." *The Journal of Asian Studies* 24: 1 (November 1964): 3-43.

Smith, Arthur H. *Village Life in China.* Boston: Little, Brown and Company, 1970.

Spence, Jonathan. *The Search for Modern China,* 2nd edition. New York: W.W. Norton and Company, 1991.

Thomson, James C. Jr. *While China Faced West: American Reformers in Nationalist China, 1928-1937.* Cambridge, MA: Harvard University Press, 1969.

Todd, Winifred, comp. *Letters from Hazel.* Fresno, CA: Liberty Printing Company, 1977.

Varg, Paul A. *Missionaries, Chinese, and Diplomats: The American Protestant Missionary Movement in China, 1890-1952.* Princeton: Princeton University Press, 1958.

Yip, Ka-che. *Reconstruction in Nationalist China: The Development of Modern Health Services, 1928-1937.* Ann Arbor: Association for Asian Studies Monograph and Occasional Paper Series, Number 50, 1995.

Zaccarini, M. Christina. *The Sino-American Friendship as Tradition and Challenge: Dr. Ailie Gale in China, 1908-1950.* Bethlehem: Lehigh University Press, 2001.

Zelin, Madeleine, Jonathan K. Ocko, and Robert Gardella, eds. *Contract and Property in Early Modern China.* Stanford: Stanford University Press, 2004.

Website Sources

Billy Graham Center Archives: Collection 187-Eleanor Ruth Elliott, T4 Transcript. www.wheaton.edu/bgc/archives/trans/187t04.htm

Billy Graham Center Archives: Collection 287-Margaret Rice Elliott Crossett, T4 Transcript, T5 Transcript. www.wheaton.edu/bgc/archives/trans/287t05.htm

Billy Graham Center Archives: The Archives Bulletin Board, March, 2003, "China Inland Mission's Call for Two Hundred Workers." www.wheaton.edu/bgc/archives/bulletin/bu0303.htm

Billy Graham Center Archives: The Archives Bulletin Board, October, 2000, "Chinese Village Evangelism Posters" www.wheaton.edu/bgc/archives/docs/chinaposters01.htm

Opentopia: "North China and South China" http://encycl.opentopia.com/term/North_China_and_South_China

School of Oriental and African Studies Library: China Inland Mission: "Chefoo School and the Chefoo Schools Association Papers" www.mundus.ac.uk/cats/4/904.htm

About the Editor

Robert Gardella, Professor of History Emeritus, the United States Merchant Marine Academy, received a Ph.D. in History from the University of Washington. He is the author of *Harvesting Mountains: Fujian and the China Tea Trade*, 1757-1937 (California, 1994) and co-editor of *Chinese Business History* (M.E. Sharpe, 1998) and *Contract and Property in Early Modern China* (Stanford, 2004).